WITHOUT ENIGMA

The Ultra and Fellgiebel Riddles

WITHOUT ENIGMA

The Ultra and Fellgiebel Riddles

Kenneth Macksey

Ian Allan
PUBLISHING

Dedicated to the genius and courage of
General Erich Fellgiebel —
unsung hero and leader of German resistance to Hitler and Nazidom.

First published 2000

ISBN 0 7110 2766 8

Published by Ian Allan Publishing

an imprint of Ian Allan Publishing Ltd, Terminal House, Shepperton, Surrey TW17 8AS.
Printed by Ian Allan Printing Ltd, Riverdene Business Park, Hersham, Surrey KT12 4RG.

Code: 0011/B

Back cover, top: A three-wheel Enigma machine.
Science Museum/Science & Society Picture Library

Back cover, bottom: General Erich Fellgiebel. *Bundesarchiv*

Contents

Preface 7
1. Fellgiebel Takes the Initiative 11
2. The Schemers 17
3. Stewart Menzies' Dilemma 25
4. Garbo 31
5. Diatribe and Dissent 35
6. The Trials 41
7. The Conspirators 47
8. The Crucial Decision 53
9. Reversion to Conjecture 57
10. Without Enigma 63
11. Flash Point 67
12. Decay and Disorder 71
13. Crises in the Atlantic 77
14. Back to Intuitional Guesswork 85
15. Purple and Fish 93
16. Dramas, Threats and Sideshows .99
17. Encroaching Nemesis 105
18. Fortitude to Overlord 113
19. Surprise, Brute Force and Ignorance 121
20. Breaking Points for Field Marshals 129
21. Heroes and Bunglers 133
22. A Foregone Conclusion 143
23. The Riddles 149
Bibliography 153
Index 155

Preface

It was the late Professor Sir Harry Hinsley, author (with others) of the monumental six-volume official history, *British Intelligence in the Second World War*, who said that the effect of the famous German Enigma encoding machine had been greatly exaggerated by historians, and then added, ' . . . but there is little that can be done about it now'. This may well be true, bearing in mind that so many, including official historians, have indulged in guesswork and fantasy to justify their conclusions.

Not everybody has the time to study Hinsley's great work — to which I am personally enormously indebted for its vital assistance in the writing of this book. But the validity of Hinsley's objection is undeniable. So it seemed worthwhile, by use of a literary trick, to attempt to compress into one volume an account of Enigma's effect on both sides in the course of the war.

That is the aim of this book.

* *

In 1939 Germany went to war equipped with the most sophisticated communications organisation in the world, a system that was crucial to the victories she initially won so convincingly before things started going badly awry in September 1942. That she managed to do so was very largely to the credit of a communications genius, General Erich Fellgiebel. Crucial to the supremacy of the system he created was the adoption of a supposedly unbreakable encoding machine called Enigma.

Compared with code books, the relatively small and compact electro-mechanical Enigma machine was faster, easier to operate and, most unlike hand code books, almost foolproof. It made feasible secure radio networks which alone could make possible secret strategic and tactical command and control of ships at sea. It also, in theory, made it less necessary to use land telegraphic and telephone cable communications for the rapid transmission of secret strategic orders and information from the highest personalities of state down to the lowest diplomatic, intelligence, operational and administrative levels, civil and military.

To Fellgiebel's disquiet, all the major power-greedy organisations of the Third Reich — the Navy, the Army, the Luftwaffe, the Abwehr, the SS, the Foreign Service, the police, and the railways — demanded and obtained their own private networks of Enigma machines. In so doing, it can be argued that, besides growing over-dependent upon these revolutionary facilities, the Germans' whole system became appallingly vulnerable should an enemy work the seemingly impossible and penetrate any part of Enigma's secret. This made the role of signals intelligence — Sigint as it came to be abbreviated — all the more crucial.

Yet uncovering the Enigma secret in 1940 is precisely what the British achieved by possession of a Polish invented electro-mechanical machine known as the Bombe, thus giving rise to an historic situation, as Sigint flourished to an unimaginable degree in a state of presumed inviolability on the German part. Admittedly the effects were not immediately productive for the British — after all, the Germans' colossal conquests and almost unbroken run of initial victories over a period of three years could not be gainsaid. These successes were in fact achieved, despite Germany's enemies' intimate knowledge of her intentions, because the Wehrmacht's generalship, military doctrine, organisations, weapons and communications — above all the latter — out-matched and thus eliminated opponents who were far from ready for war.

For all we now know of its shortcomings, the adoption of Enigma machines came as a great relief to the German armed services who, as a result of their World War 1 experiences, had come thoroughly to mistrust code books of all kinds for high grade, strategic messages which had been regularly penetrated in the earlier conflict. Nevertheless, to cope with the vast number of sensitive radio messages which would need to be transmitted, the Enigma machines could never be enough; they could not manage without extensive use of medium and low grade codes for lesser messages. For example, the German Navy alone employed 27 different kinds, many of which were broken by hand. And, incredible to relate, the Army, SS and police adopted a system based on the British 'Playfair' code which the Germans knew was insecure since they themselves had broken it during World War 1.

In fact, from 1940 until mid-1942, all that the British Ultra organisation could do was make an unique contribution to an exercise in damage limitation. That is, by use of crucial Sigint and inside information, to pre-empt, without necessarily defeating, Axis strategic plans and thereby win time for Britain, with vast American aid and eventual full military participation, to rebuild its forces in order to overthrow the aggressors.

This is the point at which this book takes up the story fully. It is the theme of this book to indicate what might have happened if, early in 1943 as the Axis powers slid into decline, the Germans had discovered that Enigma was thoroughly penetrated. Almost at the moment when the tide could be perceived to have turned against the Axis, we shall see what might have happened if General Fellgiebel, head of the German Armed Forces Signals Service, had called a high-level staff meeting to announce that he had reason to believe Enigma had been broken — as well he might have done in reality if only he and others had used their wits more sharply and investigated more thoroughly that vital matter.

The extent of the rewriting of history here is kept to the minimum. Where there are 'Deviations from History' they are indicated in the style of footnotes with the letter 'D' in the text. On the other hand, where it is necessary to emphasise authenticity, far more numerous confirmatory footnotes are inserted and numbered in the usual way. Thus it is intended to demonstrate, by many instances, what effect Enigma really did impose between March 1943 and the war's end.

Simultaneously the opportunity has been taken to record the genuine activities of General Erich Fellgiebel, an unsung hero of the German resistance against Hitler and

Nazidom. Little known by the present generation of Germans for his outstanding achievements and courage, his leading role in the conspiracy is usually reduced to a derogatory walking-on part in English language histories of the period. It is a privilege to have done something to correct history in this respect.

* *

In the writing of this book I have become indebted to many people, dead and alive. Many of the former either worked in the field of intelligence or in the writing of its history: their names and works will be found in the Bibliography. Principal among them are Ronald Lewin, who first aroused my interest in this subject, and Professor Sir Harry Hinsley and his colleagues who compiled the unique and invaluable British official history upon which I have drawn so extensively.

Those among the living whom I have consulted are far fewer in number. In Britain they include, with my immense gratitude for their time and helpfulness, Tony Sales, Director of the Bletchley Park Museum and the staff of the Public Record Office; in Germany, Generalmajor Berthold Schenk von Stauffenberg and Dr Gerd R. Ueberschar of the Bundesarchiv.

Also I owe a great debt of thanks to Helga Ashworth who both translated documents from the German and gave valuable insight into the Germany in which she lived during peace and war. And to John Ashworth who critically read the first draft and finally most emphatically of all to my wife, Joan, who gave the manuscript that last essential polish.

Kenneth Macksey

1.
Fellgiebel Takes the Initiative

Three senior staff officers, one from the Army, one from the Navy and the third from the Luftwaffe, stood to attention as General der Nachrichtentruppen (General of Signals Troops) Erich Fellgiebel and Admiral Wilhelm Canaris entered the small overheated conference room in Block 88 of the *Wolfschanze* (wolf's lair), Hitler's East Prussian command post. Outside among the imposing, steel and concrete blockhouses, the January air was chill; inside the atmosphere was tense. The usual heel-clicking, hand-shaking ritual was soon disposed of as the bespectacled Fellgiebel, head of Armed Forces (Wehrmacht) and Army Signal Services, routinely introduced his colleagues to the Chief of Intelligence and Security.

'Rear-Admiral Stummel of the Naval Communications Division you know, of course, as well as my old friends and comrades, General Martini of Luftwaffe Signals and General Albert Praun, Chief of Signals at Army High Command [OKH].'

They settled and waited anxiously.

'You know why we are here. Security!' announced Fellgiebel, pausing for a glance at his notes. 'At the risk of stating the obvious, however, let me first remind you that the course of the war has changed, and not just in Russia and the Mediterranean. Three months ago we were pushing ahead in the Caucasus and at Stalingrad and were entrenched firmly at El Alamein, almost in sight of Cairo. On 9 January we had the unwelcome news that the besieged Sixth Army had been called upon to surrender at Stalingrad, the efforts of Field Marshal von Manstein's Army Group Don to relieve the city having broken down irrevocably. Meanwhile, of course, Field Marshal von Kleist's Army Group A is stalled in the Caucasus and Field Marshals Kesselring and Rommel are running for shelter in Tunisia as our enemies close in by land, sea and air in the Mediterranean. For the moment we have lost the initiative and, personally, I regard that situation as closely associated with failures in both communications security and with intelligence. That is precisely why Admiral Canaris has joined us to-day.'[D1/1]

Stummel, sensing a repetition of accusations against the Navy, made as if to interrupt, but Fellgiebel raised his hand. 'There will be discussion later, but first let me mention certain apparent lapses and breakdowns which, a year or more ago at the height of our successes, would have seemed inconceivable. Take, for example, the failure to maintain essential oil supplies to Rommel's army at Alamein. How was it that nothing reached North Africa in the first week of October? Because two large tankers had been bombed and sunk in Navarino. How was it that the safe arrival of a tanker on the 10th was the last delivery by sea until the battle was lost on 1 November? Was it by chance that, in the course of the battle which began on the 23rd, five out of five large tankers had been sunk?'

'Well, we all know why, don't we?' snapped Stummel, leaning forward. 'It's common knowledge. The Italians are not to be trusted. They're the people who are passing sailing times and the like to the enemy.'

Canaris raised his head and growled. 'Not impossible, but we have no proof and I find it hard to believe they would treat their own people that way. Besides, I gather the British seem to have uncanny knowledge of ships' courses as well as timings?'

Ignoring the question, Fellgiebel continued. 'We have been presented with the astonishing lapse that, last November, not only were we quite unaware of the objectives of the Allied invasion of north-west Africa, their Operation 'Torch', but we failed utterly to obtain the slightest indication of their convoys' approach. And do not forget that, until then, your *B-Dienst* had been reading anything up to 80% of British, American and Canadian traffic.'[2]

'We might do better if only the Luftwaffe would allocate sufficient suitable aircraft for reconnaissance,' exclaimed Stummel.

'The Reichsmarschall does his best,' protested Martini, 'but the Luftwaffe, too, has its conflicting priorities, as the Navy knows.'

'And also because,' Stummel complained in turn, 'the Reichsmarschall adamantly blocks Admiral Dönitz's every request for operational control of aircraft.'

'Gentlemen,' chided Fellgiebel, 'we are not here to recriminate. I would point out the possibility that both the Luftwaffe and Navy, when signalling to U-boats or aircraft, might inadvertently have helped the enemy divert those convoys out of danger. Or that Luftwaffe traffic when in support of the Army may easily provide a running commentary on ground operations even if the Army has imposed radio silence.'

Canaris was seeking attention. 'There is something you should all be aware of. In fact my Abwehr was told the destination of the enemy's Torch convoys in a letter from one of our best agents in England. Regrettably, however, the letter did not arrive in Lisbon until the day of the event.'

'Are you saying then', queried Stummel, 'that this excellent person was not equipped with radio?'

'Most unfortunately that is so. We are in the process of rectifying that now,' was the discomforted reply; which omitted to add that the agent concerned had been pleading since August for this vital item of communication equipment.[3]

'Please take heed,' interrupted Fellgiebel hastily, though this item of news was fresh to him. 'Here we are seeking solutions and, I repeat, are not in the business of recriminations. So let us proceed and ask how it was that the Russians caught our army totally by surprise when, on 19 November, they drove in our flanks on either side of Stalingrad and at their weakest points? I would be the last to disagree that those weaknesses might easily have been discovered by orthodox means, but my judgement warns of something more sinister. Perhaps our enemies are better informed than we might expect, and must not permit.'

'I concur,' interjected Praun, 'and would be the first to admit that we in the Army may bear some responsibility for this. Our command arrangements on the East Front were in a muddle, worsened by poor liaison with the Romanian, Hungarian and Italian

Armies, upon whom the enemy counter-stroke almost exclusively fell, and because the cover of Luftwaffe and our own ground reconnaissance left much to be desired. We were all overstretched — and still are. Nevertheless, I fear that is not the only factor which allowed this disaster. I refer, of course, to signal security and the possibility, however remote, of the enemy having significantly broken the Enigma machine codes.'

The others would have been right if they suspected that there was collusion between the two Army communications experts. Beforehand, indeed, Fellgiebel had informed Praun of his intention to focus on this vital aspect of security, as had been done on previous occasions. It was a thorny subject bearing heavily as it did upon the ability of the nation, let alone the Wehrmacht, to wage war successfully against enemies of infinitely greater numerical and, in certain respects, technical strength. Better than the vast majority of officers, Fellgiebel and Praun could claim that Germany's amazing run of victories and conquest of Europe since 1939 was the product of economies of force made possible by efficient, secure and flexible signal communications.

As Praun always insisted, 'Signal systems are the nervous system of an army. They conduct the ideas originating in the brain of the supreme command to the fist, the fighting troops, where the ideas are converted into action. The structure of the signal communications of the Wehrmacht, therefore, is to a great extent dependent on the structure of the supreme command itself.'[4]

Stummel was still leaning forward, his expression livid. 'What General Praun says is not only pernicious rubbish but also threatens to wreck our entire naval strategy. He knows full well that more than once the Enigma system has been checked and found infallible. True, our best experts admit to the faintest feasibility of breaking even the most advanced Triton four-wheel navy machine — but only in such a laborious and time-consuming manner as to make the effort worthless. To suggest otherwise is treasonable. In any case we have repeatedly amended procedures as a precaution. The U-boat war in the Atlantic would be nigh-on crippled if we stopped using our Enigma systems and denied the one hope we have of preventing the Americans transferring their full weight into Europe. We simply cannot admit to this even if it is true!'

'We in the Luftwaffe naturally agree with the Navy in this respect,' said Martini soothingly. 'Like the Navy, but unlike the Army, which can to a far greater extent make do without radio, we are vitally dependent upon radio for operational as well as administrative matters. I'll go farther. The introduction of the electro-mechanical Enigma machine, so ably developed by General Fellgiebel and his colleagues over the past decade, has positively encouraged us to neglect other more expensive means of transmission. We are wedded to radio communications and I tremble to think of the blockages and damage that might be done if forced to change our methods and systems overnight.'[5]

Praun and Fellgiebel were nodding agreement. 'Your objections are neither unexpected nor dismissed,' said the latter. 'And it is true that the Army alone, with its excellent networks of line and cable at home and in the occupied territories (where in France alone we have extended the trunk network from 6,000km to more than 10,000km)[6], is inherently the most secure. We soldiers can get along without much radio behind the front. But there are more reasons for anxiety than those I have already raised. Ask yourselves! Is there not a fairly high chance that, for some time, the enemy has been in possession of one or more Enigmas? After all, it first appeared on the civil market in the 1920s. Anybody could go out and buy it, as we did then.'

Little of what Fellgiebel then recounted was entirely unknown to his listeners. His aim, in fact, was intended not so much to inform as to drive home the magnitude of the threat and to overcome the closed minds that, as usual during such debates, had surfaced. He reminded them that, assiduous as responsible officers at sea and in the field no doubt were in the protection and destruction of Enigma machines and code books, it would be surprising if some had not fallen into enemy hands. He postulated what might happen in dire, surprise circumstances when an army headquarters was overrun by the enemy (as had occurred all too frequently since 1941) or at sea when a ship was boarded and searched by the enemy before sinking. Rhetorically he asked, 'How many missing weather ships, coastal vessels or even U-boats have yielded machines and documents to the enemy without our being aware of it?'

'Only recently, indeed, a report which appeared in the English *Evening Standard*, as long ago as 19 November 1940, has been drawn to my attention. It says that the British cruiser *Naiad* captured a Luftwaffe meteorological party going ashore on Jan Mayen. What happened to their communications equipment? And how was it that the exact time of the party's arrival was so precisely known? Furthermore, is it not just possible that the Abwehr-enciphered message detailing that important mission had been compromised?'[7]

'I cast no aspersions. Yet, incidents of this kind should make us ask searching questions. How often has complacency or sheer carelessness blinded us to revealing mistakes? Above all, how knowledgeable is the enemy about our code and cipher systems?'

Martini was first to respond by denying all knowledge of the Jan Mayen incident; this was the sort of communication failure that was common enough on the Abwehr's part and indeed throughout the Wehrmacht and Nazi Germany, due to lack of interdepartmental collaboration and poor staff work. But Canaris, forewarned by Fellgiebel, nodded his head in agreement even though it reflected on his Abwehr. Stummel, on the other hand, threw doubts on the possible loss of ships' equipment.

Praun then recalled a curiously disturbing event during the First Battle of Alamein on 10 July 1942 when, for some unaccountable reason, the Panzer Army intelligence office, complete with files and encoding equipment, had strayed close to the front line and had been captured along with its ingenious Leutnant Seebohm by a British attack.

'God knows how much compromising material they laid their hands on. And I should tell you that, within a matter of hours, our most fruitful insight into the codes of the American Military Attaché in Cairo was lost. In fact I think it fair to say that, ever since the disappearance of Seebohm, Marshals Kesselring and Rommel have been in the dark and frequently deceived.'[8]

'Gentlemen, I am no longer convinced we can afford to bury our heads in the sand.' insisted Fellgiebel. 'Of course, we all know that sometime or another codes are liable to be broken. I should know. I became involved in this business from its beginnings nearly 40 years ago! The Army, like the Luftwaffe, has profited enormously from listening to insecure enemy transmissions on all fronts. The Navy's *B-Dienst* has been immensely successful in monitoring and reading British naval signals, though the British Army and Air Force, for their part, have regularly baffled us. These things happen. The struggle goes on and we relax our vigilance at peril. Nothing said this morning leaves me with complete confidence in Enigma. And I must remind you that through Enigma machines pass material of the very highest grade and strategic importance from Armed Forces High Command [OKW] and the Führer himself. I therefore insist that, as a matter of urgency, Enigma — everybody's Enigma — must be re-examined in a far more radical manner than ever before.'

Fellgiebel's plan was nothing short of challenging. In essence he called for a controlled experiment designed to trick the enemy into revealing their mastery of Enigma, if, of course, they really did possess it. But, fundamentally, he was attacking the heart of the Wehrmacht's communications weakness which was due to rampant departmental independence and lack of centralised control.

Each service was requested to transmit a selection of carefully phrased messages designed to provoke an unmistakable enemy reaction which could be safely monitored. For example, an order tasking a U-boat to pick up an agent said to be bearing vital intelligence from a certain rendezvous at a certain time with the aim of seeing, by covert observation, if the enemy made an attempt to interfere. Or orders for a spurious Luftwaffe reconnaissance mission of a sensitive target to see what counter-measures were attempted. Or an army report of completion of a bogus ammunition dumping task which might tempt the enemy into raiding the dump.

Praun, needless to say, was in favour — as he was bound to be since he came under Fellgiebel's direct Army command. As was his way, Canaris waxed non-committal, though unobtrusively. Stummel and Martini, needless to say, raised objections; unlike Praun they were not under Fellgiebel's direct control. Their reservations concerned the very need for an experiment which threatened their autonomy; they were worried about the perils that might be thrust on the monitors involved; and they went so far as to question the practicality of drafting convincing misleading messages. As was their duty, however, they promised to inform their chiefs of the project and arrange support as quickly as possible.

DEVIATIONS FROM HISTORY
[D1] Since the summer of 1941 the German Navy, because it was far more dependent on secure radio communications than were the other services, had been most worried about security leaks, especially from treachery. No such meeting as the one described here took place, however, since faith in the integrity of Enigma remained universally absolute.

Confirmatory footnotes:
1 Hohne passim for most references to Canaris.
2 Hinsley Vol 2 p 636.
3 Hinsley Vol 4 pp 116, 117.
4 Praun p 48.
5 Wildhagen p 185.
6 ibid p 44.
7 Hinsley Vol 2 pp 677, 678.
8 Kahn pp 475, 476.

2.
The Schemers

The two senior officers with their vast complementary experience sat opposite each other, a bottle of claret between them on the desk. Very likely they were the best informed and among the most cynical men in Nazi Germany.

Wilhelm Canaris had joined the German Navy in 1905, the same year Erich Fellgiebel had joined an Army telegraph battalion. Quite by chance in World War 1, Canaris had found a niche in intelligence. In 1915, after taking part in the Battle of the Falklands the previous December, he was given the task of improvising an information network in support of the cruiser *Dresden's* raiding. Subsequently, until September 1916, he spied for German U-boats in the Mediterranean before being trained to become a successful U-boat captain.

Fellgiebel's career, on the other hand, had been less adventurous though a lot more constructive than that of the rather untidy sailor who was known now as the Little Admiral. As one of an élite of specialist communicators, the dedicated and far-sighted Fellgiebel had attended the Military Technical Academy in 1913 and spent the entire war either running a cavalry corps' radio communications or, after 1916 when he was appointed a member of the élite General Staff, serving on the staff of an army corps. Thus he obtained a profound insight into the development of sophisticated strategic and tactical telegraphic and radio networks, along with the improvisation and expansion of radio intelligence methods capable of acquiring information of the highest value, especially on the Eastern Front where Russian security was often lax. He was regarded as a brilliant organiser and leading personality in the integration of signals with the Great General Staff's operational system, including that of its intelligence branches. In the opinion of many people he was a genius.

After the war, as a member of the 100,000-man army to which Germany was restricted by the Treaty of Versailles, Fellgiebel spent four years in the Reichswehr Ministry working in the Truppenamt (the shadow General Staff) under General von Seeckt, followed by two years with a signals unit and four more on the staff until returning to the Reichswehr Ministry in 1929 to spend two years in the Abwehr department. He became involved with the creation of major projects, such as the development of secure and flexible land-line and radio networks suitable for mobile defence of the then almost defenceless Reich by fast mechanised formations and units. And, as a result of the Abwehr posting, he became caught up in espionage work. For although, under the Treaty of Versailles, Germany was forbidden an intelligence organisation, in 1920 she created the Abwehr which, covertly, was committed to counter-espionage.

Meanwhile Canaris, true to his right-wing subversive inclinations, became involved at the end of the war in anti-communist activities and misguided attempts to rebuild the armed forces contrary to the Treaty of Versailles. However, when Germany began to stabilise politically, the opportunist Canaris rejoined the Navy in 1922, dabbled briefly in intelligence matters and then reverted to conventional duties at sea, with few prospects of promotion higher than the rank of captain.

The Nazi revolution and the coming to power of Adolf Hitler in January 1933 changed everything and significantly affected them both.

Fellgiebel was soon absorbed in the heart of the re-armament process, first as a lieutenant colonel as Chief of Staff of the Signals Corps Inspectorate and then as a colonel and Inspector in the implementation of plans to expand the Army on modern lines. The latter appointment was quite remarkable since not one of the five Inspectors over the previous 15 years had belonged to the signals arm — such was the General Staff's traditional rejection of technical specialists.

Canaris, as an admirer and self-seeking favourite of Hitler, was unexpectedly appointed head of the Abwehr Department on 5 January 1935, despite strong initial reservations from Admiral Erich Raeder, the C-in-C of the Navy. Thus by political opportunism, Canaris ascended to the pinnacle of the intelligence community as a prelude to descent into the depths of political intrigue and subversion. For henceforward the Abwehr would be engaged in many other tasks besides counter-intelligence.

Promotion for these two officers of markedly disparate capabilities came quickly as, functionally, they were drawn together. Come 1938, the year in which Adolf Hitler first began openly to exhibit disenchantment with his generals, and General Franz Halder became Chief of the Army General Staff, Fellgiebel was made major-general. Working together easily in their military duties, Halder and Fellgiebel also began conspiring against the Nazis. But while Halder could never quite bring himself to act and time and again thrilled at the task of successfully planning and executing Hitler's military intentions, Fellgiebel nurtured his anti-Nazi sentiments and fostered contacts with like-minded people — and did so openly enough to attract the attention of the Gestapo which, in 1938, began tapping his telephone conversations, though without hearing anything incriminating.

On the eve of war Fellgiebel was appointed head of OKW Communications and Intelligence, an all-embracing yet flawed organisation due to its lack of direct authority over the Navy and Luftwaffe. Yet it was remarkably efficient due largely to his founding work as Inspector in the best General Staff tradition — for it was the Inspectors who had carried preponderant authority in the Reichswehr. In February 1940 he was promoted lieutenant-general and six months later general. Yet Gestapo suspicions continued and in 1942, even though Hitler had once referred to him as 'my most trustworthy general,' an attempt was made by SS Reichsführer Himmler to unseat him. This failed for the excellent reason that, as General Rudolf Schmundt (since September 1942 the Head of Personnel) said, 'we have no successor.' Fellgiebel, with his unique knowledge and grasp of Reich communications was that rare officer — an indispensable one.[1]

Meanwhile Canaris had risen to admiral, even though the Abwehr over which he presided was also gravely flawed, due to poor internal communications. This made it similar to many another organisation run by a Hitler nominee; but its problems were also the result of other, divisive, internal causes — Canaris was neither the first nor the last mediocre sycophant promoted by Hitler to high military office. As Sir John Wheeler-Bennett has emphatically pointed out, the Abwehr under Canaris displayed no very great efficiency either as an intelligence agency or as a focus for conspirators. Yet Canaris frequently benefited from the many items of information acquired by the immensely powerful civil and military communications system that had been created since the mid-1920s.[2]

It had been in 1926 that the first major electronic change was brought about. The old and inefficient damped radio equipment began to be replaced by small, portable, undamped long-, medium- and short-wave sets for tactical use, which were not so sensitive to interference. Progressively more powerful sets were developed that could be operated from moving motor vehicles. In harness, a decade later, came quad-cable that could be laid at 150km per day. This could carry telephone, telegraph or teleprinter messages that made the teleprinter moderately secure and often made radio transmissions unnecessary for the Army. Moreover, in due course, radio communications would be further improved by the introduction of directional micro-wave beam sets which were extremely difficult to intercept.

Of most strategic importance, however, was the national trunk underground cable network which, in conjunction with the over-centralised Reichspost system was expanded, prewar, to the frontiers and, in due course, linked to the systems of allies and the occupied territories. In effect a dense system of telephone tentacles was spread throughout the Reich which for simplicity and flexibility was always preferable to strategic Enigma-encrypted radio traffic. Nevertheless, the more complicated and less reliable Enigma was thought essential for rapid and, supposedly, unbreakable transmissions of high grade content.

First adopted by the Navy in 1926 to save itself from the disasters of the previous war (when the British consistently broke their code books), Enigma was taken up by the Army in 1929 (when Fellgiebel was serving in the Abwehr). Then, in 1934 at Hermann Göring's insistence, 'his' newly-formed Luftwaffe, at great cost, set up its own lavish line and radio network for information and administrative as well as operational purposes. This met fierce opposition from Fellgiebel on the grounds of waste by unnecessary duplication of the Army's system. Fellgiebel also came intensely to dislike Göring on account of his predilection for extravagance and for his involvement in the murder of a number of distinguished Army officers besides the leaders of the Nazi Sturm Abteilung on the so-called Night of the Long Knives of 30 June 1934.[3]

Demands for prestige possession of Enigma-secured radio links amounted to an addiction Fellgiebel and the Army could not resist. Soon the diplomatic corps along with the Abwehr were hooked in attempts to reduce their reliance on couriers and less reliable radio code books. And in due course Heinrich Himmler's SS, the police and logistic organisations possessed their own facilities, too.

* *

The office door was firmly shut and Fellgiebel had forbidden any interruptions. Canaris studied his old comrade over the rim of his wine glass and stated, 'I am uncertain what you hoped to achieve from to-day's confrontation.'

'Let me then ask you a question in reply', riposted Fellgiebel. 'How do you imagine we can avoid losing this war?'

'Only by defeating the enemy.'

'Yes, but by what means? Do you really think by force of arms? Because, with our special insight, that is hardly a realistic proposition is it? We both know the Fatherland is hopelessly outnumbered and, in terms of industrial output, overborne. And, so I am told, even the Führer sometimes admits it in his saner moments. After all, was it not you who said, after witnessing one of his rages before the war, "I have just seen a madman."?'

Canaris, ever intent on self-preservation and fully aware of Nazi ruthlessness, inwardly shuddered at indiscreet utterances such as occurred ever more disturbingly on Fellgiebel's part. 'But how can a tentative trial of this sort, even if it does produce a semblance of proof, improve the Fatherland's situation decisively?'

'By restoring to us the information advantage provided by communications systems that offset the numerical and industrial inferiority we have suffered from since 1940,' said Fellgiebel. 'Listen! We both know how in the last war everybody penetrated everybody's else codes almost with impunity. Intelligence was reduced to a guessing game. Remember how the British read your naval codes for years, and therefore were forewarned of the High Seas Fleet's movements? Nobody thought then to challenge their mastery which, I remind you, came about because in 1914 they had seized the code books from one of our cruisers. Largely as a result of that we lost the war at sea. Which is why the Navy seized on the Enigma machine as a way to being a secure jump ahead of its enemies.'

'So?'

'We still make the old mistakes believing our signals are invulnerable. There remain those, like Stummel, who cannot accept the possibilities of anybody having seized possession of a machine with its instructions intact, along with fully wired wheels. Arrogantly we accept that a machine which manages to select a daily-changing key with 150 million million million solutions is perfectly secure.'

'Quite!' agreed Canaris sardonically, pouring himself more wine as Fellgiebel waved a dismissive hand. 'Let me remind you that the British navy is still using old-fashioned code books and the like. Can it be because they are ignorant of a machine like Enigma?'

'Then how is it that their army and air force seem to possess one which we cannot yet break?' retorted Fellgiebel. 'Wilhelm, listen to me. Everybody, especially you sailors with your enviably efficient communications system, chants how that wonderful four-wheel Triton Enigma machine of yours is so much more impregnable than the original three-wheeler. How dare we despise the enemy so? Just think: Enigma is no more than an unreasoning electro-mechanical gadget and therefore, in theory, penetrable by electro-mechanical gadgets.'

'Meaning?' queried a puzzled Canaris.

'Meaning that it might, *just might,* be possible to devise a machine which, somehow or other, can solve the Enigma key. Though how to make it produce at the necessary high speed I have not the remotest idea! Nevertheless, because I am extremely worried about the Fatherland's situation, I can justify anything to satisfy myself that Enigma is safe.'

'And therefore make our situation even more awkward if you are right. Because you still will not know how they do it, where they work and therefore how to counter them.'

'That is no reason for living in a fool's paradise. We must persuade the Navy and the Luftwaffe to take part in the trial — though that will be struggle enough in itself. Oh! What a mess this so-called, "wonderful unified" Oberkommando der Wehrmacht, this High Command of ours is in! Cast your mind back to that meeting a few minutes ago. Who would think we were on the same side? The same old jealousies, bickering for position and obstructions leading to waste and, far worse, serious failures in interdepartmental collaboration. Again and again over crucial matters we falter and suffer because the one man who might make Göring and Raeder abandon their precious independence and join with the Army in a unified communications organisation refuses to do so. Worse, as we both know from daily observation, it is the Führer who, for his own political survival, prefers to exacerbate situations by playing people off against their comrades. Result? Chaos! There is hardly an OKW communications problem that does not call for wearisome negotiations for an agreed solution.'

'But suppose Enigma has been broken? Can we then prevent a downhill slide all the way to our inevitable destruction?'

'Not unless we find out — and without delay — how the enemy does it and then turn that knowledge to our advantage. And to do that we must first identify and then locate the code-breakers themselves. Which means, if theirs are anything like ours, searching for top-grade enemy mathematicians, chess players, crossword addicts, electricians and the like. So, Wilhelm, what if anything did your people turn up?'

At short notice it had been a struggle to identify anybody of that category. Prior to the war the Abwehr had spent little time or effort preparing for hostilities against Britain; least of all rummaging for arcane geniuses of the kind Fellgiebel described. And, indeed, it was in a brain-storming session with one of Fellgiebel's bright younger officers on the Intelligence side that the most promising lead had emerged. In 1938, sponsored by the German military attaché in London, he had spent a few months on a 'goodwill mission' in London, Oxford and Cambridge, keeping his eyes and ears open when mingling with scientifically and technologically oriented people in the services and in the universities. At Oxford he met a Professor Lindemann, who had been born in Germany (and seemed to resent it) and who was involved as a scientific adviser to Winston Churchill, then in the political wilderness. Mainly, however, he had been involved with younger people of whom two had stuck fast in his memory.

At Oxford, and of most interest to him personally, was a robust Dr R. V. Jones; aged about 26, he thought, who apparently was studying radio and infra-red radiations, although reluctant to discuss the subject. The other, at King's College Cambridge, was lacking the same presence as Jones, but already regarded as of quite astonishing brilliance. For Alan Turing, at the age of 22 in 1934, had become a Fellow of Kings, and in 1936 had gained a prize for his thesis on Gaussian Error Function. Mathematician and expert in electromagnetics, he was talked about as the inventor of a theoretical 'thinking computer', referred to as the Turing machine.

What chiefly had made one of Canaris's researchers sit up and take notice was a chance remark suggesting that Turing was following in the footsteps of a 19th century English mathematician called Charles Babbage, who had built, but never completed, two different kinds of mechanical calculating machine. The first worked to eight places of decimals for the purpose of removing inaccuracies from logarithms. Far more promising for Canaris's needs, however, was the second machine — a computer (or so-called 'difference engine') programmed by Jacquard punch cards to create what Babbage visualised as a sort of brain. Of compulsive inspiration to Fellgiebel and Canaris, however, was the revelation that Babbage not only had been a Cambridge professor but also an enthusiastic, inspired cryptologist. To the Germans the credentials of Turing were too coincidental to do other than make him the man they sought. Surely Turing in his studies had been inspired by Babbage?[D1]

'Both your discoveries intrigue me,' said Fellgiebel in some excitement. 'But this Turing fellow seems much more promising. I don't suppose you know where he is and what he is doing just now?'

'No, but there are ways of finding out and I have already set the wheels in motion. I am putting one of my best England agents on the job — the same, incidentally, who obtained that excellent though delayed information about the Torch convoys. We are telling him it is urgent. But I am warning you, don't expect instant results. And don't be too hopeful either. Remember, these are top men he'll be chasing. The British will value them highly and protect them for all they are worth if they really are engaged on important work. So my man has been instructed to proceed with the utmost caution. Oh, and I hope you do not mind, but I am opening enquiries into this fellow Jones as well. He may not mean much to you, but the Navy are deep into infra-red for all manner of uses and you never know what might turn up.'

Probing into another indirectly connected matter, Fellgiebel sought Canaris's opinion about the current power struggle between Admiral Raeder and Hitler. What might be the outcome, in the aftermath of the defeat of a force of cruisers and destroyers which had attempted to intercept a Russian-bound convoy on 31 December 1942? Both were aware of the Führer's rage when, due to a signalling failure, he had been left in ignorance of the set-back until informed by a British news broadcast, and had seen the minutes of a conference on 6 January when Hitler, for 90 dreary minutes, had lectured Raeder on rudimentary naval history, though also exposing his ignorance of the principles of naval strategy. They knew, too, that the upshot had been a threatening Führer order, prompted by Reichsmarschall Göring, to make proposals for the decommissioning of the Navy's remaining battleships, and abandon construction of three aircraft carriers.[4]

Canaris guessed Raeder might keep his job along with some of his precious capital ships. Fellgiebel demurred. Raeder had been C-in-C since 1928 and was tired. In the wings stood Admiral Dönitz, well regarded by Hitler and straining to take over in order to win a better deal for his U-boats. Maybe, Canaris acknowledged, the current unpleasantness at OKM (Naval High Command) was why Stummel had been so touchy. Moreover, Dönitz was not without problems. With more U-boats at sea than ever before it was worrying that convoy sightings that month were few and far between and sinkings scanty. The possible reasons haunted Dönitz, and would be accentuated when he heard news of an incident which occurred at almost the same time as the Canaris–Fellgiebel meeting.

On 12 January the captain of *U459*, a *milch Kuh* supply boat, was surfaced at a pre-arranged rendezvous 300 miles to the east of St Paul's Rock — some 800 miles from Freetown and far removed from convoy routes. At any moment the Italian submarine *Kalvi* was due to rendezvous and replenish. All was quiet, with no cause for alarm, when the sonar operator reported sounds from more than one vessel heading quickly their way. 'Perhaps destroyers,' the operator said as the alarm was shouted and the boat crash dived. Then the rumble of screws nearby and the deathly wait for the blasting of depth charges. But happily nothing as the vessels proceeded on course without taking action. Biding his time, *U459's* captain rose to periscope depth to be delighted by the sight of two destroyers departing.

The arrival of *U459's* report of this inexplicable incident caught Dönitz at a sensitive moment, coinciding as it did with the tensions of the Raeder crisis and the decline in sightings and sinkings. Not for the first time, Dönitz's doubts and suspicions about signal security were aroused. Again he quizzed the Director of the Signal Division and, as previously, received stock replies: Italian treachery, coincidence and mischance, enemy radio direction finding (DF) and/or radar — anything but Enigma and especially the latest model. And, of course, the arrogant suggestion that if the British navy lacked a machine encoder, how likely was it to appreciate Enigma?

This time Dönitz rejected the old excuses which had been blocked over the years. In 1941, he pointed out, sources of enemy intelligence from other than sightings were ruled out and the betrayal of U-boats put down to leakages in the German Admiralty and Commands, and excessive use of radio by boats, making British DF possible. Attempts to reduce the last of these, however, failed to stop chatter. In 1942, after a long wrangle, it had taken a personal visit by Stummel to convince 'the experts' in Berlin that homing by airborne radar was even possible. And even then the experts were tardy developing counter-measures.[5]

Stummel's well-timed mention of Fellgiebel's request for a trial persuaded Dönitz to take the matter to Raeder for permission to take part. Whereupon the C-in-C, eager to impress the Führer with a show of determination, readily agreed, even though the Director of the Signal Division 'persisted in his view that the enemy would not be able to decrypt the U-boats' radio messages, which were enciphered with Key M.'[D2/6]

At once Stummel passed the news to both Martini and Fellgiebel, making it justifiable for the former to persuade General Hans Jeschonnek (Chief of Staff of the Luftwaffe) to conform, without bothering to consult Göring. Meanwhile Dönitz broadcast orders to U-boats underlining the need for minimising radio transmissions.

DEVIATIONS FROM HISTORY

[D1] The information about Jones, Turing and Babbage is factual, but that about the German research into them and the task set their agent by Canaris imaginary.

[D2] Although it is true that Dönitz harboured strong doubts concerning Enigma's integrity and did impose some transmission restrictions, he did not take the matter further. Therefore Fellgiebel's trial would not have taken place.

Confirmatory footnotes:
1 Wildhagen p 295.
2 Wheeler-Bennett pp 597, 598.
3 Wildhagen pp 184, 205.
4 Anon *Fuh* pp 306–8.
5 Anon MOD Vol 2 p 88.
6 Anon MOD Vol 2 pp 77–9, pp 25, 26, pp 86, 87.

3.
Stewart Menzies' Dilemma

Sir Stewart Menzies studied the piece of paper laid before him with a mixture of dismay and disappointment. As 'C', the Head of the Secret Intelligence Service (SIS) over the past three years, he had grown accustomed to receiving far more bad than good news. Now, when at last the tide seemed to have turned in Britain's favour, this was most unkind, most unwelcome, not according to the rules and awkwardly timed. But the fact that it had been delivered in person by Sir David Petrie, Director General of MI5, was an indication of its gravity.

'You read this the same way as I do, I take it? They've woken up to Ultra at last?'

Since seeing the first short messages decrypted by GC&CS (Government Code & Cipher School) at Bletchley Park towards the end of 1939, Menzies and Petrie had struggled to prevent this dreaded moment which threatened the killing of the goose which laid a million golden eggs of priceless intelligence about the enemy.

'I think we must take it seriously, Chief. Mare's nest it may be, of course, but it cannot be ignored. Especially since the Abwehr have addressed it to Garbo, one of their most trusted agents we are led to believe. Besides, their targeting of Jones and Turing, both of whom work at Bletchley, shows insight — or something far more threatening.'[D1]

Old Etonian, Household Cavalryman, holder of the DSO and a member of Field Marshal Haig's staff in World War 1, with contacts at the highest level of society, Menzies was a moneyed and imperturbable Scot with a sense of humour, whose appointment as C on the death of his predecessor in November 1939 had been singularly appropriate. For not only was he then Deputy Head of the SIS but also the officer responsible for running the fledgling organisation later called Ultra. Since then he had expanded it vastly, especially in 1942 with the vital Y Services which not only intercepted enemy radio transmissions worldwide but also, through what was known as Traffic Analysis, interpreted the meaning of many uncodes or thinly disguised messages to amplify the high-grade material provided by Enigma for Ultra. For these crucial assets he had fought tenaciously to guard their essential, deep secrecy. Among other things this had led him to object most strongly when, in November 1942 on the eve of the Russian counter-offensive at Stalingrad, the Prime Minister pressed him to help the Russians by sending them information provided solely via Enigma at the very moment the Germans were tightening radio security. 'I am always embarrassed at sending the Russians information only obtained from this source, owing to the legibility of many Russian ciphers', he had written. And soon the PM's practice was curtailed.[1]

So far the strictly applied control system seemed to have held water: largely through rigorous enforcement of a system keeping the number of people (British and

American) with access to the secret and its products to a minimum, as well as setting up restrictions on a need-to-know basis to the 12,000 rigorously sworn-in people working at Bletchley, of whom perhaps only four knew just about everything that was going on there.

Ever since that thrilling moment at Victoria station on 16 August 1939, when a French officer had handed his predecessor a Polish-built Enigma machine and the technical drawings of the so-called Bombe decoding machine, Menzies had left the work of developing technology to others, above all to brainy cryptanalysts like Turing, who dominated the team which struggled to build a Bombe with vastly higher speed and capacity than the primitive Polish version. It was sufficient for Menzies to know that the arrangement of internally-wired wheels interconnected with plugs to a typewriter keyboard could select the right one out of millions and millions of alternative code-settings, sometimes within minutes and often within hours. Like the vast majority of ordinary mortals, the mathematics and technology and how the Bombe could rapidly, every 24 hours, solve the Enigma riddle, based on 'indicators' or settings transmitted in clear before encipherment for the day, was beyond his comprehension.

Indeed, it had taken a genius to solve that riddle and that master mind belonged to Alan Turing, ably assisted by a few dedicated colleagues with complementary skills. The Abwehr and Fellgiebel had hit the nail on the head when they guessed Turing's machine was related to Babbage's; and they might have done even better if they had followed up the opinions of some of their experts who surmised such a computer might be feasible. But, after all, they no doubt reasoned, if we Germans cannot do it, who else can? And how sick they would have been if they had known it was the racially despised Slavic Poles who had done so.

When GC&CS recruited Turing to improve on the Polish Bombe's rate of decryption, they simply presented him with a heaven-sent opportunity to pursue the expensive research needed to turn his theoretical machine into a high-speed working model. The specification for what became known as the Turing Bombe was drawn up in July 1939, after he and Dillwyn Knox hit on the possibility of developing a Bombe to cope with 'the beginnings of cipher text', and also for use against the indicators.[2] To over-simplify a very long and complex story, the idiosyncratic Turing (who chained his mug to a radiator to prevent people stealing it and buried his money in the grounds but forgot where) dominated affairs due to 'his ability to handle abstruse mathematical concepts' which were 'innate, spectacular and creative.'[3] Creative those concepts certainly were since, before the war, he had used two machines to assist in his work on mathematical problems, including 'an electrical, binary multiplier'; in other words, an embryo of a fast modern computer, though without a memory.[4]

So far as the rapid breaking of Enigma settings was concerned, however, the speed of electricity was only one fundamental aid. Punched paper and cards, â la Babbage, were also used. In addition, acceleration of the first magnitude was assured when, in May 1940, Turing fathomed that the rapid 'testing' of 26 hypotheses (one per letter of the alphabet) could be achieved by 'simultaneous scanning' of the wheels. On 8 August, the first big day of the Battle of Britain, one of these radical machines was installed at Bletchley Park, with dramatic impact on the war and the future of humanity.[5]

Of prime importance among the problems facing Menzies and Petrie at that moment in early 1943 were the instinctively subjective and painful questions, 'who has blown the secret and how?' But next came the more sceptical query, 'has it really happened?' Leading to the reactive, logical dilemma, 'what should we do about it? Jump to the worst conclusions, or wait and see?' And 'what to do about Garbo', since the long-disputed departmental rules for employment of double agents did not take into account using them as private investigators.

'But above all,' ruminated Menzies, 'there's the politics of the matter which, I suppose due to the gathering of all the Great at Casablanca, has been to some extent simplified. The Prime Minister will want to inform the President and the Combined Chiefs of Staff. As to that, my initial instinct is to be soothing and not alarmist. Let's think about it for an hour or two. Meanwhile, could you find out if there are any signs of unusual enemy radio activity which might indicate his genuine concern? And you had better call in Masterman of the Twenty Committee, without yet telling him why.'

There was just one scrap of relevant information available when they met again after lunch. Something from Naval Intelligence, via the 'Y' radio monitoring service, suggested the U-boats were chattering slightly less than usual, though still using the four-rotor naval Enigma, which most profitably had at last been cracked in December 1942, courtesy of Turing's brilliant work.

The draft message to the Prime Minister (then attending the summit meeting with President Roosevelt in Casablanca) describing the German initiative and the counter-action proposed, in essence summarised C's plan without going into detail or mentioning Garbo. In effect, he aimed to discover the underlying intention of the hunt for Turing and Jones, in conjunction with an investigation to see if any internal leak had occurred and how it had come about. 'No doubt you will be informing the President and Chiefs of Staff,' it added. 'In which case it is desirable to state that these are early days and there is no known connection with related operations of theirs', by which he meant the American Magic operation which, since before Pearl Harbor in December 1941, had deeply penetrated the Japanese codes.

Radioed by unbreakable one-time-pad (OTP) or Typex codes, as was the practice with all Ultra-related signals, the message, according to drill, was instantly destroyed once read. The reply was not long delayed and typical of Churchill in its thoughtfulness. 'Approve your plan. President and Cs-of-S told. Spare no efforts and keep me closely informed. See that everything possible is done to ensure the safety and well-being of those two excellent young scientists to whom we owe so much.'

To be fair, Menzies had given thought, admittedly from a purely military angle, to the personal safety of Jones and Turing — and maybe even to the unlikely possibility of their complicity in what had happened. But he had forgotten that Churchill knew both men and, like the entire nation, owed them much. For it had been Jones who, for twenty minutes on 21 June 1940, had briefed a Cabinet meeting about the function and grave threat posed by German radio beam bombing aids, and a day later had threatened to report direct to the PM if the latter's order for a trial flight to locate the beams was cancelled. The beams had then been detected that very night. Jones had since been a member of the SIS and was now an Assistant Director of Intelligence (Science) in the Air Ministry and therefore well known to Menzies who also knew of Jones's continuing contacts with Bletchley Park.[6]

As for Turing, Churchill had met him and had been much impressed by his grasp during a visit to Bletchley in August 1941. And on 22 October Churchill had received (over C's head) a 'For Prime Minister only' letter from Turing and three vital colleagues. They had pleaded for his personal intervention in overcoming the rigid bureaucracy which was denying them much-needed materials, preventing recruitment of various support personnel for Bletchley and threatening the removal by call-up for military service of various skilled operatives. Churchill had responded instantly with one of his 'Action this Day' memos that overcame the difficulties within three weeks.[7]

MI5 had the unenviable task of investigating possible sources of the alleged leakage. Long before present-day positive vetting procedures, this was a fairly hit-and-miss business which yielded little of value. The prime suspects, whose patriotism was beyond doubt, were easily eliminated. The only common denominators connecting Jones and Turing were mathematics, electro-magnetism and their working together at Bletchley early in the war. In any case, Jones had nothing to do with cryptography, though he was a major customer of Bletchley's services. There was the known Oxbridge connection, of course, which the Abwehr's letter to Garbo had suggested might be a starting point for his investigations; but nothing to suggest a universities link except through Professor Lindemann. Circumspectly MI5 decided not to bother a close friend and colleague of the Prime Minister!

As for Bletchley Park itself and the thousands working there, that was another matter. The spacious grounds and various huts were virtually impossible to make intruder-proof. Such guards as there were acted mainly as a deterrent. Furthermore, most of the staff, including the key cryptanalysts, were billeted in the surrounding countryside and therefore free to come and go almost as they chose, subject to keeping their counsel in public and not attracting attention.

Anonymity and unobtrusiveness were, indeed, Bletchley's best safeguards. That was one reason for locating all the 'Y' Service monitoring stations with their aerial arrays at a distance and having the products of their non-stop eavesdropping on the enemy's radio nets brought in by teleprinters, couriers and despatch riders. Moreover, another concealment gradually created as the war progressed, was the arrival locally of many American organisations which occupied nearby residences and thus helped distract attention from Bletchley Park. Nevertheless, MI5 did what it could by observation and vigilance to detect intruders, especially in the vicinity of the wooden huts and buildings that had been built on the lawns and which housed the crucial decoding machines of ever greater sophistication.

A study of past scares about possible leakages due to the misuse of Ultra and its output showed that this was the most alarming threat. From the start in 1940 decrypts of German signals had been monitored for signs of the compromising of Ultra or of enemy insight into Allied codes. It was during the earlier stages, when unpractised users were learning from experience, that the dangers of compromise were highest.

And then that Allied Sigint sometimes detected evidence of enemy success in reading the high-grade ciphers — without knowing if the enemy had drawn the right conclusions.

Fundamentally there were the dangers, notably at sea where the Navy managed without secure Typex machines, of reactions which could only have come about due to information obtained through disclosure via Enigma decrypts, or due to revelations from insecure means of transmitting verbatim or unscrambled ex-Enigma messages. The investigators were aware of the disastrous fate of 15 German supply ships that

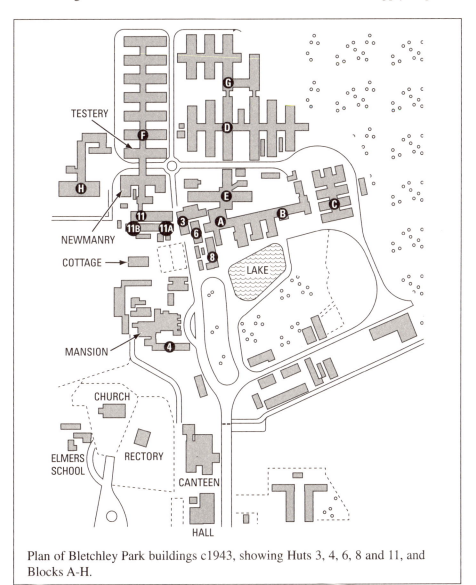

Plan of Bletchley Park buildings c1943, showing Huts 3, 4, 6, 8 and 11, and Blocks A-H.

were intercepted and sunk between 7 May and 11 July 1941. Of these, eight could have been disclosed only through Enigma and two had been attacked despite an Admiralty attempt to reduce suspicion by letting them escape. Then there was the error of repeating the position of three U-boats reported in a relayed Ultra signal and a signal sent to a submarine from Malta, exactly copying a GC&CS decrypt, giving precise information of Italian convoy sailings. Similar slips would occasionally happen and incur very strong official rebukes.

At the same time, there was the struggle to deter the Prime Minister's indiscretions when he was tempted to break the rules as it suited him. For example, he complained in April 1941 when GC&CS paraphrases seemed to him to lack the full flavour of indications that Hitler was taking a personal interest in Rommel's attack on Tobruk. Churchill needed guidance to save him killing his golden geese. On the one hand, as in the Stalingrad incident previously mentioned, he could demand dangerously excessive disclosure, and on the other call for an investigation and hand down a tough rebuke to General Montgomery when, in September 1942, it appeared from decrypts of German signals that the enemy knew of British awareness of Rommel's forthcoming unsuccessful offensive at Alam Halfa.

Of most recent concern was the lapse concerning the Naval Officer in Command (NOIC) at Bône in Algeria who, on 11 December 1942, using a suspect code, delayed a convoy and gave indications that an E-boat attack was expected. To begin with, the NOIC was not an authorised Ultra user and to make matters far worse, ' . . . the cipher used by the NOIC was being read by the enemy: the enemy cancelled the E-boat attack and it was an Enigma decrypt ordering the cancellation which brought the incident to Whitehall notice.' Very recently and also alarmingly careless, C's investigators noticed how the captain of the 10th Submarine Flotilla at Malta had signalled information about a convoy sailing that was subsequently cancelled. For this the captain concerned received a severe reprimand from the First Sea Lord.[8]

It was incidents such as these which suggested to the investigators and to C good reasons why the enemy had become so suspicious. And therefore why Masterman, chairman of the Double Cross, XX or Twenty Committee, should be called in to consider the risks of compromising the double agents under his control. The matter was rated that serious.

DEVIATIONS FROM HISTORY

[D1] This is the first fundamental British deviation from history in response to the notional German initiative.

Confirmatory footnotes:

1 Hinsley Vol 2 p 62.
2 Hinsley Vol 3, Pt 2 pp 954, 955.
3 Lewin *Ultra Goes to War* p 57.
4 Hinsley Vol 3 Pt 2 p 956 and Hodges pp 138–40 and pp 155–8.
5 Hinsley Vol 3 Pt 2 pp 954, 955.
6 Jones pp 101, 102 .
7 Hinsley Vol 2 pp 655–7.
8 *ibid* pp 643-647.

4.
Garbo

C had good reason to think very hard indeed about employing Garbo, one of his prime double agent assets, to deal with the Abwehr letter. For if Ultra was the most prolific of golden geese for obtaining vital and prolific intelligence in the struggle for victory, the flock of double agents under British control could reasonably enough be rated silver swans in mounting crucial attempts to 'mislead the enemy on a big scale at the appropriate moment' — meaning in most people's minds the invasion of Europe.[1]

Since 1938, when, according to Hinsley, the Foreign Office had at last awakened to the vital need to expand the SIS greatly from its derisory headquarter's strength of 30 people, among the tasks for C and his predecessor was dealing with the large and potentially extremely dangerous number of hostile activists at large in Britain, each of whom could side with Nazi Germany and its Abwehr. Fascist Italians of the Axis partnership were obvious targets, as were neo-Nazi groups with freedom to operate aggressively alongside the British Union of Fascists (BUF), which at one time was 50,000 strong. Fewer in number, but liable to collaborate with others of left-wing leanings (especially after August 1939 when Germany and Russia signed their fatal pact) was the expanding Communist Party of Great Britain (CPGB) supported by Russia. Then there was the IRA which opened a bombing campaign in England in January 1939 and was being wooed by the Abwehr. Finally there were some 70,000 Germans in the country, although many of these were refugees from Nazi oppression and likely to be anything but hostile.

In the event, within a short time of war breaking out, the SIS, MI5 and Scotland Yard Special Branch had reason to be modestly satisfied with their grasp of the subversives situation, above all with having immediately interned four of the six inept Abwehr agents then circulating, and picking up a fifth in December 1939. They had been especially happy to receive into voluntary custody on 4 September a spy code-named by them as Snow.

Snow was a Welshman whom the Abwehr had made their chief agent in England, but who had been working with the SIS and Special Branch since 1936. Most loyally during the so-called Phoney War, as the first of many double agents, he continued, under MI5 control, to travel abroad to maintain his German contacts, while sedulously delivering up several Abwehr agents to MI5. Subsequently many more would be pointed out by other MI5 contacts and dealt with in various ways. The point is that MI5 had achieved virtual control of all subversive organisations and people in the aftermath of the defeat of Norway, Holland, Belgium and France in June 1940, and in the process had created a cadre of double agents whose presence and status obviously demanded exploitation and a regulating organisation.

September 1940, on the eve of the intended invasion of Britain, was indeed a crunch month. It began with the landing on the south coast of four rather naive Abwehr agents, equipped with radios. Each of these was captured immediately; three were subsequently executed and the fourth interned. The fate of a fifth agent, parachuted in on the 6th and also swiftly captured, was kinder, however. In return for his life, he agreed to become double agent Summer and as such operated until January 1941, when, after escaping from his lodgings and prompting a vast man-hunt, he was captured before trying to reach Holland, where he would have blown Snow, among others.[2]

Initial discussions led to the formation in October 1940 of Masterman's Twenty (XX) Committee, to be composed of representatives of the SIS, the Navy, Army and RAF Intelligence Directorates, GHQ Home Forces, the Home Defence Executive and MI5. Its objectives, as laid down by MI5 at the first meeting, were principally defensive: to retain the enemy's confidence in the double agents; control them sufficiently to deter the sending of any more; and, in due course, mislead the enemy on a big scale. In the months to come the policy governing the aims and functions of double agents evolved slowly and, at times, painfully. Interdepartmental disagreements were sometimes acrimonious. Yet, come the end of 1942, the *modus operandi* adopted had moved steadily, in company with the improving strategic situation, towards increasingly aggressive methods — and to no small extent this was due to the contribution of Garbo, a disillusioned Spaniard called Juan Pujol.

Garbo became a British double agent via the Abwehr, which he joined in Madrid in February 1941 on the pretext of going to England. Instead, after they had code-named him Arabel, trained and equipped him, he went to Lisbon in July where he stayed, composing for the Abwehr highly imaginative and lively messages as if he were living in England. Not until January 1942, after trying four times in good faith to join the British and being rebuffed, he at last came, as a consequence of his reports 'of superb inaccuracy', to the notice of the SIS and, a month later, MI5. Brought to England in April, his fantastic competence, flair and unique accord with the Abwehr was a source of wonder to C, Masterman and the entire Twenty Committee, to the extent that, in order to make full use of his genius and initiative, it was deemed essential to change the Committee's terms of reference.

Teamed with Thomas Harris as a sort of assistant and minder, this pair set about creating, ironically to the great satisfaction of both Canaris and Menzies, a ring of 14 notional agents and 11 informers, spread about the United Kingdom in London, Glasgow, Harwich, Methil, Dover, Brighton, Exeter and Swansea. All were approved and funded by the Abwehr which eventually, in 1944, awarded Garbo the Iron Cross. Guided by the Twenty Committee and using their imaginations to the full, Garbo and Harris employed their notional network to send accurate as well as deceitful information, not only to fool the Germans about events in the UK (such as the movements of Torch convoys already mentioned in Chapter 1, with a deliberately delayed letter) but also to extract details of newly arrived agents ready for the catching.[3]

But when C and Masterman sat down to consider how Garbo might perform as a 'private investigator' of two real celebrities working in the highest and most sensitive reaches of the intelligence and security sector, the perils of a unique situation, including the dangers of initiating another departmental row, were forbidding even to them.

'Let us be clear about one thing,' stated C. 'Until proven beyond a shadow of doubt, we do not admit to the Germans having broken Ultra. This whole business might yet be a try-on, a trap.'

'And one which could also blow Garbo and perhaps my whole Double Cross set-up,' concurred Masterman.

'So we must not give the Germans a hint that we are aware of their discovery?'

'Ye-es. Assuming, that is, that you place Ultra, even if it *is* blown, above Garbo and the others in order of priority? After all, the double agents could become a more valuable intelligence and deception asset if we were no longer able to rely on what comes out of the Bombes.'

'Or if the Germans cease using Enigma. Have you thought of that? No, I aim to hang on and procrastinate as if nothing has happened for as long as possible. And that is why I want your Garbo chap to keep the Abwehr in play without blowing the gaff.'

'Well, I suppose that is feasible,' conceded Masterman. 'We can spin things out in all sorts of ways. Put yourself in the place of making enquiries about anybody these days? Before you know where you are somebody will get suspicious and report you as a Fifth Columnist. Oh, I can visualise all sorts of fun and games when Garbo's investigators run into common or garden busybodies! Come to think of it, I wonder how real private detectives fare these days when nosing into connubial infidelities?'

'Don't ask me', said C with a prim grin. 'Anyway in time of war such people would be better employed working for the National Effort!'

'Nevertheless, I think it might be worth taking advice from that kind,' said Masterman making a note on his pad. 'I take it Jones and Turing are men of incorruptible moral character?'

'Well, Jones undoubtedly is. Happily married and recently a proud father. But Turing . . . ? Well, I know him, too, of course. Rather an eccentric type, and not one for the girls either, so I'm told. Although they certainly like and admire him.'

'In any case, there seems nothing to be gained dragging them into our game. Quite the opposite if it distracts them from their tasks. It will make my job a lot easier to keep them in ignorance. So, what I have in mind is building up convincing life-like personalities and occupations, as we do with our notional agents, but based in these two cases on their known characteristics and likely employment.

'That sounds about right to me,' agreed C. 'You'll have to find them appropriate employment, of course. You must keep at a distance from Bletchley and their real work. You should not have much difficulty losing them in London or somewhere in the industrial north. But I'd also keep 'em at a distance from the universities and the academics. You know how they all know each other and how they gossip. Meanwhile I think I'll arrange for an unobtrusive watch to be kept — just for safety's sake.'[D1]

DEVIATIONS FROM HISTORY

[D1] Needless to say, this was one operation in which neither Garbo nor any other double agent took part.

Confirmatory footnotes:
1 Hinsley/Simkins Vol 4 pp 41—4.
2 *ibid* pp 91, 96, 97, 102.
3 *ibid* pp 112—17.

5.
Diatribe and Dissent

For Captain Alexander Stahlberg, 6 February 1943 was a day to remember vividly. This was the moment when, for the first time, Germany's parlous state was revealed to him in much of its stark reality.

Since November 1942 he had been Field Marshal Erich von Manstein's ADC and since then he had been the field marshal's shadow, constantly in his company and in duty bound invariably monitoring his telephone calls and office conversations. He had therefore been privy to all Manstein's operational decisions as C-in-C Army Group Don both in the abortive attempt in December to relieve General Friedrich Paulus's surrounded Sixth Army in Stalingrad and in the January withdrawal when the Army Group was itself in danger of envelopment. With admiration he had witnessed at first hand the finesse of the commander many German officers rated the Army's finest strategist.

The job of ADC had come Stahlberg's way after his predecessor had been killed. It was at the recommendation of his cousin, Lt-Col Henning von Tresckow, who had been on Manstein's staff — and was done with a purpose transcending military duty. When Stahlberg asked Tresckow why he had recommended him for the job, the reply had been evasive, 'Because you are not scared of big game'. Assuredly the well-connected Stahlberg was accustomed to rubbing shoulders with the great. In 1933 he had been on the staff of Vice-Chancellor Franz von Papen and, on the eve of Hitler's becoming Chancellor, had taken the man he regarded as 'a poser' to Papen's study. That was when, surprised at the weight of Hitler's raincoat, a search of its pockets uncovered two Walther pistols.[1]

At times during the meeting, Tresckow had been enigmatic, especially when pointedly warning Stahlberg that Frau von Manstein was a committed member of the Nazi Party, and also when giving instructions to memorise two names without writing them down. The first was General Erich Fellgiebel, whose fine reputation Stahlberg was well aware of, the other a Major Claus Graf von Stauffenberg, whose name meant nothing. In the event of either of these officers visiting Manstein they were to be 'reliably protected', said Tresckow — meaning they were not to be overheard by anybody other than Stahlberg.[2]

Not until 26 January 1943 did either of these designated officers approach Manstein, but Stahlberg registered a significance in the brevity of Fellgiebel's 10-minute meeting with the field marshal shortly prior to Stauffenberg's arrival. As Stahlberg was to learn, Manstein and Fellgiebel were very old friends and comrades who addressed each other intimately as *Du*. As instructed, Stahlberg arranged for both meetings to be private. Through a half-open door he alone could see and partially overhear what was said. Of Fellgiebel's conversation he heard nothing, but much of Stauffenberg's long talk with

35

Manstein was audible. It covered the current adverse military situation and then moved on to extremely shaky ground, concluding loudly and passionately in a disagreement connected with Stauffenberg's oblique suggestion that the time had come to end the war by the creation of a *fait accompli*. This plainly was abhorrent to the field marshal who, on a later occasion when invited to join the conspiracy to remove Hitler, made the emphatic remark, 'Prussian field marshals do not mutiny.'[3]

On 30 January Paulus had been promoted field marshal by Hitler along with instructions, as befitted a defeated German field marshal, to commit suicide before Stalingrad fell. To the Führer's disgust, Paulus had declined the ultimate honour and, as would soon become known, had chosen to emulate German generals of the past who had defected to the Russians. Moreover, in the months ahead, he would become an active member of a Federation of German Officers, formed by Sixth Army officers as an off-shoot of the anti-Nazi, Russian-inspired National Committee of Free Germany.

The last Germans at Stalingrad surrendered on 1 February. Five days later Manstein was bidden to Rastenburg for a conference with Hitler and General Kurt Zeitzler, the Army Chief of Staff, in the Wolf's Lair (*Wolfschanze*). Cunningly, to disarm Manstein, Hitler opened the meeting with a frank admission of his responsibility for the Stalingrad disaster — though taking the opportunity also to blame Göring. 'It was,' recorded Stahlberg, 'the politician speaking'.

Zeitzler outlined the current situation, showing how Manstein's Army Group Don was in dire peril from Russians advancing in mass towards Kharkov. Manstein gave his appreciation of the situation in military jargon which Hitler 'simply did not understand,' recalled Stahlberg. 'I still have a clear picture in my mind of Hitler's uncomprehending face when Manstein had the floor . . . Manstein's manner was amazingly carefree, almost as if he were facing a seminar of young trainee General Staff Officers . . . the atmosphere was frosty. Hitler seemed suspicious, or at least I observed in his face something that I was often to see at later briefing sessions: with his eyes still stubbornly fixed on the situation map.'

Suddenly Manstein, who had failed to turn the debate to the long-term strategic future, sprang his big surprise. He addressed the explosive question of lack of unified command and the need to abolish 'the dualism created by Hitler between OKW [Armed Forces High Command] and OKH [Army High Command].' Such as, for example, the OKW-run theatre of war in Tunisia and the OKH theatre of the Eastern Front, which created similar problems to those afflicting Fellgiebel's fragmented OKW Signals organisations.

'With Hitler, however, the subject fell on deaf ears. He did not contradict, he simply behaved as if he had not heard the question . . . it simply seemed to me that Manstein was dismissed with distinct coolness and reserve.'[4]

Afterwards at the well-appointed OKH guesthouse on the Mauersee, a small group of old comrades from Reichswehr days, including Zeitzler, a senior staff officer of his, Colonel Adolf Heusinger, Manstein and Fellgiebel, sat in comfortable armchairs taking a snack and drinking burgundy, plentifully served by old soldiers, and smoking cigars. The subject of Admiral Raeder's replacement as Navy C-in-C by the Hitler-admiring and intensely ambitious Admiral Dönitz may well have been touched upon.

But centre stage was seized by Fellgiebel as the wine quickly worked on him and he 'simply went for his old friend Manstein as if there was no cause for restraint.'

Making no secret of his contempt for Hitler, Fellgiebel challenged Manstein on almost every issue from the overall military situation and adverse strategic balance through the current state of the economy and production to revelation of the most appalling administration of internal affairs. Again and again he exposed the field marshal's ignorance and misconceptions of vital matters. At first Manstein attempted to restrain his old friend, but to no avail as Fellgiebel grew more excited. Stahlberg and the others listened in trepidation. What were the servants thinking — or reporting?

'Suddenly Fellgiebel got up and headed for the door to the passage. It had scarcely closed behind him before we heard loud imprecations from the corridor. I jumped up and ran after him. As I opened the door I saw him disappearing into the lavatory, but inside the large tiled room his anger swelled. I can still hear his furious outburst today, "That liar! That swine! That destroyer of our Fatherland! That murderer! That scoundrel! . . ."'

'I jumped at him from behind and, as I held his mouth closed with both hands and all my strength, I could feel him weeping uncontrollably.'

Gradually the tension left his body and he became quite calm. He apologised and thanked me, "Ah, Stahlberg, if you only knew what we signals officers hear you would not believe me. It is ghastly!"

When they returned to the sitting room the others had gone to bed, but as of that moment Stahlberg was unwittingly caught in the conspiracy against Hitler, and not just because, 'I felt very close to Fellgiebel from that day.'

Two days later Hitler held another momentous meeting, this time with his new C-in-C Navy, Admiral Dönitz. Present were Vice-Admiral Kranke and Albert Speer, Minister for Armaments and Munitions. Top of the agenda was a disappointing report of the submarine campaign in which Dönitz explained why it was that, with a record number of U-boats at sea, only 15 enemy ships had been sunk in January.

'Of course bad weather had much to do with it, Führer. Although the worrying fact is that the enemy's convoys are evading our groups and, so far as we can understand, the reasons for this derive from three sources — treason, undetected reconnaissance planes locating the formations and the breaking of our codes. So far as treason is concerned, all necessary steps are being taken. Reconnaissance aircraft are hard to deal with, especially because the Luftwaffe, most regrettably, has no aircraft suitable for interception over the Atlantic and, unlike the enemy, we have no aircraft carriers. Indeed, I have to say, as I have before, that the complete lack of any type of air support, especially reconnaissance, is the weakest point of our conduct of the war at sea.'

'Now, as for the Enigma codes, our experts advise they are unbreakable. I certainly hope so because we will be in serious trouble if they are being broken. But I have reservations and have agreed to collaborate with General Fellgiebel in OKW's attempt to trick the enemy into disclosing if he actually has broken Enigma. That trial is in progress now and, as you probably know, the Army and the Luftwaffe are also participating.'

The minutes of the meeting go on to record concurrence with Admiral Raeder's plan to decommission the three surviving battleships and four cruisers. The Führer expressed his complete and definite approval to employ the big surface vessels offensively if a worthwhile target appeared. There is no record of any comment by him on the subject of codes or if he had heard of the Fellgiebel trial — or even if he appreciated the vital importance of signal security to naval forces.[D1/5]

The questions of treason and treachery, associated with a creeping paranoia and loss of confidence in Hitler in the aftermath of Stalingrad, were present in people's minds. Reports were mounting of lowered morale and war weariness — and even dissent. The possibility of losing the war was mooted as Russian radio propaganda reached into homes, giving the names and addresses of the dead and prisoners among the 200,000 casualties of Sixth Army. At the same time realisation of the mass transportation of Jews to the death camps could not wholly be concealed. One source of leakage, needless to say, were Fellgiebel's telephone exchanges whose inquisitive operators habitually listened into the conversations of top Nazi Party and military leaders after making connections.

Traditionally the universities were clearing houses for anti-Nazi Party news and informed opinion, exacerbated to some extent on this occasion because many of the students were embittered ex-servicemen who had been incapacitated by war wounds. The University of Munich was the distribution centre for anti-Hitler Youth pamphlets called 'White Rose Letters' and in contact with the Berlin conspirators. Inevitably copies of these reached the Party faithful, prompting the Gauleiter of Bavaria to harangue the student body on 16 February on the subject of their national and patriotic duty.

As the worst kind of crude Nazi, with a caustic tongue, Paul Giesler let himself go. Threatening to return crippled male students to the front, he reserved masochistic vulgarity for the girls. 'They have healthy bodies, let them bear children . . . There is no reason why every girl student should not for each of her years at the University present an annual testimonial of a son. I realise that a certain amount of co-operation is required and if some of the girls lack sufficient charm to find a mate, I will assign to each of them one of my adjutants, whose antecedents I can vouch for, and I can promise her a thoroughly enjoyable experience.'

Spontaneously enraged, the students shouted him down and poured into the streets where they protested in a way never before seen in Nazi Germany. There were demonstrations and serious acts of sabotage in the Munich marshalling yards, the telephone exchange (out of action for three days) and the radio station which, probably in order to prevent spread of the dissident virus, was off the air for a week. A state of emergency was declared in the city. But news got out and triggered demonstrations in Vienna, Mannheim, Stuttgart, Frankfurt and the Ruhr where, it is said, the SS fired on the crowds.

Leaders now appeared, chief among them Professor Kurt Huber, Hans and Sophie Scholl and four other students who distributed leaflets in Munich University calling for people to 'Resign from the Party Organisations' and to 'Fight the Party', and declaiming, 'The dead of Stalingrad are calling you. The German name is dishonoured for all time if German youth does not rise now to take its revenge.'

This could not go on. Clamping down hard, Giesler arrested the Scholls who were beaten up under interrogation, Sophie suffering a broken leg. Tried by a special People's Court and ferociously treated by judge Roland Freisler, of awful reputation, Sophie replied to his browbeating with undaunted courage. 'You know as well as we do that the war is lost. Why are you so cowardly that you won't admit to it?'

The Scholls were found guilty and condemned to death on 18 April and hanged on the 22nd, as later were Huber and the other four. On the 22nd on the wall of many Munich houses were painted the words *Ihr Geist lebt weiter* — Their spirit lives on. These brave, if ill-advised, martyrs went to their doom unsupported by the other groups of conspirators. For the latter, as will be seen, had insurmountable difficulties of their own.[6]

DEVIATIONS FROM HISTORY
[D1] There was no mention of suspect codes or of the Fellgiebel trial.

Confirmatory footnotes:
1 Stahlberg pp 15, 16.
2 *ibid* pp 203, 204.
3 *ibid* pp 240–6.
4 *ibid* pp 251–5.
5 Anon *Fuh* pp 308–10.
6 Wheeler-Bennett pp 540, 541 and footnotes which provide numerous references about this almost forgotten incident.

6.
The Trials

The Fellgiebel Enigma committee next met on 22 February, a few days earlier than had been anticipated in January. Those present were as before, with one significant substitution. Canaris sent in his place his deputy, Major-General Hans Oster, an officer he rated a man of action, albeit hot-headed, many of whose activities he preferred to distance himself from.[D1]

Fellgiebel opened the meeting in up-beat mood with a resume of Manstein's on-going counter-stroke south of Kharkov that was overrunning the Russian spearheads before they reached the River Dnieper, and the encouraging increase in sinkings in the Atlantic, compared with January's poor figures. Next, Praun reported on the Army's efforts on the Enigma tests. These chiefly consisted of attempts to dupe the enemy into attacking pseudo targets in the Mediterranean, mainly in Tunisia.

'As you can see from my report, Russia was given consideration but produced nothing of significance, seemingly confirming our belief that the Western Allies are being sparing in the supply of intelligence to their communist friends. The offerings of promising targets for raiding in France provoked zero response. Maybe they lacked sufficient temptation.'[1]

'Tunisia, where the initiative rests with us as a result of General von Arnim's minor offensive operations in the north and, latterly, with Field Marshal Rommel's strong thrust to smash the Americans at the Kasserine Pass, offered opportunities to draw a sensitive enemy,' continued Praun. 'Of course it was only prudent to select targets of sufficient importance to justify use of Enigma. The enemy must know that we use lower grade codes for tactical events. For us suddenly to depart from that mode would only make him highly suspicious. So therefore we concentrated on transmitting messages of a strategic nature. Some concerned the building of spurious logistic and field maintenance facilities related either to actual or notional thrusts. For example, one of them disclosed the location of Rommel's headquarters in such a place as to indicate an imaginary thrust line. Another ordered a bogus raid against the enemy's lines of communication in the north.'

'I have to admit that only the pseudo logistic targets provoked any recognisable reaction of the sort which could have been prompted by anything other than knowledge of Enigma messages. In one case a notional dump was bombed with commendable alacrity by the Americans — to the delight of our observers until they too were strafed! In another, enemy patrols diligently scoured a range of hills in the hunt for a non-existent maintenance area, which, in fact, at one time had been a French Army training area. Hardly conclusive, gentlemen, but evidence of a sort, I think you will agree.'

'I have more to offer than that,' said General Martini. 'We in the Luftwaffe make much more extensive use of Enigma than our comrades in the Army, as you know. In consequence we had a wider field in which to experiment with a variety of activities. In summary, and rather like the Army, we achieved the most interesting results in North Africa. Orders for spurious sorties by transport aircraft from Sicily to Tunisia, which actually were started and then cancelled or changed at the last moment, drew signs of counter-action. The same applied to attacks against shipping off Algiers, except that on one occasion, so deluded was the enemy, we actually put in an improvised strike that sank a ship. Logistic targets certainly proved productive. On one occasion the enemy bombed a dummy fuel dump where we simulated a few fires. And twice we provoked him, so far as we can tell, into hastily reinforcing notional targets with anti-aircraft guns.'

'Surely you had some difficulty observing results?' queried Praun.

'Yes, we did. There was an occasion when our spotting aircraft seems to have attracted undue and nearly fatal attention. But in other operations it was our radar which provided the best evidence of enemy sorties. Which leads me to our attempts against England. Here, as over Tunisia, we successfully monitored enemy reactions to Enigma orders by radar in connection with low-level sorties which, at the last moment, were changed or cancelled. More than once we listened to RAF pilots asking plaintively where our machines were, even though they had not taken off.'

'So, Martini, you conclude that the enemy did read — and read with remarkable speed — our Enigma transmissions?' asked Fellgiebel.

'Yes, against all my instincts and with obvious reservations concerning the impossibility of guaranteed verifications, General Jeschonnek and I have drawn that conclusion.'

When Stummel spoke, the others already were aware of Dönitz's profound concern about radio security in the past, recently amplified by the results obtained from the naval aspects of the trial. 'Frankly,' he began, 'the C-in-C was already extremely suspicious. Let me remind you of events that had gone before: the Jan Mayen incident mentioned by General Fellgiebel at our previous meeting. Then that strange business the Admiral well remembers from 28 September 1941 when a submarine attacked *U67* and *U111* in the Bay of Tarafal in Cape Verde Islands. His diary states, "Either our ciphers have been compromised or it is a case of leakage. A British submarine does not appear by chance in such a remote part of the ocean." As a result we tried to reduce the quite ridiculous number of people with access to Enigma in depots, dockyards and research places, as well as surface vessels, and a few months later introduced into service the superior four-wheel Triton Enigma.'

'Yet since then have ensued the quite remarkable, and decisive, enemy successes against our tankers sailing to Cyrenaica last September and October; our failure to intercept the Torch convoys; the almost total evasion by enemy convoys of our Atlantic U-boat groups in January; and the *Kalvi/U459* incident at the end of January. The cumulative effects of these major adverse events cannot be overlooked. The law of averages cannot be ignored, gentlemen.'

Fellgiebel nodded. 'And the trial?'

'We followed the same principle of realism as the Army and Luftwaffe. For the

Channel and North Sea we transmitted Enigma messages ordering spurious E-boat attacks, and observed clear indications on radar and by air reconnaissance of related enemy actions which may or may not have been coincidental.'

'Farther afield we broadcast messages to raiders, but unfortunately nothing came of that. We would have liked to have tried something with blockade runners, but for the moment everything is on hold with them.'[2]

'It was to the Atlantic that we paid most attention and where we were best placed to attempt elaborate, observed diversions of enemy convoys. We took the opportunity, coincidental with the sailing of two boats in company, to have them locate and report a convoy's heading and then remain in touch without molesting it. The captains had written instructions to simulate, in conjunction with our headquarters, a typical assembling of two U-boat groups ahead of the convoy. Which they managed to do twice, resulting on each occasion in a major diversion of the convoy away from our boats and, fortuitously as it happened, in the direction of another of our groups. Finally an attack was launched for the sake of realism and one of the boats abandoned the hunt.

'Gentlemen, the timing of the diversions left us in no doubt that the enemy was reading our Enigma. As did subsequent evidence when the remaining boat reported substantial reinforcement of the convoy from afar. I should add that both captains took considerable risks in so effectively carrying out this subterfuge.'

Fellgiebel intervened. 'Can we be sure that the enemy was not made aware of the meaning of those manoeuvres?'

'Yes. Discreet code words only were used to report anticipated events or give foreseeable orders.'

'So there it is,' said Fellgiebel with a sigh. 'To my mind there is sufficient evidence to show that somehow or other the enemy has broken the unbreakable.'

Nobody dissented. All nodded, including Oster who looked less glum than the rest.

'The question now is what action needs to be taken? How do we proceed? Do we abandon Enigma altogether? Or double-encode messages — which will take time to implement? Or do we, in order not to alert the enemy to our insight, continue as we are and use this flawed medium to distract the enemy with false information on Enigma, while sending vital information by other more secure means?'

The ensuing debate naturally reflected acute self-interest. On behalf of the Luftwaffe, Martini held out for the status quo on grounds of the disruptive effect the abandonment of Enigma would have on current operating procedures and the overall flexibility and mobility of air power. He did concede, however, the detrimental effect this would have on the other services and suggested a radical minimising of radio for strategic and administrative purposes — provided OKW (meaning Fellgiebel) could rapidly reinforce land-line links to Luftwaffe facilities.

Stummel, not surprisingly, was adamant that Enigma must be banned in relation to all maritime operations (including those of the Luftwaffe) until it could be made more secure or replaced by something better. Lacking those facilities, the strategic/tactical control of individual U-boats, as well as groups, would be so seriously limited as to induce collapse of the system and loss of the Battle of the Atlantic.

'And therefore,' he added grimly, 'loss of the war, since in those circumstances the Americans will be free to pour men and material into Britain in overwhelming quantities. Even as it is, we must now carry out a crash programme to re-indoctrinate captains and staff with tactics that cope with the new situation,' he announced. 'That means bringing home many boats earlier than anticipated and therefore temporarily reducing our scale of effort at the very moment when we seem to have established a significant advantage in numbers and techniques over the enemy.'

By far the best balanced opinion was contributed by Praun, whose views, as usual, reflected those of his old friend and comrade Fellgiebel. Reminding the conference that the Army could manage quite well in a strategic sense without Enigma-guarded radio messages, he pointed out that more stringent control of priorities would reduce the volume of high security traffic. 'From a recent check I can quote an enormous number of over-graded messages which might just as well have been sent by courier or by land-line teleprinter. And need I add that we increasingly have the Lorenz and Siemens *Geheimschreiber* (Secret Writer) coming into service down to army group level, including a link to von Arnim at Tunis?'

From the expression on his face it seemed that Oster was the only person present in ignorance of Secret Writer. Fellgiebel smiled indulgently. 'It is a radio or line appliance, Hans. I'll tell you about it later. But it could be that, unlike Enigma, this system has not been broken since it employs a different technology and probably would be even more difficult to break even if the enemy is aware of its existence.'[3]

'Which we must assume he is,' said Praun. 'But a word of caution. Unlike the Enigma machine, Secret Writer is bulky and not all that technically reliable. We should not depend on it absolutely nor, from a security point of view, deploy it below corps level — preferably it should be at army group level.'[4]

Now spoke Fellgiebel. 'Unsurprisingly, I consider it apparent that there is no simple, overriding solution to our respective dilemmas. There will have to be give and take. I have to say, however, that the Navy's case is so strong as to make it impossible to carry on as if nothing has happened. Measures are needed which inevitably will signal to the enemy that we are aware of his astonishing achievement. It would help if we knew how he does it — although there can be little doubt that if this man Turing is involved — and we still have not traced him — some sort of thinking, analytical machine is at work.'

They waited respectfully while he peered dramatically at them through his spectacles. 'But there is one crucial aspect you have not considered — and I say this in the realisation that our recommendations will have to be put before the Führer at the earliest possible moment. Gentlemen, so far we have been departmentally inward looking. We have not addressed the matter of the highest and most sensitive communications generated by the diplomats and — let's face it — by the Führer himself, and his ministers and all the top commanders, discussing and disclosing to the enemy matters of the greatest and most sensitive importance. I am appalled and believe you will agree that this cannot go on.'

Hastily Stummel intervened. 'You do realise that C-in-C Navy has a meeting scheduled with the Führer in four days' time? Is that not the moment to present the proposals we agree to-day?' And, he might have added, when the Navy had both a rank and numerical advantage in council.

'I am aware of that meeting and have already sounded out General Jodl [Hitler's Chief of Operations at OKW], saying this might be our wish. No doubt all services will be represented at the appropriate level. So I now propose that the Führer should be requested to authorise a radical curtailment of Enigma until methods to solve the present difficulties can be evolved. This will call for intense research besides reorganisation of communication methods and growth of several facilities. I foresee extensions to the huge expansion of the land-line facilities we already have made in the conquered territories, with some priority to the Luftwaffe. We must improve and raise production of Secret Writer — while maintaining a close watch for any indications that the enemy has broken into that as well.'

There was a nodding of approval round the table. For once, thought Fellgiebel and Praun in unison, a matter is sufficiently serious to forestall the usual bickering. Praun it was who seized a heaven-sent opportunity.

'It seems to me that this is the moment when closer co-ordination of all signals users is highly desirable — indeed essential. Is not this the moment for a central tri-service committee to be formed here at OKW under General Fellgiebel's chairmanship? It might monitor technical progress, keep an eye on hold-ups and lead to a better pooling of resources and ideas than at present is the case.'

Everybody recognised the meaning of that suggestion. Always, Praun had been an enthusiast for centralisation and sharing of intelligence — and habitually the heads of services, made jealous of each other by Hitler's deliberate tricks of divide and rule, had avoided whole-hearted collaboration. Nobody now objected and it was left to Fellgiebel to close the meeting with the remark that he 'would do what he could', knowing perfectly well that politics — Hitlerian politics — would eventually rule and probably in the most abstruse way.

DEVIATIONS FROM HISTORY

[D1] The entire report of this meeting is, needless to say, a fabrication.

Confirmatory footnotes:

1 In fact, had Praun but known it, at that moment raiding by commandos of British Combined Operations, with minor American involvement, and by agents of the Special Operations Executive (SOE), were held virtually in suspension. The reason was a profound disagreement among C, and the Chiefs of Staff over policy and priorities as the Allies' emphasis on offensive operations veered from small scale pin-pricks to major invasions of Europe in 1943. Macksey *Commando Strike* pp 172–7.

2 The Allies never broke the raiders' Enigma key so that aspect of the plan could not have worked. Stummel would, however, have been appalled had he but known that the most prolific source of information about blockade runners was the American Magic intercepts of Japanese diplomatic codes. Hinsley Vol 2 pp 539–42.

3 Hinsley Vol 3 Pt 1 pp 477–82.

4 Praun pp 36–8.

7.
The Conspirators

'Before I describe Secret Writer to you,' Fellgiebel said to Oster as they drank wine in the former's office, 'please tell me, how is your man Arabel getting on in England? Has he run down either Jones or Turing?'

'Not very well, I regret to say. We received a report yesterday. Not as flamboyant as usual. He's got three people working on it and they've all drawn a blank. It's like looking for a needle in a haystack, and a lot more dangerous, he says. The trouble is that, in wartime Britain — as here of course — if you start asking suspicious-sounding questions the chances are you will be reported to the police. Apparently one of his people had a very frightening time talking his way out of trouble when somebody thought he might be a fifth columnist. Another ran into difficulties by becoming involved in some sort of domestic dispute. He says, and I quote, "The people are consumed with terror of the oppressive authorities as well as with the day of reckoning when the victorious German Army invades their perfidious island."'

'He'll go on trying, of course, no doubt about that. Arabel is a very persistent fellow. It seems he has somebody working through telephone directories. But they are very out-of-date and it appears that in England the name Jones is as common as Müller here in Germany. Turing may be the better bet, so we might strike lucky with him before we can run Jones to earth.'

'How about the Universities? Has he tried them yet?' asked Fellgiebel.

'Yes, but without much luck. At Oxford they are aware of Jones and his connection with Professor Lindemann, but nobody seems to know what he is doing now except that he is married and working for some ministry or other in London.'

'And Turing? That's the one who really interests me.'

'More and more mysterious. Nobody has seen him for a long time, though there is a rumour that he is somewhere out in the country. A strange bird it seems. Not all that many friends. He may be the more difficult to find.

'Well keep me closely informed,' said Fellgiebel. 'Though I have to admit that, even if we do find them, I have no idea what good will come of it. Alright, it might take us to where they work and it could give a lead as to how they work, but what then? It would be fascinating to know how they do it and with such speed. It might even give us a lead in the direction of how to baffle whatever method they have, but it will not make the problem go away. They've clearly got a big lead over us. Which brings me on to Secret Writer, with which, I trust, unlike Enigma, we have a clear lead over the enemy if only because it has not long been in service.'

'That is,' interjected Oster with a hint of sarcasm, 'if they really *have* broken Enigma!'[D1]

Fellgiebel stared at his old comrade, paused and laughed. Then, 'I make no comment on that, old friend, other than say that nothing I may do is any more likely to be reprehensible than some of your activities in the common cause! So, to Secret Writer!'

The story had begun in the late 1920s when the firm of Lorenz approached the Army with a radio device capable of transmitting non-morse unenciphered teleprinter impulses. Development was slow. It was not until midway through 1940 that a machine, code-named *Sägefisch*, was capable of sending and receiving, by radio on long- or short-wave, simultaneously enciphered/deciphered messages. The next step by a Lorenz SZ 40 machine was in the form of a three months proving experimental service between Vienna and Athens in mid-1941. That was sufficiently successful to initiate the construction of a slowly increasing number of Lorenz links for the Army, plus Siemens T 52 links for the Luftwaffe, as well as a few for the SS and the Navy, although not for use at sea.[1]

'There have been difficulties with *Geheimschreiber*,' reflected Fellgiebel. 'But I'd stake my life that it is even more difficult to crack than Enigma — and that is saying something. You see, it transmits teletype mechanically with the help of perforated tape at a speed of 25 letters per second. Hence, I must assume it is currently unbroken since the method would surely have to be very different from that applied to Enigma and, as I say, we must have a considerable lead. So one of my recommendations will be to step up production of Lorenz machines for the diplomatic and Army links, the latter, at the moment, having only a very few from the transmitting centres of Berlin and Königsberg to Tunis, Athens and Army Group A in the Caucasus.'

'Therefore, in the meantime I take it, making us mainly dependent on land-line and courier for the most sensitive communications?' asked Oster.[D2]

'Exactly! Provided our beloved Führer can be made to understand. Which, I gather, might actually happen,' said Fellgiebel as Oster's eyebrows rose. 'You see, Tresckow visited me yesterday [from HQ Army Group Centre]. He says there are indications that the Supreme Commander is very unsure of himself. Well, he certainly has every reason to be so, what with the goings-on with those White Rose Letters in Munich and the Russian breakthrough nearing the Dnieper. You know, I suppose, that when he visited Manstein at Zaparohze he exhibited unusual signs of irresolution? The man's shaken!'

'Who or what makes Tresckow think that?' snapped Oster.

'Manstein's ADC, Stahlberg. I've met him. A trustworthy fellow, closely related to Tresckow. Worked for von Papen before the war and has told Tresckow he regards Hitler as a criminal. He also said he had stood opposite Hitler for hours on end and several times had the chance to shoot the man! Tresckow was furious. He said we'd been looking for an opportunity like that for months. Waiting for it. Longing for it. Each time it's no use or something goes wrong.'

'Why didn't he do it then?'

'That's what Tresckow asked. It seems Stahlberg replied, "Firstly, because I don't yet know what is supposed to happen when Hitler is dead. And secondly I haven't the strength for this kind of job. I have taken part in plenty of attacks with my division. I also have the assault badge, but I have the great good fortune of never having had to shoot a man face to face . . . I wondered once or twice if I could manage to shoot him down across the table, because it would have been easy to bring my Walther PP in, ready to fire, in my right trouser pocket. But I was sure I would have been so nervous that I would definitely have missed and did and do believe that one could theoretically remove Hitler, as a single agent, but all one would end up with would be Göring or Himmler taking command immediately. And in my eyes they are just as villainous as Hitler."[2]

'I suppose he has a point or two there,' admitted Oster grudgingly. 'We've discussed it often enough. Well there now is our Operation 'Flash', at last agreed by General Beck. The brothers Boeselager are to be flown into Berlin to take command of the assassination when the moment comes. It might work, and it could not have been activated that way if Stahlberg had taken it into his head to act without warning us, even if he had killed. Yet, if I were Stahlberg, I would have had a go and hoped for the best. You see, I now hold the well-grounded suspicion that the top gangsters would turn on each other. You know how consumed with personal jealousies and rivalries are Ribbentrop, Göring, Himmler and the rest of the gang. And how Hitler has driven them to love and trust each other so dearly! I believe that if internecine war broke out, the generals, freed from their oath to a dead Führer, surely would have the opportunity to move in. And, given Beck's leadership, might well take it.'

Fellgiebel, with experience of Oster going back over many years, was prepared to believe the Abwehr chief of staff capable of anything; a man who had variously been labelled 'brash, cynical, volatile and a womaniser', but also 'a man among men'. As a frequently decorated infantryman during World War 1, Oster had remained in the Army and by 1931 had risen to lieutenant-colonel on the staff of 6th Division, at about the time he struck up an association with Captain Canaris. But on 31 December 1932, on the eve of the coming to power of the Nazis, a court of honour forced him to resign his commission on the grounds of 'irresponsible carelessness' in an adulterous affair.[3]

No Nazi, Oster had spent the next few months as a phone tapper on Hermann Göring's staff, prior to joining the Abwehr as a civilian. But shortly after Canaris took command of that department in 1935, he was re-employed in the rank of major. In 1938 Canaris promoted him to colonel and placed him in charge of the Abwehr's key organising and administering Z Department (*Abteilung Z*). Both were already committed to covert resistance to Hitler and the Nazis. Oster then had developed this position as a cover for conspiracy, filling the staff of sub-departments (such as records, filing and foreign policy) with men of similar persuasion. By the time he became major-general and Canaris's chief of staff in 1939, he not only was the spider at the centre of a web of espionage and intrigue but was also eagerly plotting a *coup d'état*. Moreover, he was in close touch with General Beck (a disenchanted former Army Chief of Staff who had been forced into retirement by Hitler); with General Halder, the new Chief of Staff; and with Fellgiebel, among several other soldiers and civilians.

Canaris appears to have been seriously concerned about Oster's obsession with the *coup d'état*, to the neglect of other duties, let alone the vital matter of precautions against the danger of detection by the Gestapo. Prior to the invasion of Czechoslovakia and following the outbreak of war, his conspiratorial activities certainly covered a wide front. They had included the encouragement of anti-Nazi generals to take the law into their own hands by seizing Hitler and ousting the Nazis, and the exploitation of medical evidence of Hitler's insanity to prove his unsuitability to govern. But always these attempts failed to materialise for one reason or another, of which the officers' reluctance to break their oath of allegiance to the Führer was not the least.[4]

In desperation, before news had broken about the impending Russo-German Pact and ensuing invasion of Poland (and therefore the start of what he considered must be a disastrous European war for Germany), Oster launched secret efforts to warn intended victims. Through an envoy he left the British and French governments in no doubt of Hitler's determination for war, in the hope it would stiffen their resolve — perhaps to the extent of scaring hesitant German generals into rebellion. Poland needed no warning; her fate was sealed, to the approval of many Germans. But when in 1940 it was the turn of Holland and Belgium to be ground underfoot and the generals had lost their will to resist, it was Oster alone who, in November 1939, personally warned their legations.[5]

Fellgiebel was aware of these events, with their attendant possibilities of weakening Germany's chances of victory. Just as he was aware of Oster's half-hearted attempt to revive the plot in December 1939. Failure then had doomed Germany to the consequences of such stunning victories in 1940 and 1941. Not until the set-backs of the winter of 1941/42 could the conspirators be motivated with any conviction — and then only amateurishly and without much hope of encouragement from leaders, field marshals and generals above all, who mattered. In fact, not until the aftermath of Stalingrad, the harbinger of ultimate defeat, could the plan for assassination (as opposed to abduction) Tresckow had mentioned to Stahlberg be shaped with any hope of acceptance by men of good conscience.

'Will you update me about Flash, please?' requested Fellgiebel.

'We are ready; it is time for Flash. It only requires a few final touches at a conference of intelligence officers at HQ Army Group Centre in a few days' time. As soon as possible the Führer will be lured to Army Group Centre at Smolensk. Where, all being well, Field Marshal von Kluge will permit Tresckow to arrange the assassination. It will be carried out by Lieutenant-Colonel von Boeselager's cavalry officers with their usual efficiency. Then Boeselager and his brother will fly to Berlin to help Beck and our comrades throughout the Reich to take charge.'

'And the Field Marshal? Can we rely upon him? He has a reputation for running out at the crucial moment, after all.'[6]

'We must hope for the best.'

'Hmm. Well just bear in mind that when Carl Goerdeler [one-time mayor of Leipzig] spoke to Heinz Guderian and mentioned Beck's role, the General was strongly opposed to somebody so indecisive, and there is something Tresckow told me about an occasion he, too, tried to recruit "Schnelle Heinz". Beforehand he had been warned not to mention Kluge's involvement, but he did and Heinz exploded! Said he could not work with somebody so unreliable — and you cannot deny his qualifications for holding that opinion![7] In any case, now that he has, surprisingly, been given the job of Inspector General of Armoured Troops it is unimaginable that he will join us. He's a Prussian who genuinely imagines he can persuade Hitler to adopt a more rational strategy to extract the Fatherland from its difficulties. And as a Prussian the Oath to him is absolutely binding.'

Oster sighed as Fellgiebel continued, 'And don't forget, too, that Manstein has condemned Paulus for his disobedience to Hitler when declining to commit suicide instead of surrendering at Stalingrad. I do hope Flash does not misfire!'[8]

'Then I have a question for you, Erich. Two questions. First, are you *really* convinced that the English have broken Enigma? And second, if not, why have you pushed it so hard?'

Once more Fellgiebel stared hard at Oster, 'You doubt me?'

'Yes. You're up to something and I'd like to know what's behind it.'

'Well, the answer to your first question is no. I am not absolutely certain. But as to the second, even if totally unsure, I would still attempt what I am doing if I could.'

'For God's sake why? You of all people must realise the appalling consequences to the Fatherland.'

'Indeed I do — and the most important reason is that, like your past activities to warn the enemy and, I suspect, your indulgence in espionage on their behalf, I, too, aim to spoil and weaken our own efficiency and resolve. That way we might hasten the end of this ghastly war along with the collapse of a criminal government.'

'But in so doing you could cause the very opposite effect!'

'Not if the U-boat campaign fails. No, hear me out,' pleaded Fellgiebel as Oster shaped to interrupt. 'True, the enemy will be embarrassed by loss of Enigma, but not nearly as badly if his shipping losses cripple or seriously delay the build-up from the other side of the Atlantic. Why do you think Dönitz has taken such a positive line? Obviously because he knows that, as of now, the ability to find and attack convoys will diminish. January was a miserable month for him. February so-so, although, so far, he seems to have lost over 15 boats.[9] If March and April don't improve hugely, he's failed and is beaten.'

'But the enemy will be just as seriously handicapped — if not more so — through deprivation of crucial intelligence about our strategy and intentions. He, too, will suffer — badly. And that might prolong the war in a most costly manner.'

'There's a fundamental difference. Dönitz forfeits more than the supply of intelligence. He loses command and control of his striking force. He will forfeit the essential ability to manoeuvre flexibly with quick responses to every enemy ploy. Lacking secure radio communications and air reconnaissance, the U-boat groups will become a headless rabble, groping in the Atlantic wastes for an elusive prey who grows bigger and more dangerous with every day that passes. As it is, just when he hoped to reinforce his packs, he is being compelled to withdraw units for retraining. March will not be the stunning month he expected. April little better, since, by then fully aware that we know he has broken Enigma, the enemy will have won the initiative, for he will have benefited from the time granted to mount counter-measures that may pre-empt and defeat Dönitz's forthcoming new tactics.'

Oster pondered out loud, 'So you think that if Flash succeeds it will be all the easier to convince the saner members of the Party, as well as OKW, that the game is up?'

'Yes. And if it fails or does not take place, at worst there will be a further undermining of our's and Hitler's self-confidence and morale. Don't you see?'

'Maybe more than you do. I see no reason why the enemy should be totally robbed of strategic intelligence. Just think, Germany is infiltrated on a large scale by thousands of hostile workers forcibly recruited to keep the economy running. And the occupied territories are seething with discontent, populated by potential spies who, we know, are supplying unknown quantities of intelligence to our enemies. Of course they don't have access to much high grade strategic information. Or do they?'

'Meaning they could find out through my telephone operators?'

'Of course. Don't forget, I once was one of Göring's telephone tappers! What I am suggesting is this, the provision and passing through your facilities and mine of vital, select messages to the enemy via neutral countries, like Switzerland, Sweden, Spain, Portugal and so on.'

'I'll give it more thought than I already have,' said Fellgiebel. 'But first let's try to get the Führer on our side on the 26th.'

DEVIATIONS FROM HISTORY

[D1] A wholly imaginary discussion, but containing elements of truth.

[D2] Although this conversation about Secret Writer is imaginary, there can be no doubt that, at this time, some acceleration of its installation was contemplated.

Confirmatory footnotes:
1 Hinsley Vol 3 Part 1 p 477 and Praun p 31.
2 Stahlberg pp 280–2.
3 Hohne, *passim* for pre-1943 biographical details about Oster.
4 Wheeler-Bennett pp 396, 406, 407.
5 *ibid* pp 440, 472, 477, 485.
6 *ibid* pp 560, 561.
7 Macksey *Guderian* pp 181, 182.
8 Wheeler-Bennett p 534.
9 Anon *Fuh* p 316. Actually 19 U-boats were lost in February.

8.
The Crucial Decision

The Führer, uplifted by his visits to Zaparohze, had suddenly developed a taste for leaving behind the safety of the Wolf's Lair. Such forays were designed to demonstrate for propaganda effect his astute generalship and close personal control of vital operations — even though his destinations, like Vinnitsa and Zaparohze, were far behind the front. Usually these visits were arranged and often altered at very short notice. For the Führer and his minders were obsessed with dread of his abduction or assassination, such was their consciousness of his unpopularity in certain circles and his conviction that virtually nobody could be trusted. This to some extent lay behind the logic of holding his conference of 26 February with Admiral Dönitz at the elaborate, heavily guarded headquarters at Vinnitsa. It was a meeting which, at General Jodl's urgent request, was widened significantly to tackle the Enigma crisis, as described by Fellgiebel to Hitler's Chief of Operations.

The minutes of the meeting show that, in addition to the Führer and Admiral Dönitz, the following were present: Lt-Gen Jodl, General Fellgiebel, Admiral Kranke, General Jeschonnek and Captain von Puttkamer (Naval adjutant to the Führer).[D1]

To quote from the minutes and Fellgiebel's subsequent oral comments to Praun (marked in italics):

'1. General Fellgiebel, Chief of Wehrmacht Communications and Intelligence (CWCI), reported that there is convincing evidence, following an exhaustive investigation, of breaking of the Enigma ciphers by the enemy. This means that, for an unknown period, he has read a substantial volume of the highest level messages sent by radio, including diplomatic, OKW, Army, Navy, Luftwaffe and SS signals. The Führer expressed his deepest concern and asked who was to blame for this laxity. CWCI explained that frequent investigations in the past by experts have never revealed grounds for suspicion and that, even now, it was impossible to say how the enemy had succeeded in doing the impossible by breaking the assumed unbreakable. At the Führer's request CWCI explained the workings of Enigma and the problems facing anybody attempting to break it very rapidly.'

[Hitler seemed utterly baffled. I don't think he really grasped it. Just kept looking down at his papers and didn't make any comments or ask questions.]

'2. There was discussion about the consequences of this extremely serious event. C-in-C, Navy, reported that there was no doubt that the insecurity of Enigma was the reason behind the failure of U-boats to find their quarry and for the sometimes astonishing enemy ability not only to locate and attack U-boats but also our own convoys. Treachery, as previously suspected, could be ruled out to some extent now. At the Führer's request he explained how the strategic and tactical command and control of U-boat packs was exercised.'

[Again my impression was of the Führer's inability to grasp the subject. But that's how Dönitz and Raeder have always got away with matters beyond Hitler's landsman's comprehension. He hates exposing his ignorance!]

'Chief of Staff, Luftwaffe, (COSL) concurred with C-in-C Navy, admitting that radio transmissions by his service probably revealed vital information about land and sea operations as well as purely air matters. CWCI concurred with C-in-C, Navy, and COSL but stated the Army was less seriously affected than naval and air forces.'

[I was asked to explain the reason for this. I guessed that the man, as usual, would blame the Army and probably thought I was endeavouring to cover up and disclaim responsibility. But once again he remained unusually subdued, even though Jodl must already have briefed him of what was coming.]

'3. At the Führer's request, CWCI proposed measures for rectifying the current disadvantage.' *[These, of course, were those recommended by our Committee.]* 'The Führer criticised the need for such extreme measures, stating that there must be better ways to mitigate their effect. C-in-C, Navy, said that the matter was extremely urgent if the Battle for the Atlantic was to be won. It was imperative to withdraw U-boats for the retraining of officers and communicators to operate new code systems being developed. At the same time it was also imperative that air support should be greatly increased and improved. COSL reported that the Reichsmarschall had promised his support but the construction of various types of long-range reconnaissance planes would have to be given priority. The Führer sharply criticised promises which were readily made regarding the performance and range of certain types of reconnaissance planes, which later proved illusory. He does not believe that much will be gained by rebuilding the He 177. At the request of C-in-C, Navy, the Führer promised to find out whether three BV 222s could not be made available immediately for convoy reconnaissance in the West.'[1]

[Jeschonnek then, as ever, shrank like a schoolboy before Hitler's reprimand. Once more the man had got himself off the hook by cleverly diverting attention from the vital problem of abandonment of Enigma. For a moment I wondered if the whole problem would be deferred for one of his typical, temporising, post-conference decisions that would fudge the issue and play people against each other — this time, and not for the first time, Göring against Dönitz. But Dönitz was ready for that one.]

'4. C-in-C, Navy, reports as follows. The Führer has previously decided that we cannot afford to let our large ships lie idle, since they are not in a position to engage in combat . . . The C-in-C, Navy, is however of the opinion that the Archangel convoys would make excellent targets for the large ships and he considers it his duty, in view of the heavy fighting on the Eastern Front, to exploit these opportunities to the fullest extent. He also considers that, in face of the radio security problems now hampering the U-boats, every other available weapon should be used in compensation.'[D2] He therefore considers it essential to send the *Scharnhorst* to Norway to strengthen the forces there. The *Tirpitz*, the *Scharnhorst*, and for the present the *Lützow*, together with six destroyers, would be a fairly powerful force. The Führer, however, is strongly opposed to any further engagements of the surface ships since, beginning with the *Graf Spee* in 1939, one defeat has followed the other. Large ships are a thing of the past.

[Dönitz, nevertheless, persevered and a rambling debate ensued on the possibilities (or otherwise) of the big ships ever finding action. Dönitz said within three months, and shrewdly kept returning to the Enigma problem and the as yet unsurmounted difficulties of controlling the U-boats at sea in the new situation. To my surprise Hitler relented, but with the smug comment, "Even if it should require six months, you will then return and be forced to admit that I was right about the ships."[2] The meeting then took a turn I had not anticipated. After Hitler had stated there was no point in asking the Italians to provide submarines as supply ships, Dönitz mentioned a Japanese Navy request, via Ambassador Oshima and Ribbentrop, for two U-boats. Dönitz opposed this for technical reasons and Hitler thought it might be diplomatic to let them have one in payment for the rubber they have sent us. Then suddenly Hitler asked how, due to the Enigma problem, in future we will communicate urgently with the Japanese? It occurred to me that nobody else had thought of this because everybody present looked at me!]

'5. CWCI reported that using Enigma it would no longer be possible to communicate securely by radio with Japan. Until new code books were distributed this problem might be overcome by arrangements with the Japanese who use, presumably, equivalent Enigma-type machines which might not have been broken. He wondered if the Japanese would be prepared to allow us access to their most important confidential diplomatic material? The Führer promised to take this up with Foreign Minister von Ribbentrop and Ambassador Oshima as a matter of the utmost urgency. In reply to a question from the Führer, CWCI confirmed that very likely even the most confidential radio messages originated by the Führer in person, as well as the Abwehr and SS, might frequently have been intercepted and read by the enemy.'

[I had the distinct impression that this reply came as an awful shock to the man. My mind went over some of the horrifying communications concerning the treatment of Jews, Poles and Russians in concentration camps with which he and the SS were deeply implicated. Only at that moment, I suspect, did the full meaning and menace of the breaking of Enigma hit him personally.]

'6. The Führer asked CWCI how he proposed preventing further breaches of security. CWCI replied that until alternative encoding methods were developed and in place there was need for strictest control from the highest level of all radio communications. This temporarily would lengthen the time required for transmission of all communications and cause severe congestion of existing systems. He suggested that this vital matter might best be managed by a special committee under his control. The Führer said he would consider the matter and give his decision later.'

[For one intoxicating moment I dreamt of all our co-ordination problems at last being solved under my hand. But, as Jodl warned me after the meeting, "Dictators cannot afford to be contradicted and thereby forfeit power." Well, he should know and still I wait. Meanwhile the Army, the Navy and the diplomats have decided to abandon Enigma, the Luftwaffe is still making selective use of it, as are the SS, and the Abwehr is keeping its counsel.]

He had to wait three days. And when the answer came the name of the person appointed to take charge in the new situation surprised him — but not the organisation for which that person worked.

DEVIATIONS FROM HISTORY

[D1] Anon *Fuh* pp 311, 312. The contents and sequence of the original minutes have been substantially amended to take into account the effect of the inclusion on the agenda of the Enigma problem, as has the list of those present to include Fellgiebel and Jeschonnek.

[D2] This sentence was not included in the actual minutes.

Confirmatory footnotes:

1 Anon *Fuh* p 311.

2 *ibid* p 312.

9.
Reversion to Conjecture

Nobody was more struck, or depressed, by the drying up of high grade intelligence from Enigma than Winston Churchill. For nearly three years he had relished the opportunities it offered and frequently drawn comfort in hard times when leafing through 'the golden eggs' regularly delivered to him by Ultra. Their absence, save for a thin trickle, left a gap in his hectic life. Moreover, lack of them deprived him of a priceless opportunity to look into Hitler's mind as well as providing intimate forewarning of intelligence with which to match in debate the professional expertise of the Chiefs of Staff and of the Chief of the SIS.

'He is disgruntled,' said Stewart Menzies to David Petrie. 'History and ancestry have him by the throat. Yesterday he reminded me of how his great ancestor was able to read Louis XIV's mind through remarkable letters written by some unknown spy in the French court during the War of the Spanish Succession. You've read his biography of Marlborough I suppose?'

'I am afraid not,' admitted the head of MI5.

'Well you could do worse than scan through all four volumes — if you've the time. It's brilliantly written and will tell you a great deal about our Prime Minister. Now let's consider what we are going to do about this Enigma business and yesterday's meeting with the PM and Chiefs.'[D1]

The meeting had been tense. Each member had read a paper by C summarising the possible consequences of likely counter-measures by the Germans if they actually had discovered that Enigma was broken; it went on to ask them to consider the effect these might have on future developments and operations. Each had studied the matter carefully in the sincere hope that it was only a scare. The realisation, made plain by the sudden enormous reduction in the number of Enigma encoded messages and certain significant naval redeployments, now removed all doubts in everybody's mind that the worst had befallen and that some very hard thinking was demanded.

C had requested the Chiefs to examine the matter under two main headings. First, with regard to known, highly threatening technical developments such as atomic explosives, chemical weapons, jet-propelled aircraft, rockets and submarines. Second, concerning the feasibility of future strategic plans, of which, top of the list, was winning the Battle of the Atlantic, second the plans approved at Casablanca for the invasion of Sicily and the massive Bomber Offensive against Germany, and finally, of lesser urgency, the future likely invasions of Italy and North-West Europe. Based on their answers C intended to devise ways and means to compensate for the loss of Enigma information and search for ways of exploiting the enemy's discomfort caused by the disruption inflicted — some of which was already detectable.

The nuclear threat with the possibility that the Germans were working on an atomic bomb was regarded, especially by the Prime Minister, with dread. It was known that the Americans, with help from Britain and physicists from all over the place, were moving closer to building an atomic bomb. Furthermore, from spies, agents and European physicists, there had emerged convincing evidence of German activity, although no indication of how far they had progressed. Attention was focused on German possession of the important heavy water and uranium materials.[1] There was immense relief at the success only a few days previously of a Special Operations Executive (SOE) raid on the Norsk Hydro plant at Vermork in Norway.[2] Intelligence therefore was reasonably good; noteworthy, however, was a total lack of it from Enigma.

Enigma's contribution to intelligence about chemical weapons and gas was also extremely sparse. Until the previous month it had contributed only one decrypted item of indirect importance in the form of an estimate of the number of replacement gas masks that would be required by all units of the German Army, other than those in Germany, Poland and Czechoslovakia, as at 1 April. General Sir Alan Brooke, the CIGS, had agreed with the Prime Minister's concern that this might mean the introduction of a new type of gas.[3] There always had been, of course, innumerable rumours, suppositions and guesses about German intentions to use gas; probably several of these were threats to deter the Allies from taking that same step. But the consensus ruled that Hitler, even in the role of mad dog, was unlikely to take the plunge at this moment.

Information about jet-propelled aircraft, the performance potential of which was well recognised by the British from their own successful Gloster Whittle experimental E1 machine, was also only fragmentary. There had been a report in December 1939 of a jet machine with rocket assisted take-off and in May 1942 aerial photographs had disclosed a Heinkel machine on the ground. This was followed in November by intelligence of Heinkel and Messerschmitt activity in this area. Enigma contributed nothing.[4]

Rockets, despite knowledge of German activity in this field since 1939, had attracted little serious attention until very recently when, in December 1942, SIS sources within Germany began repeatedly mentioning advanced trials with long-range rocket-propelled missiles.[5] 'The latest we have,' said Menzies, 'is from a chap who says that there's an experimental factory at Peenemünde on the Baltic coast. He says he has seen a rocket with a range of 100km and a 10-ton warhead. Moreover, he has heard that it will be fired at England from the French coast.'[6]

As for U-boats, the most important Enigma contributions came in the strategic field, from statistical returns giving production of new boats.[7] The vast majority of intelligence, in fact, was gleaned from the interrogation of prisoners of war (POWs) and the study of captured documents. Of the latter, the most important prize was that of a gridded chart from *U110* which opened the door to understanding how the Germans disguised the position of U-boats in Enigma signals.[8]

'Perhaps the most recent important nugget for our naval colleagues is confirmation by a POW of 1941 Enigma intercepts mentioning acoustic homing torpedoes,' said Menzies. 'Apparently reference in December 1942 to 80cm horizontally polarised radar (whatever that is!) mounted on U-boats has been extremely helpful since it helped our interrogators to learn everything about it from a co-operative POW.[9] Which all rather goes to show that, in the technical field, Enigma has rarely produced anything to match good old-fashioned methods of conjecture. So now let me tell you the guidelines emerging from the operational world.'

As Chairman, General Sir Alan Brooke (CIGS) had spoken for them all after Admiral Sir Dudley Pound (First Lord of the Admiralty and Chief of Naval Staff (CNS)), Air Marshal Sir Charles Portal (Chief of Air Staff (CAS)) and Vice-Admiral Lord Louis Mountbatten (CCO) had expressed their own opinions.

Pound, rather like Dönitz had he but known it, was possibly the most worried — although nothing like as badly as his German counterpart. He regretted being deprived of the movements of blockade runners with vital supplies for the enemy. Much more worrying, in the sense that the Battle of the Atlantic was nearing a crisis, he feared deeply the consequences of deprivation of the positions and intentions of U-boats which provided vital information to enable the diversion of convoys and the appropriate positioning of anti-submarine resources to combat them. On the other hand, it was pleasing to notice the first signs of premature withdrawal of some U-boats to port. From analysis of the copious signals they sent and received, he could well imagine Dönitz's dilemma as his command and control became tentative and stood on the verge of collapse. Moreover, Pound had mused, valuable time was being gained to deploy the latest long-range American Liberator bombers to help close, in company with more light aircraft carriers and better equipped submarine hunters, the mid-Atlantic air gap.

'Far from incidentally,' he had remarked, 'it must not be forgotten that it is not only the content of the decoded messages from which we profit. It is the mere transmission of those messages by the enemy which, due to the excellence of our latest direction finding (DF) equipment, instantly leads our ships and aircraft to the U-boats' positions. Nor can I visualise their being able to operate effectively under total wireless silence. Who knows, but that this discovery by the Germans of our capability may be of greater assistance to us than to him? Add to that the results coming from 10cm radar and you have an encouraging picture.'

To begin with, the normally phlegmatic Portal had seemed more upset than Menzies had expected. It just happened that recent Enigma decrypts were advertising a fairly significant redeployment of Luftwaffe bombers and fighters from the Eastern Front to the West. Knowing how quickly the Luftwaffe could switch from one place to another, it was all the more desirable for ample prior warning of this sort. Yet the bomber offensive against Britain that had started in mid-January was proving quite modest by previous standards. On reflection, however, Portal had remarked that, apart from the strategic warning, Enigma contributed little else except the revelation of the Luftwaffe's post-Stalingrad shortage of trained men and machines.[10]

Only very rarely did Enigma give adequate warning of raids. Mainly it was the low- and medium-grade codes (decoded with some ease by hand) which contributed the best information. Frequently the enemy achieved a measure of surprise (regardless of radar) and all the more so when he abstained from using the radio telephone — as now was common.[11]

Likewise Enigma contributed but little to the mounting Allied Bomber Offensive. In the main, estimates of damage caused were based on agents' and neutral observers' reports, photo-reconnaissance (PR) and calculations founded on earlier British experience. Enigma did, however, indicate the enemy's reactions to measures and counter-measures in night-fighter combat, although in truth far more information was obtained from bomber crews' post operation reports and expert monitoring and interpretation through the Y Service of enemy aircrews' conversations. And very much the same can be applied to operations by the American Eighth Air Force as it stepped up its daylight offensive.[12]

'So I conclude by saying that, much as Enigma would be missed, its demise will not be fatal. And thank God we so extensively expanded those Y Services of ours last year', said Portal.

'I will miss it, too,' Mountbatten said, 'because it often stimulates ideas and points to targets worth raiding. On the other hand, like CAS, I can get along without it since I depend far more on the traditional sources. Besides, in my line of business, I am never on the defensive and invariably hold the initiative.'

Brooke, on the other hand, had grave misgivings. 'For one thing it is the only way I know about Russian dispositions through German messages which we intercept.[13] But nothing that I can imagine will replace the superb strategic intelligence coming from the highest level in profusion.'

'That is so,' replied Menzies. 'Without making any promises I will do what I can to rectify that. But as of now I hope to hear of any likely changes to current and envisaged operations. Then I can formulate better ways of obtaining information. For example, I must decide not only on where to attack the enemy but also the priority allocated to each task. Do I, for example, give lower priority of effort to Enigma and higher priority of attack on other sources, such as medium-grade codes or Secret Writer?'

Brooke's reply, conforming to the strategy worked out during hard bargaining with the Americans at Casablanca, was unyielding. In his crisp staccato style of delivery he declared, 'No change that I can see.' First priority remained attached to winning the Battle of the Atlantic, ' . . . which, amazingly, seems nearer to being in our grasp.' There seemed no reason to modify the Combined Bomber Offensive. With the concurrence of the Americans the main Allied effort against the Germans would focus on the Mediterranean. Only in the event of a sudden enemy collapse would any attempt be made to invade France. Moreover, with a steely glance at his colleagues, 'Once we have thrown the Axis out of Tunisia within the next couple of months, the next objective is Sicily.' He had no desire for a re-opening of the protracted 'hammer and tongs battle to keep the team together' at Casablanca when, having persuaded the American Chiefs of Staff to go for Sicily, they had plumped for Sardinia. To do otherwise, as he had told his own Chiefs, 'would irrevocably shake their confidence in our judgement.'[14]

Brooke continued, 'I think CCO has put his finger on it. It is not only he who holds the initiative. We all do, except perhaps at sea, or if the Huns come up with a truly effective secret weapon, such as an atomic bomb. But we already have heard that

Enigma has made no great contribution in that field. Therefore it seems to me that, in answer to C's request, he should continue to work on the lines of 'no strategic change to our plans' while doing everything in his power to restore a measure of insight into Hitler's thinking. At the same time I think we should endeavour to turn the present situation to our advantage. You see, I cannot imagine the enemy is exactly happy. The change of strategy and tactics forced on him — especially on his navy — must be very embarrassing. That already appears from the erratic movements of his U-boats. But it must be without compromising such resources as might be vital when we commence major operations on the Continent next year. In the meantime I will see to it that the Prime Minister and our American allies are kept fully in the picture.'

A satisfied Menzies retired from the meeting. He now could develop his own strategy with the Chiefs' approval. But in his pocket was a note from Brooke asking for a briefing on the Secret Writer which, he had written, had not been mentioned during his contacts with Bletchley Park.

DEVIATIONS FROM HISTORY

[D1] No such conferences as those mentioned in this chapter took place, of course, but the facts noted are authentic and often indicate, especially regarding the developments of new weapons, how small was Enigma's contribution to intelligence compared with that of other sources.

Confirmatory footnotes:
1 Hinsley Vol 2 pp 116, 122, 123.
2 *ibid* p 127.
3 *ibid* p 119. In fact (and unknown to the Allies) the new equipment was required to give protection against Tabun, the deadly nerve gas then coming into production.
4 Hinsley Vol 3 Pt 1 p 334.
5 *ibid* p 360.
6 *ibid* p 361.
7 *ibid* p 240.
8 Hinsley Vol 2 pp 681–2.
9 *ibid* pp 683–5.
10 *ibid* pp 509, 510.
11 *ibid* p 512.
12 *ibid* p 515.
13 Fraser *Alanbrooke* p 280.
14 *ibid* p 323.

10.
Without Enigma

'The Secret Writer — or *Geheimschreiber* — first came to the notice of the Foreign Office in 1932 when the Metropolitan Police wireless organisation and the GPO 'Y' Station detected unusual German non-morse, teleprinter radio transmissions,' explained Menzies to Brooke. 'They were intermittent and seemed experimental and unenciphered — until the autumn of 1940, that is, when enciphered signals were picked up. In due course we discovered that the Germans called this *Sägefisch* — so GC&CS, by this time very interested, code-named it Fish. Also we discovered that, like German on-line cipher machines, *Sägefisch* could provide simultaneous reception and decipherment of radio or teleprinter messages based on the international teleprinter code. And this, it soon was realised, might be extremely difficult to break.'

The CIGS's attention was seized as Menzies went on to explain how, given the plentiful provision of intelligence from Enigma, only limited priority of attention had been paid to the Secret Writer until mid-1941, when some improved Enigma machines became more difficult to break. In mid-1942, therefore, GC&CS had stepped up its efforts to break a German Army Secret Writer, code-named Tunny, that was coming into increasing use. Towards the end of 1942 a new reception station had to be opened at Knockholt in Kent to overcome the difficulties of detecting the associated weak radio signals, many of them beamed and therefore hard to intercept. Moreover, the high speed transmissions were often of great length and being churned out at 25 characters per second.

'To begin with,' went on Menzies, 'the staff had to decipher the teleprinter characters by hand from the tape on which they were received. Only after that was done could a master tape be produced for decryption, again most laboriously by hand, at Bletchley Park. Last June, however, a new deciphering machine was installed and that helped. From then until the end of October we were reading almost currently many of the messages sent on a link the Germans had established between Vienna and Athens. It was no mean achievement, CIGS, but clearly not good enough. And recently the Germans have so improved it that we no longer can read their messages concurrently. Therefore our best people at Bletchley, several of whom, including Dr Turing, you have met, are now engaged in the design of high speed machinery to cope with what is to come. For already, last November, we found that the enemy had opened a Tunny link to their Army Group A in the Ukraine, and another in January to their Panzer Army in Tunis.'

'Where, therefore, do we stand now?' asked Brooke.

'At present there's a machine called Heath Robinson under development at the GPO Research Station at Dollis Hill. It's a bit of a slow-speed lash-up of tape drives and sprockets — hence the name — but the Prime Minister, quite rightly in my opinion, has ordered top priority and we hope the prototype will come into operation in May. Meanwhile we make do with a combination of methods — anything from minor machines of varying complexity to simple hand counters. It is a struggle which will get no easier until Heath Robinson is ready and proven. The best news is that, for the present, the Germans keep the basic Fish setting in force for a month at a time.'[1]

On the pretext of discussing the latest Enigma situation, Menzies now took the opportunity to sound out the CIGS's views on the subject of forthcoming deception plans, in which he was deeply involved through contacts with the so-called London Controlling Section (LCS). This organisation had come into being in June 1942, under Lt-Col J. H. Bevan. It was tasked to work for the Chiefs of Staff, ostensibly as part of the Joint Planning Staff, to:

a. Prepare deception plans on a worldwide basis;
b. Co-ordinate deception plans prepared by commands at home and abroad;
c. Ensure that 'cover' plans fitted into the general framework of strategic deception;
d. Watch over the execution by the service ministries, commands and others of approved deception plans prepared by LCS;
e. Control the support of deception schemes originated by commanders-in-chief by such means as leakage and propaganda.[2]

Menzies was seeking Brooke's current reactions to LCS's proposals on the shape and nature of deception operations now that the real major operations were to be centred on the Mediterranean and not in Western Europe. For at that very moment Colonel Bevan and his team were elaborating the deception schemes which, at the request of the Combined Chiefs of Staff, they had outlined in the aftermath of the Casablanca Conference. Since it had now been decided Sicily was to be the primary objective it was not only desirable to convince the enemy that some other place, such as Sardinia, Crete, Greece or the Dodecanese, was the intended target, but also that some sort of major invasion from the United Kingdom was impending.

With some reservations, under heavy pressure from Churchill, the Chiefs had conceded the principle of the launching from the UK of 'such limited offensive operations as may be practicable with the amphibious forces available', and had agreed to assemble there 'the strongest possible force . . . in constant readiness to re-enter the continent as soon as German resistance is weakened to the required extent'. Their reservations concerned the problem of how to make compatible with spurious activities three kinds of operations actually intended. These were raids aimed at provoking air battles that would wear down the Luftwaffe's strength; raids to reduce German strength sufficiently to permit the seizing and exploiting of a bridgehead; and preparations to make possible an invasion of the Continent, with whatever forces were available, in the event of impending German internal collapse.

With memories of the Dieppe debacle of August 1942 fresh in mind, the first of these three was not contemplated with enthusiasm. The third was generally regarded as wishful thinking since there was little evidence to hand of a really effective German resistance movement or signs of a genuine collapse of morale despite the defeats at Stalingrad and in Africa. Only the second course, a projected attack on the Cotentin peninsula early in August, had real substance, although the availability of sufficient forces, especially amphibious craft, was regarded as unlikely to make this practical.

To his delight, Menzies discovered that Brooke's reception of the LCS's solution to the demands of the Casablanca Directive was favourable. The CIGS went along with the concept of a cover story suggesting that many thrusts would be made in 1943 — into the Balkans, in the central Mediterranean theatre, across the Channel and into Norway. The beauty of LCS's plan lay in the fact that, apart from Norway, offensives of this nature actually were in prospect. The danger that a spoof might be to the detriment of reality was declared to be an advantage on the grounds that it would be impossible for signs of the reality to be concealed from the enemy. Moreover, timing and scale might make it possible to employ the spoofs as distractions from the reality.

'It therefore becomes feasible,' elaborated Menzies, 'to simulate the build-up for an invasion, timed for September, of the Pas de Calais, an operation which would also comply with the Casablanca Directive's requirement for an air offensive designed to wear down the Luftwaffe. In conjunction with this there can be suggestions of a major amphibious raid in August which could, ostensibly, later be stood down until September, by which time Sicily ought to have been captured and a real invasion of Italy projected.'[3]

'Work along those lines,' ordered Brooke. 'and develop them in close collaboration with the Supreme Allied Commander's staff when it takes shape under Frederick Morgan in the near future.' (Major-General Frederick Morgan had been appointed Chief of Staff to the Supreme Allied Commander [COSSAC] to lead preparations for the genuine invasion of Europe until such time as the supreme commander was actually chosen.) Brooke then added, 'The PM's not going to like it, but I see no prospect of a major amphibious operation against the Cotentin peninsula in August — or at any other time this year, if only because of the landing craft situation. After all we've yet to win — and might even lose — the Battle of the Atlantic.'

Menzies nodded. 'I think it should be possible to lay on a very convincing distraction, given the resources at our disposal. The double agents will be very useful, though they'll need very careful handling for fear of killing them off before the day we really do invade. I do have one regret with regard to the loss of Enigma information, of course. Until now it has been very comforting to learn from the enemy the effect of our distraction measures. That's now lost to us.'

'Well, in that case you will have to find other ways,' said the CIGS grimly. 'I've no doubt you will make do. After all, you do have the likelihood of help from a largely friendly populace in Europe and the other occupied countries. And I would like to think that there are some Germans who, in the current state of gloom, will be forthcoming.'[D1]

DEVIATIONS FROM HISTORY
[D1] A pious hope to end a make-believe meeting which, nevertheless, contains much actual fact.

Confirmatory footnotes:
1 Hinsley Vol 3 Part 1. pp 477–81.
2 Hinsley/Howard Vol 5 p 243.
3 *ibid* pp 71–4.

11.
Flash Point

Any hopes the Allies might have harboured about the prospects of a German internal collapse in 1943 were badly undermined by the Enigma effect. Hitler's choice of the man to co-ordinate code and cipher policy was guaranteed to send ripples of alarm through the resistance and intelligence communities, let alone the Wehrmacht signals and intelligence branches. For the man nominated was not only a member of Himmler's SS but one of its most ruthless and able officers. He was none other than the 32-year-old Walter Schellenberg, acting chief of the RSHA (Reichssicherheitshauptamt — a department which comprised the secret police [Gestapo], the criminal police [Kripo] and the Sicherheitsdienst [SD, the Security Agency] under a criminally minded thug and lawyer called Ernst Kaltenbrunner).

Sturmbannführer Schellenberg was also a lawyer, though, unlike Kaltenbrunner, a man of considerable charm. He had joined the SS in 1933 and taken a post in the SD a year later. Highly regarded by Himmler and a close associate of the sinister Reinhard Heydrich in the formation of the RSHA in September 1939, he was by then well versed in security and counter-intelligence work. His reputation was established beyond challenge when, in November 1939, he engineered the kidnapping of two high-ranking British intelligence officers at Venlo in Holland. This exploit fundamentally weakened MI6/SIS and other allied services. Since then he had been involved, in successful collaboration with Canaris's Abwehr, in the attack on the communist-run European-wide Rote Kapelle spying, which, at the end of 1942, was in tatters and virtually crippled.

His collaboration with the Abwehr reflected a long-standing friendship with Canaris, with whom he was in almost daily contact from their habit of taking early morning horse rides together.[1] This companionship naturally caused concern to Oster and Fellgiebel for fear it would lead to exposure of their resistance activities. Yet, for the moment, Schellenberg hardly posed a threat to the Abwehr and its double role — Canaris grew far more worried when Himmler made Kaltenbrunner head of the RSHA on 30 January 1943. He had good reason, since Kaltenbrunner was almost universally detested and feared by those who knew him; a calculating maverick who arrogantly menaced everybody from Hitler and Himmler downwards.[D1]

Thus the Admiral's enforced closer formal association with Schellenberg in his new job as Reich Signal Security Co-ordinator (RSSC) actually held prospects of becoming something of a safeguard. For Canaris was keenly aware that his SS friend's loathing of the new head of the RSHA was akin to his own. Indeed, apart from the fact that one was a Nazi and the other not, they shared many beliefs, even if some were never mentioned during their many conversations. Most fundamentally taboo were opinions touching on the improbability of Germany winning the war.

In the summer of 1942 the travelled and extremely well-informed Schellenberg, unlike the vast majority of his parochially minded SS colleagues, had come to certain conclusions that simply could not be raised in safety with anybody in government circles: 'At this moment we still stood on the dizzy heights and the Nazi leaders still believed that victory was in sight. I felt, however, that for me this was the real turning point. I was forced to the conclusion that the idea of "total victory" and its later version, "final victory" could no longer be realised. This brought me to the problem of how to inform our leaders of these unpleasant facts, since they rigidly refused to consider their possibility . . . I came to the conclusion that as long as the Reich had the power to fight, it would also have the power to bargain.'[2]

The upshot of this catalytic reasoning had been a private meeting with Himmler. Schellenberg boldly asked the Reichsführer SS, 'in which drawer of your desk have you got your alternative solution for ending this war?' A question which initiated a long, rambling discussion that, amazingly, terminated with Himmler granting Schellenberg authority most secretly to put into action a plan designed to remove the war-mongering Ribbentrop from his post as Foreign Minister by Christmas 1942. The result would, optimistically, clear the way for the start of diplomatic negotiations 'directed towards extricating Germany from her present situation with a minimum of territorial loss.'[3]

Inevitably this naive scheme was doomed to failure by the adverse march of events for Germany in Russia and Africa and by Himmler's characteristic vacillation when faced with difficult decisions in the Byzantine world of Nazi politics. Schellenberg, however, retained his idealistic notions even as he unwittingly encountered the equally Byzantine machinations of Abwehr activity, though, out of personal regard for Canaris, he concentrated only on the glaring shortcomings of the Abwehr's legitimate work, without trying too hard to uncover the activities of Oster and his fellow resisters.

Sensing that Canaris 'was bedevilled by his anxiety about the outcome of the war and the muddle of his own plans,' Schellenberg was embarrassed in 1942 gradually to uncover the Abwehr's glaring flaws. 'He was over-inflating his organisation, indiscriminately enrolling serious workers and dubious riff-raff; reforms were feebly attempted and then allowed to peter out. To me his whole organisation was a nightmarish oppression (sic). For how was the general situation to develop if no efficient work was done in this important sector of military intelligence? How were we to reach a position from which to influence the leaders and, if need be, change the direction of their policy?'[4]

How astonished might Schellenberg have been, as he began in March 1943 to forge working arrangements with Fellgiebel on code and cipher co-ordination, to realise that at that very moment the Wehrmacht Chief of Signals and Intelligence, along with Oster within the Abwehr, was on the verge of launching Operation 'Flash' — a scheme which aimed to change policy in a far more radical manner than anything Schellenberg dreamed of.

The initial concept for the cavalry officers under Lt-Col von Boeselager to assassinate Hitler when on a visit to HQ Army Group Centre at Smolensk had been abandoned for precisely the cause that had turned Guderian against involvement with any dealings with Field Marshal von Kluge. Entirely to form, 'clever Hans' (*kluge*

Hans) as he was nicknamed, had refused permission to act in that manner. He could not condone a premeditated killing of his supreme commander, he explained by way of excuse to Lt-Col von Tresckow, who now had assumed leadership of the assassination attempt.[5]

Tresckow and his aide, Fabian von Schlabrendorff (whom he light-heartedly called his 'guardian and political conscience') thereupon decided to plant a bomb with a time fuse in Hitler's Condor aircraft when the Führer was returning to Rastenburg after paying a visit to Smolensk on 13 March. The explosive and timer were packed and disguised as two bottles of brandy as a present from Tresckow to his old friend (and fellow conspirator) General Helmuth Stieff at OKH. It was handed to a Colonel Brandt shortly before take-off, already set to explode 30 minutes later. Meanwhile Schlabrendorff had alerted Oster, Beck and Fellgiebel and they were standing by in readiness to seize power when news of the crash was received. Unhappily, as the hours ticked by, they went on waiting until it was reported that the Condor had landed safely. The fuse had failed. At any moment the deadly package would be handed to Stieff and the game might be given away. A telephone call from Tresckow to the fortunate Brandt, explaining that an error with the date of presentation had been made, gave time for Schlabrendorff to fly to Rastenburg next day to substitute real bottles for the faulty bomb and save the Flash plotters from exposure.

Undeterred, Tresckow planned to try again on 21 March at an exhibition of captured weapons when Hitler, Göring, Himmler and Keitel would be present. This time a 10-minute fuse would be needed and it turned out that there were none available. Whereupon Oster, in consultation with sceptical colleagues, decided to abandon Flash for the perfectly sound reasons that the sketchy plans for exploitation of the demise of the Führer needed elaboration. Common sense had prevailed at last.[6]

* *

The tensions and strains bearing down on Fellgiebel throughout March were increasingly distractingly intense. To the normal pressures of everyday work had to be added those of coping with the menacing presence of Schellenberg, with his SS security-minded attachments, plus the machinations of Oster and Tresckow as they blundered their way to the demise of Operation 'Flash'. Its cancellation must have come as a distinct relief. Yet there emerged a quite unexpected abatement for Fellgiebel as, in the course of dealings with Schellenberg, a remarkably constructive rapport developed. Dreading any attempt by the SS officer to lay a heavy personal hand upon the co-ordination of codes and ciphers, he found himself being consulted in a civilised manner by a man who, like himself, was prepared to listen and to delegate. Quick to grasp the security and technical implications of the breaking of Enigma, Schellenberg equally surprisingly declared his sympathy with Fellgiebel's long-standing difficulties. He concurred with Fellgiebel's endeavours economically and efficiently to rationalise and control the sprawling Reich communications system's operational procedures.

Schellenberg smiled to himself when the outspoken Fellgiebel lashed out at the inherent waste created by the independent, uncontrolled services — citing above all Göring and 'his' Luftwaffe as the principal offenders in this respect. Neither did he absolve some of the Abwehr's deficiencies when Schellenberg touched on that subject. Towards the end of their first meeting an accord had been reached. At the conclusion of the second a policy and plan had been hammered out.

With immediate effect Schellenberg's Reich Signal Security Office (Reichsignalsicherheitsdienst — RSSD) would assume responsibility, implemented by Fellgiebel's Wehrmacht Signal and Intelligence Office, for the control of code and cipher policy throughout all government departments and armed services. As interpreted by Fellgiebel on the basis of Schellenberg's oral remarks, this conferred an almost free hand in matters beyond codes and ciphers. It seemed to him that, played dextrously, opportunities might be devised to strengthen his grip, under the aegis of SS authority, over certain other communications areas.[D2]

Meanwhile Germany's situation worsened as the adverse Enigma effect Fellgiebel had injected expanded its ramifications and the perils of his own central role in resistance activity multiplied.

DEVIATIONS FROM HISTORY

[D1] Fictional as is the notion of a very senior SS officer in the imaginary role of RSSC, there is about it a certain logic at a time when Hitler was progressively expanding the SS's functions as a state within the state, of which the appointment of Kaltenbrunner as head of RSHA was a most significant move.

[D2] A totally imaginary organisation and situation which, under pressure from Kaltenbrunner, epitomised the actual, gradually oncoming merging of Abwehr and SS intelligence functions.

Confirmatory footnotes:
1 Schellenberg p 85.
2 *ibid* pp 122–3.
3 *ibid* pp 129–35.
4 *ibid* p 157.
5 Wheeler-Bennett p 561.
6 *ibid* pp 562, 563.

12.
Decay and Disorder

Prospects for the month of April, as contemplated by Hitler and the sycophantic staff of OKW, looked a trifle rosier than at the beginning of March. Manstein's victories in the Ukraine and the recapture of Kharkov had driven the Russians back to Kursk and put an end to Russia's post-Stalingrad exploitation. The alignment of the vast salient to the west of Kursk now offered the Germans an opportunity to deliver a great, perhaps decisive, envelopment of Russian forces as soon as the weather and state of the ground permitted. In Tunisia, too, for a fleeting moment at the beginning of the month, the front seemed to have stabilised in mountainous terrain. Furthermore, although the weight of night attacks by the British Bomber Command on cities was growing disastrously in scale of devastation, the badly run-down Luftwaffe was showing signs of a recovery which might help redress the balance of air power. At the same time, moreover, under the efficient drive of Albert Speer, industrial production was rapidly expanding and the development of new weapons showing signs of promise, and at sea the Battle of the Atlantic hung in the balance as an increasing number of U-boats strove desperately to sever the Allied lines of communication and seal the blockade.

To the best informed pragmatists, above all to Canaris, Oster and Fellgiebel, disaster loomed grimly ominous, not only in the military and civil operational spheres but also within their own rickety resistance movement. On 5 April, in the course of the arrest by the Gestapo of one of the conspirators (Hans von Dohnanyi) on suspicion of smuggling Jews into Switzerland, evidence was also uncovered which threatened to point at the leaders of the conspiracy, including Oster, who was caught attempting to conceal an incriminating document. For ten hair-raising days, while Dohnanyi brilliantly won delay under interrogation, Canaris struggled to save Oster while evidence of the conspiracy was destroyed. But on 15 April Canaris realised that the continued employment of the security-careless Oster was no longer prudent. He dismissed his deputy and put him under house arrest even though, at a single stroke, this left the resistance movement leaderless and many of its members petrified for their own safety.[1]

It would be another seven months before a leader of sufficient dedication and fire would emerge to replace Oster, and it was not without significance that the future self-appointed assassin of Hitler was at that very moment struggling to recover from serious wounds received in Tunisia. During the months of convalescence ahead Lt-Col Claus von Stauffenberg would compose the philosophy that generated the sense of burning duty which drove him unreservedly to undertake that crusade.

Meanwhile Fellgiebel kept his fingers crossed and did what he could to maintain a basic resistance network in being. At the same time he pursued his normal duties in the service of the Fatherland, of which imposition of control of the new code security system was foremost — a job for which he was ideally qualified and placed.

* *

Fellgiebel's supreme position at the centre of the German communications web allowed him unlimited opportunities to travel freely to all corners of the Reich and the occupied territories. He was frequently on the move, thus making it easy for him to stay in personal touch with almost everybody involved with resistance. Moreover, he could freely use the peerless radio, telephone and teleprinter networks he had created, even to the extent of using a private code of his own for clandestine purposes.

The foundations of the military signals network were the special headquarters constructed for the Führer and the highest military staffs. The prototype was called *Felssenest* and located in concrete emplacements set in difficult terrain near Munstereifel to control the 1940 campaign in the West. Its principal disadvantage was the lack of land-line links due to the impossibility of access by cable. This made excessive use of radio and greater use of codes inevitable. Far more sophisticated and better located were *Wolfschanze* near Rastenburg, and two long-range main signal centres called *Zeppelin* (not far from Berlin near Zossen) and *Amt Anna* (near Angerburg within 20km of Rastenburg).

Wolfschanze had been designed to control the campaign in the east in 1941. It consisted of numerous large bomb proof bunkers built on the surface and set in a large area, and was served by rail as well as by road and air. Profiting from the lessons learnt at *Felssenest*, it incorporated at its heart a true wonder of signal communications. The most modern technology was introduced and it was staffed by highly trained personnel. Priority was given to cable communications of very clear performance and high security. The cables radiated in all directions, thus facilitating switching in the event of interruptions or breaks.[2]

The spacious internal layout of *Zeppelin*, dug in 20 metres below ground, was well described by General Albert Praun. 'The subterranean accommodation contained telephone lines for local and long-distance communications, the teleprinter exchange, amplification equipment, frequency and alternator telegraph installations, emergency current supply and the control rooms, as well as sleeping accommodation, kitchens and bathrooms.'

As the war progressed the demands on *Zeppelin* and *Amt Anna* imposed almost unbearable loads and strain. 'The increase in personnel and the countless amplifier valves diminished the supply of air far beyond the original calculations for air conditioning. In the teleprinter offices and other equipment rooms there was a constant temperature of 40 degrees C.' When describing *Zeppelin* Praun claimed. 'The working conditions for the ladies were most difficult below ground. But they worked bravely and their precise and pleasant voices on the telephone contributed greatly in bringing human features to the grim circumstances.'[3]

Wildhagen (Fellgiebel's biographer) called him 'a modern man' who made the best of everything at his disposal. In 1940 he had approached Frau Göring for assistance in recruiting from her Red Cross organisation the first 600 ladies for the Wehrmacht's Signals Corps. By the end of the war their number would rise to 85,000. They were all well educated and volunteers since, in Hitler's Germany where women were encouraged to stay in the home, they could not be conscripted. The pay-off amounted to the release of two men for every three women for other duties in all three services. The girls were usually billeted in nearby civilian houses, although some were accommodated in barracks.[4] They were sometimes known as 'the grey mice'.[5]

Fellgiebel, blessed by an ever youthful personality, was never happier than when in the company of young people. Frequently after supper he would surround himself with those who, unlike their superior officers, were not so overworked. If transcripts had been made of those conversations they would have given ' . . . a complete picture of the war's development with appropriate optimistic, critical, pessimistic or catastrophic undertones and comments. Fully informed through reliable sources and himself disposed to clear and logical thought, Fellgiebel argued repeatedly with the "Young People" who had been influenced by Nazi dogma or Nazi Propaganda. He spoke with reckless frankness, knowing full well that not only his telephone conversations were tapped, but that his demeanour and remarks were carefully recorded by the Gestapo.'[6]

'Fellgiebel wore his heart on his sleeve and this would become increasingly dangerous. Aware of this he once said, at the beginning of 1943 in the Paris officers' mess, "Well, one simply has to risk one's head." Everyone knew in which camp he stood and everyone felt saddened by a worrying future.'[7]

Predictably, despite the authoritative support of Schellenberg, the imposition of the new strict discipline and rules governing high grade codes did not proceed unopposed. Inevitably it was the Luftwaffe which, for practical as well as prestige reasons, protested the most vehemently. Geared for command, control and logistic purposes to the prolific use of radio and Enigma, it found itself in extremely serious operational difficulties. Fellgiebel did what he could to satisfy the priority needs of Göring's pet service, but the linking of its sprawling airfields, command and control centres by additional cable could not be arranged overnight, if only because of the shortage of materials needed, such as scarce metals like copper.

Priorities for allocation of cable links were promulgated and concessions made when they proved impractical. All low security traffic was diverted to special courier and Reichspost. Endeavouring (with ill grace) to placate Göring, Fellgiebel permitted the Luftwaffe limited use of Enigma for internal purposes only. Specifically, however, nothing that might compromise the security of other services was permitted. Even so, occasions did arise when the Reichsmarschall, in a towering rage, would appeal direct to the Führer — as he did when Fellgiebel insisted on integrating the Luftwaffe's own information service with the Army's. Then it would be Schellenberg, briefed by Fellgiebel, who stood in the firing line and more often than not (as with this matter) won the day. For Göring had already forfeited his pre-eminent position with Hitler while the minions of Himmler's élite SS were acquiring more and more influence and power.

For their part the SS and the police, as minor users of Enigma, complied quite readily with the new regime, and the Army had relatively few difficulties in adapting since it always had been fairly security conscious and made extensive use of cable and courier.[D1] As suited an inherently secretive organisation, the Abwehr made least fuss, although Canaris was horrified when he plumbed the depths which the penetration of Enigma had made into the Abwehr's most delicate espionage and security arrangements. Even without investigating in detail, it was obvious that the enemy might well be in possession of intelligence of the most damaging kind. Fortunately it was possible to put existing code books into use almost immediately.

Meanwhile the Diplomatic Service and Navy were so hard hit that crisis points were reached immediately. They, worst of all, would now suffer from the penalties of the self-inflicted tyranny of radio until approved code book systems could be prepared and distributed to all users.

Fellgiebel wanted to adopt a standard Wehrmacht high grade code book to replace Enigma, fully aware as he was of the inherent vulnerability of such systems. After all, the various Wehrmacht signals agencies had all along been penetrating the British, Canadian and American code books, in December 1942, for example, reading no less than 80% of their naval traffic.[8] Therefore he and Schellenberg opted to spread the risk by permitting each service to produce its own high grade code books to avoid a wholesale compromise. Even this could not be done overnight, and in the meantime there was enormous potential for errors which would almost inevitably be of help to the code-breakers of Bletchley Park.

* *

It had come as a considerable shock to Joachim von Ribbentrop and the Diplomatic Service when they learned that, for an unknown length of time, their communications with Continental and overseas embassies and consulates had been thoroughly compromised through use of Enigma. With no nation was this more damaging than Japan, with whom communication by radio was the only practical means. Not only was it revealed that the enemy had been privy to the most sensitive diplomatic, military and technical intelligence but it was also plain that secure contact with connections outside the Reich were virtually prohibited since nearly all were carried by radio. It would be many weeks, maybe months before diplomats in distant countries, such as those of Central and South America and Japan, received new non-Enigma codes delivered in absolute safety.

There was a certain irony about this. For years the foreign military attachés' offices and some embassies in Berlin had been rented to their occupants at an exorbitant charge and the premises systematically bugged by the Germans for the benefit of their security services.[9] Now the Germans would have to close down their own diplomatic radio links and, in some cases, go cap-in-hand to their clients to arrange alternative encoding and decoding facilities. Needless to say, the diplomatic repercussions were enormous. All of a sudden at a moment of declining German military prestige, appalling, incalculable flaws in the vital German communications system were revealed. The detrimental effects on confidence were colossal.

Links with Japan were not only the most important but also the most difficult to restore. The distance between their nearest outposts was far beyond the range of aircraft. The journey by sea from France via the Cape of Good Hope or Cape Horn was of extremely long duration. Carriage by post or courier through neutral countries was little faster and wide open to interception by the vigilant enemy — as indeed were all other methods. Under these conditions the time needed to issue new code books was embarrassingly long but unavoidable. As a stopgap it was suggested that the Japanese might be willing to permit use of their machine code system, but this was rejected as thoroughly insecure. In no way were the Germans willing to consign their closest secrets into Japanese hands. So, for the time being and with much loss of face, the Germans admitted the difficulty to their most important Axis ally and begged to be kept informed through Japanese channels — which themselves were penetrated.[D2/9, 10z]

The frustrated Ribbentrop was infuriated and hunting for scapegoats. Naturally he first blamed Canaris and Fellgiebel for having permitted the situation to occur, but this got him nowhere since it was pointed out that every user of Enigma (including the Diplomatic Service) had adopted it independently on the advice of experts. These same experts remained baffled by the cause of the debacle. So Ribbentrop then attacked Schellenberg for his alleged tardiness in providing a solution, but that only induced a row with Himmler who leapt to the defence of a cherished underling.

To Fellgiebel's almost undisguised delight a classic internecine squabble among Hitler's top Nazi Party comrades broke out to sour relationships more than ever. For the time being, therefore, the exchange of diplomatic and military information between the Axis partners was cripplingly restricted, not that this was nearly as serious as some might think since close co-ordination of German and Japanese strategy had never really been a reality of the partnership. Both sides tended to keep their own counsel, especially when it came to providing advance information of such major intentions as the German invasion of Russia and the Japanese attack on Pearl Harbor.

The diplomatic storms were damaging enough, yet nothing like as harmful as the turn of the tide in the Atlantic struggle which induced capricious reactions well beyond even the highest flights of Fellgiebel's fertile imagination.

DEVIATIONS FROM HISTORY

[D1] These are major deviations. Yet there is little doubt that, even if Enigma had remained in full operation, some such restrictive economy measures would have been beneficial to the German war effort as well as to signals security.

[D2] Which, had it been done, would have availed nothing since, prior to Pearl Harbor, the Americans had broken the Japanese Typewriter 97 encoding machine. Called Purple by the Americans, Type 97 was not, as sometimes stated, similar to Enigma, although both had sprung from known commercial sources. The method of encryption was totally different and so, too, therefore, was the method of decryption. The credit for this went to a team of brilliant mathematicians, headed by Frank Rowlett, under the leadership of a highly strung cryptanalyst called William Friedman, who broke down under the strain.

Confirmatory footnotes:
1 Wheeler-Bennett pp 565, 566.
2 Wildhagen p 191.
3 *ibid* p 191.
4 *ibid* p 191.
5 Author's observation at Dönitz's HQ in May 1945.
6 Wildhagen p 205.

7 *ibid* p 206.
8 Hinsley Vol 2 pp 555, 556, 636.
9 *ibid* p 204.
10 Lewin *The Other Ultra* pp 35–43 which describes Type 97 (Purple) in admirably clear outline.

13.
Crises in the Atlantic

At the beginning of March 1943 both the contenders in the Battle of the Atlantic dwelt in a state of intense crisis, even without taking into account the Enigma dilemma.

On the British part there was the realisation that, despite the massive and rising American construction, shipping losses still exceeded replacements and that the ever-increasing number of U-boats operating was approaching the point at which they could almost saturate the convoy routes, above all in the so-called mid-Atlantic gap where it was still not yet possible to provide the essential air cover to hamper and kill U-boats. On the other hand, the breaking of the Triton Enigma (Shark) code by Turing and the Bletchley Park team in December 1942 was providing valuable information which was making feasible the crucially important diversions of convoys out of harm's way. Significantly, however, during a single week in mid-February when Shark could not be broken, losses increased dramatically.[1]

As for the Germans, they also were under appalling pressure in the knowledge that, if they were defeated in the Battle of the Atlantic, the war most certainly was lost. True, the number of U-boats at sea in the North Atlantic at any one time had risen from about 40 in December to 66 in February and in those months the number of sinkings had improved to 34 from 19 in December and 15 in January.[2] However, it could not be gainsaid that nearly all those losses were inflicted on two unlucky convoys while, as a result of rerouteing, a vast quantity of shipping got through scot-free. This was despite the fact that *B-Dienst*, having concentrated almost its entire effort against the so-called convoy code (British Naval Cipher No 3 which had resisted breaking since 15 December) was reading it once again.[3]

Everything changed after Dönitz abandoned Enigma and introduced drastically revised emergency measures and new doctrines. It was a process demanding the phased recall of boats for the briefing and retraining of key officers and men, which could only be arranged secretly on shore and had to be done piecemeal over a period of time, especially the issue of new code books.[D1]

Anxiously the Allies on both sides of the Atlantic awaited the form of German reaction. In the Submarine Tracking Rooms of Britain, America and Canada it was realised that alterations to the extremely strict enemy operational procedures and standing orders, which had evolved since 1940, could only be gradual and empirical. By now the Allied commanders, especially the British ex-submariner, Admiral Sir Max Horton, had entered into the German minds. So familiar were the officers in the Tracking Rooms with how their German opponents worked, they could often recognise who was on duty at any time and confidently predict how they and some of the most experienced U-boat commanders (whom they identified by name) might react in any particular situation. For example, Harry Hinsley, Bletchley Park's leading expert on U-boat Command, always knew when Dönitz was on duty. 'I could tell from the way he planned it. He was good. Mind you, he had a fairly rigid mind.'[4]

When a U-boat put to sea its commander was in possession of numerous instructions, the majority of which were related to command and control as applied by U-Boat Command. In addition to the four-wheel Triton Enigma machine, through which all secure traffic was channelled, they carried code books and squared charts designed to improve the security of messages. Not until clearing the Bay of Biscay or crossing the 60 degrees North line, however, would he receive by radio his encoded destination point and orders. Adopted for security reasons to avoid the risk of compromise by careless talk on shore, this procedure thus ironically announced to the enemy his boat's identity and mission.

Previously U-boat Command had imposed very rigid tactical control. Only with special permission could these orders be disobeyed. Standing Orders demanded that every time a boat transmitted it must give its position. A typical transmission, prefaced by the commander's name and boat's number, would contain a minimum of 20 words (taking at least a minute to transmit) comprising information about a convoy's size, position and course, number and type of ships sunk, attacks by enemy aircraft or surface vessels, present position (obligatory with all transmissions), fuel and torpedo state, weather conditions and meteorological data. This was sufficiently long to facilitate effective enemy DF action.

Based on messages such as these and on decoded intercepts of enemy convoy signals, U-boat Command would decide the exact deployment of patrol lines spread across a convoy's path and direct the concentration of boats to the attack from the apparently most advantageous positions. It could also give precise orders arranging a rendezvous with a supply U-boat in a safe area, or decide when a boat should return to port. Finally, whenever a boat failed to report for several days, U-boat Command went on calling until hope had to be abandoned.[5]

Once the compromising of Enigma was recognised, these procedures had to be drastically modified and curtailed — and quickly. Fundamentally U-boat Command could no longer transmit detailed tactical instructions by radio. Fellgiebel spent a day with Dönitz and his staff hammering out the new drills. Most unwillingly Dönitz had to relinquish centralised tactical control. Henceforward such radio messages as were sent had to be very brief and carefully disguised. Commanders had to be granted far greater freedom of initiative and action. What emerged could hardly have been better calculated to undermine the submarine campaign that, alone, might have been fatal to the Allied cause. For in his determination to shorten the war and limit the appalling damage inflicted on his beloved Fatherland by the enemy bomber offensive, Fellgiebel contributed significantly by hampering vital command and control.

To begin with, the practice of issuing orders of destination and mission by radio was replaced by delivery of instructions by hand-of-officer at the moment of departure. Secondly, each boat would be allocated to a specific group, commanded by a senior officer who had been sent to a carefully selected area where convoys were expected. His orders would as often as possible be transmitted through high frequency radio, although it was over-optimistically hoped that visual signals might sometimes be feasible. Thirdly, the elaborate format of messages was reduced; no longer could any indication of the boat's number be sent, nor details of sinkings, fuel and torpedo states and meteorological data. Until new codes were issued transmissions were to be restricted to a very short daily Enigma-enciphered boat's position message and to the positions and course of convoys when found.

At the same time U-boat Command almost abolished directives that repositioned boats from one Group to another.

What was known by the Allies as the 'address book' system continued in use to disguise position. It had been introduced in June 1941 and was keyed to an imaginary person's name. By March 1943 it had been developed progressively into a complicated, yet vulnerably decipherable, code — notably when operators made errors in enciphering.[6]

Thus, with Fellgiebel's approval, Enigma continued in naval use but in very attenuated and more secure form, thus depriving the Allies of the luxuriant flood of strategic information that once had been theirs. Yet it still provided enough basic data for the trackers to divine the intentions and pattern of U-boat tactical manoeuvres. However, these movements tended to be more erratic than under the old regime as individual commanders used their intuitions and initiative.

The immediate effect of the Germans' counter-measures did far more than reduce the number of U-boats operating. They also created awful dilemmas, confusion and dismay among commanders at sea. Suddenly, without warning, to be deprived of clear and profuse guidance and be instructed to minimise all radio transmissions, they lost cohesion in a welter of indecision. No longer could patrol lines be formed, let alone in an orderly manner. All at once the supply of essential information virtually dried up. This denial was made all the more damaging by the chronic lack of information from air reconnaissance, the Luftwaffe being as absent as ever from the scene and totally incapable of survival either for observation of convoys or for the interception of the increasing number of Allied aircraft which, at last, could operate most effectively even in the mid-Atlantic gap.

Consequently, throughout March, the Allied Tracking Rooms enjoyed outstanding successes in diverting convoys from U-boats which no longer operated in large organised packs and only rarely made contact, let alone launched serious attacks. It was a decisive month in which, by use of new weapons, the hunters became the hunted.[D27] The sheer number of U-boats available for establishing long patrol lines of observation had been close to making evasive routeing impossible but, under the new German command system, it was extremely difficult to form and control those patrol lines to cover all approaches. More critical still, however, were the quantity and quality of Allied escort vessels, aircraft and weapon systems and the operational systems polished by improved training.[8]

From the increasing number of British, Canadian and US Navy anti-submarine ships could be formed crack mobile support groups to hunt and destroy U-boats, in addition to more convoy close escort vessels. In association with improved depth charges (dispensed by multi-barrelled, forward-firing mortars called Hedgehog), there were coming into service 10cm (short wave) radar sets which could be mounted in ships or aircraft to detect U-boats running on the surface by night or day even in foggy weather. By now, too, nearly all escort ships were equipped with a very efficient HF/DF set that provided accurate bearings on transmissions even of the shortest duration.

Most important of all, light aircraft carriers (CVE) were becoming available, of which the USN *Bogue* was the first into action as centrepiece of a support group in March. Gradually, too, Liberator very long range (VLR) bomber aircraft were also helping to fill the mid-Atlantic gap. Fitted with 10cm radar aligned with a powerful searchlight (the Leigh Light), a VLR aircraft sent to attack a surfaced U-boat which had been detected either by surface vessels or DF could home in on the target, commence its attack at low level and illuminate the U-boat with total surprise before dropping its bombs.

Against these powerful weapon systems the U-boats had no capable and assured reply. Unable for operational reasons to maintain complete radio silence, they were vulnerable to DF. Compelled to move on the surface either for tactical reasons or the need to re-charge batteries, they could never feel safe, for the Germans had failed absolutely to discover the nature and power of enemy radar. Arrogantly assuming that their opponent could only possess low frequency sets like their own, they concentrated on the useless *Wanze* detector to the virtual exclusion of *Naxos*, a higher frequency scanner. Furthermore, they handicapped their sailors to only very cautious use of the effective (though electro-magnetically 'active') *Metox* detector. To complete this chapter of incompetence it was the failure of German scientists and technologists to realise that a strange electronic valve found among a crashed RAF bomber's electronic equipment held the key to the radar puzzle. For the Luftwaffe, with typical departmental over-independence, had not bothered to notify the Navy or Fellgiebel of the discovery of this British-invented cavity magnetron valve which made 10cm radar feasible.

With the technological scales insidiously tipping against them, the Germans only gradually introduced their new tactics into action. There was a somewhat tentative transitory phase which, to the listening and watching Allied trackers, indicated only too obviously the dilemmas being encountered by an opponent who had been robbed of radio plenty. In his Liverpool headquarters Admiral Horton rubbed his hands with satisfaction as evidence accrued of discontent among U-boat commanders and their frustrated controllers at Wilhelmshaven. Horton naturally regretted the loss of access to each boat's sailing instructions, since this posed strategic problems and hampered planning of counter-deployments of resources. Nevertheless, from deciphering of the extremely sparse U-boat Command change-of-position orders, from boats reporting their positions, and from escort ships detecting and locating U-boat positions by DF of their radio transmissions, the trackers learnt how to formulate current deployment patterns which pointed to likely enemy tactical intentions. Almost at once they recognised the decentralisation of control to group leaders. Soon, too, they knew that they were continuing to establish patrol lines in the manner of old. This was inevitable, bearing in mind the paltry scale of Luftwaffe reconnaissance and its frequent inaccuracy. The patrol line remained the only worthwhile way of finding approaching convoys. At the same time it was noticed that, when assembling, those lines were often

Above: General Erich Fellgiebel.
Bundesarchiv

Above right: General Wolfgang Martini.
Bundesarchiv

Right: General Albert Praun.
Nachrichtentruppe

Left: A three-wheel Enigma machine complete in its wooden transit case and with its original German battery. *Science Museum/Science & Society Picture Library*

Above: A four-wheel German Enigma cypher machine, introduced on Atlantic U-boats in February 1942. *Science Museum/Science & Society Picture Library*

Overleaf: A British Bombe code-breaking machine, front and rear views, photographed at Bletchley Park 1943.
Bletchley Park Trust/Science & Society Picture Library

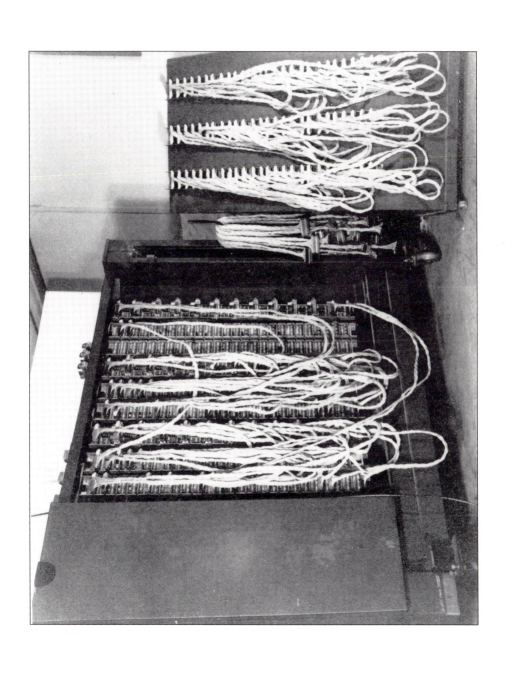

Above: Dr Alan Turing (right), photographed working on another early British computer after the war. *Science Museum/Science & Society Picture Library*

Below: Left to right: Dr Albert Speer, Admiral Karl Dönitz, General Alfred Jodl. *IWM*

Above: Adolf Hitler with (left to right) General Alfred Jodl, Field Marshal Walter von Brauchitsch, Admiral Eric Raeder and Field Marshal Wilhelm Keitel. Reichsmarschall Hermann Göring is with his back to the camera. *Macksey*

Left: General Sir Alan Brooke. *IWM*

Above: Left to right: President Franklin Roosevelt, General Charles de Gaulle and Prime Minister Winston Churchill. *IWM*

Left: General Hans Oster. *Stahlberg*

Right: Field Marshal Eric von Manstein in front, followed at the rear by Captain Alexander Stahlberg. *Stahlberg*

Right: General Henning von Tresckow. *Stahlberg*

BB/AM/WO/ PSE -=KKKKKKK

CX/MSS/2499/T 14

EASTERN EUROPE

=========================

TO : /OP. ABT.   AND TO OKH/FOREIGN ARMIES EAST ,
FROM ARGROUP SOUTH IA /01, NO. 411/43, SIGNED VON WEICHS, GEN/
GENERAL DMARSCHALL, DATED 25/4 :-

COMEHENSIVE APPRECIATION OF THE ENEMY FOR ''ZITADELLE''

IN E MAIN THE APPRECIATION OF THE ENEMY REMAINS THE
SAME AS PORTED IN ARMY GROUP SOUTH (ROMAND II A, NO. 0477/43
OF 29/3 D IN THE SUPPLEMENTARY APPRECIATION OF 15/4 .

THEAIN CONCENTRATION , WHICH WAS ALREADY THEN APPARENT,
ON THE NTH FLANK OF THE ARMY GROUP IN THE GENERAL AREA
KURSK-SDSHA --VOLCHANSK--OSTROGOSHSK, CAN NOW BE CLEARLY
RECOGNIS : A FURTHER INTENSIFICATION OF THIS
CONCENTRIION IS TO BE EXPECTED AS A RESULT OF THE CONTINUOUS
HEAVY TRISPORT MOVEMENTS ON THE LINES .YELETS --KASTORNOYE --
KURSK, AN POVORINO --SVOBODA AND GRYAZI --SVOBODA , WITH A
PROBABLE B% INCREASE) IN THE AREA VALUIKI--NOVY OSKOL --
KUPYANSK. AT PRESENT HOWEVER IT IS NOT APPARENT WHETHER THE
OBJECT OFTHIS CONCENTRATION IS OFFENSIVE OR DEFENSIVE .
AT PRESEN' , (B% STILL) IN ANTICIPATION OF A GERMAN
OFFENSIVE ON BOTH THE KURSK AND MIUS DONETZ FRONTS , THE ARMOURED
AND MOBILE FORMATIONS ARE STILL EVENLY DISTRIBUTED IN VARIOUS
GROUPS BEHIND THE FRONT AS STRATEGIC RESERVES.

THERE ARE NO SIGNS AS YET OF A MERGING OF
THESE FORMATIONS OR A TRANSFER TO THE FORWARD AREA(EXCEPT FOR
(POMAND)II GDS ARMOURED CORPS) BUT THIS COULD TAKE PLACE RAPIDLY AT
ANY TIME
END OF PAGE ONE

Above: Reichsmarschall Hermann Göring with Field Marshal Albert Kesselring to his right and Field Marshal Erhard Milch on the left of the group. *Kesselring*

Left: Field Marshal von Weich's Operation Citadel appreciation sent by FISH. *PRO*

Overleaf, left: Colossus I. *Bletchley Park Trust/Science & Society Picture Library*

Overleaf, right: Ladies at work on codes in the machine room in Hut 6 at Bletchley Park. Note the enigma wheels on the tables and in the box. *Bletchley Park Trust/Science & Society Picture Library*

Above: Signallers three in 1941: left to right General Eric Fellgiebel, General Heinrich Guderian and Colonel (later General) Albert Praun. *Nachrichtentruppe*

Left: Colonel Count Claus von Stauffenberg. *Stahlberg*

quite accurately positioned to intercept convoys. This seemed to indicate what had previously been disclosed by Enigma, that the Germans were generously supplied with information from the convoy code.

Fascinating to Horton was clear evidence that U-boat group leaders were having appalling difficulty assembling and directing their subordinates as required. To begin with, the lack of clear directives and intelligence from U-boat Command made extremely hit and miss their assessments of a local situation and the formulation of effective plans of attack that were not matters of chance. Usually each group included several commanders who were inexperienced and timid. Far too frequently, just as in Enigma days, their reporting of contacts was no more reliable than that of the Luftwaffe. Other commanders were older hands to whom freedom of initiative was not always understood or acted upon. Then there were the wild hawks who, revelling in the new freedom, tended to rove too far and wide in their own individualistic way. And always there were those who claimed imaginary sinkings.[9]

The reporting of convoy contacts and the responses to them were of variable quality, leading to the opening of wide gaps in patrol lines. Occasionally Horton even saw no necessity to order diversions, knowing that his convoys could easily slip through the German net. He understood full well, as an ex-submariner, the virtual inability of a boat left behind to catch up — especially if the enemy threat prevented it running on the surface, even at night; as now, as now, more then ever before, was the case.

Fear of radar by night, allied to inhibitions associated with *Metox*, trapped commanders and crews in a constant state of nervous tension. Boats in close vicinity to a convoy were forced to remain submerged for most of the time. Therefore they found it extremely difficult to penetrate the defensive screen. Co-ordinated attacks were well nigh impossible to arrange even if the group leader were fortunate enough to have more than a pair of boats at his disposal. To harassed commanders, the ocean seemed to swarm with ships and aircraft which attacked by surprise with alarming frequency, even at a distance from a convoy, although, due to the radio restrictions, news of this phenomenon did not reach U-boat Command until a boat returned to port and the commander was debriefed. So not only was operational command and control inflexible and vague, vital immediate analysis and response to changing trends was seriously delayed.

Not surprisingly the number of ships sunk in April was far fewer even than in March as the U-boat casualty rate began to rise. The point was indeed imminent when the construction rate of Allied ships exceeded losses, although this, too, for the time being, was concealed from Dönitz by a combination of delayed reports and gross over-claiming by individual boat commanders. As also was concealed from both sides the state of declining morale among the crews which, in Enigma days, most certainly would have been disclosed.[D3/10]

May was the crunch month. With a record number of U-boats at sea, Dönitz in days gone by might have expected a highly rewarding killing.[11] As indeed there was — of U-boats — with only sparse pickings of ships put down to their credit. Solitary boats, playing an ever weaker role, groped for an elusive enemy and never fully achieved anything like a satisfactory concentration of effort. At the same time, as losses mounted horrendously in the North Atlantic, better results at lower cost were achieved against less heavily escorted convoys in remote areas.

Come the end of May, Dönitz was forced to the conclusion that defeat in the North Atlantic stared him in the face. In ignorance of the number of ships sunk, he was all too shatteringly aware of the U-boat losses. Hardly a day passed without yet another boat falling silent. Finally the total reached such numbers that it was unrealistic to continue so damaging a contest. For example, on each of five days three boats went missing and on another no less than four. Bowing to reality on the 30th, in consultation with Fellgiebel, Dönitz sent in clear language to all boats his decision to withdraw from the North Atlantic, without, of course, disclosing what he believed to be the true reasons, since that would divulge far too much to the enemy.[D4]

In conference with Hitler, Field Marshal Keitel and General Warlimont on 31 May, Dönitz spelled out the reasons (which inevitably in the circumstances were seriously inaccurate and deficient) for his retreat and the disastrous extent of his losses, which amounted to 37% of boats at sea. 'We must conserve our strength, otherwise we will play into the hands of the enemy' he said. 'I have withdrawn from the North Atlantic to the area west of the Azores in the hope of encountering less air reconnaissance there . . . With new submarines now becoming available I shall proceed to more distant areas in the hope that the planes there are not yet as fully equipped with the modern location devices. I intend, however, to resume attacks on convoys in the North Atlantic at the time of the new moon, on condition that the submarines have additional weapons at their disposal by that time.'

No clearer admission of abject defeat could have been uttered. If spoken by an Army general it probably would have brought down a fiery diatribe from Hitler. As it was, there ensued a lengthy discussion on new weapons systems, counter-measures and the usual demands for better air support. There was no rebuke for failure. Probably because, as reported on 2 May to Tokyo by Oshima, the Japanese ambassador, Hitler already surmised the worst when he admitted that, because the war had started too soon, 'we have been unable to dominate the seas.'[12]

Dönitz then turned to the future of submarine warfare, quoting statistics demonstrating how average sinkings per boat had fallen from 1,000 tons per day in 1940 to 200 tons at the end of 1942. 'This shows clearly the growing effectiveness of anti-submarine defence and the diminishing effectiveness of submarines. Nevertheless I am convinced that submarine warfare must be carried on, even if great successes are no longer possible.'

The Führer interrupted, 'There can be no talk of a let-up in submarine warfare. The Atlantic is my first line of defence in the West, and even if I have to fight a defensive battle there, that is preferable to waiting to defend myself on the coast of Europe.'

The discussion turned to increasing U-boat production from 30 to 40 per month; though how they were to be manned in face of an acute shortage of crews was not touched upon. Instead the meeting moved on to consideration of the shape of naval operations to come in the Mediterranean in the aftermath of the ejection of Axis forces from Africa at the beginning of May.[13]

Ten days later further disaster struck when *B-Dienst* reported it could no longer break the enemy convoy code. Henceforward locating convoys would become almost entirely a matter of chance. This was at a moment when the Allies decided that, so significantly had the Battle of the Atlantic swung in their favour, ships with a speed in excess of 15 knots could be allowed to travel out of convoy. So confident of victory now were the Allied navies that Admiral King (Chief of US Naval Staff) felt that the time had come to attack the supply U-boats, even if that meant disclosing the fact that the 'address group' system had been to some extent broken. Try as he might, Admiral Sir Dudley Pound (British First Lord of the Admiralty) failed to veto this proposal. King had his way and the hunt was on, starting with a first kill on 15 May.

With the threat to transatlantic convoys removed at the end of May, Admiral Horton could go onto the offensive. Now his hunter groups and their aircraft began to blockade the Bay of Biscay, intercepting U-boats on their way into and out of port. This compelled U-boat Command to adopt new tactics. Frequently tackled above and below the surface by day and night, the U-boats were ordered to fight their way through on the surface. Boats equipped with multi-barrelled anti-aircraft guns tried, at first with success, to shoot down aircraft which needed to deliver their bombs from low level to be sure of scoring a killing hit. But their assailants also soon developed new tactics. Instead of operating singly, they worked in co-ordinated groups, shooting up the gun crews as the bombing run commenced.[14]

Among the victims in the Bay blockade were three supply boats as they endeavoured to reach the relative safety of the remote South Atlantic refuelling areas to the southwest of the Azores. But even these places were no longer safe. In July a fourth supply boat was sunk by aircraft, followed in August by four more victims of the same kind, all to British and American aircraft, and a further two to the same killers in October. So disparate, however, were the circumstances of these losses that it was not until October (when few supply boats survived) that the Germans at last concluded that the enemy were in possession of several different means of detection. For example, they could pick up and DF vital radio transmissions (like calling for a doctor), or use radar and infra-red detection as well as disguised Enigma to locate refuelling places. This brought to an end the use of the supply boats and contributed to the hampering of sustained operations in remote waters.

Long before that, however, Dönitz had been forced by intolerable losses to abandon use of the Bay ports, group tactics and attacks on convoys. The Enigma factor was only a lesser cause of the loss of 17 boats in June and 46 in July — no less than seven were sunk on 30 July.[15] In any case the integrity of the new code book did not long survive due to a by no means unique circumstance in the transition phase from one system to the other. As had happened in the past, a U-boat's operator made the mistake of linking the new code with the old, an error that was gratefully seized upon rapidly by the cryptanalysts at GC&CS in order to break the new.

Without this disaster, however, the U-boat campaign was doomed to failure. For the principal cause of defeat was not lack of a secure code but the compound effect of the concentration of overwhelming numbers of ships and aircraft fitted with the latest detection equipment, and the destructive power of deadly weapons applied by expert Allied commanders and crews.

The future was to be a chapter of retreats as, progressively, the U-boats were withdrawn from most distant waters because of the loss of the supply boats as well as unsustainable casualties among the main force itself. Already the Allied rate of building replacement shipping exceeded losses. The Battle of the Atlantic had been lost not only at sea but also in the shipyards. And as the Japanese reeled from a series of defeats at American, Australian and British hands in the South Pacific, the German Navy was consigned to only a minor role in World War 2 as the Third Reich dropped into the abyss of defeat.

DEVIATIONS FROM HISTORY

[D1] Here the strategic and tactical story diverges fundamentally from what happened, although it must not be overlooked that the introduction of new and improved Allied weapon and security systems continued apace and with deadly effect.

[D2] This was very different to the actuality of March 1943 when 66 U-boats hunted twice as many ships as had crossed the Atlantic in February. In March the Allies lost 42 ships from Atlantic convoys (no less than 21 from two disastrous convoys in return for the sinking of only one U-boat) against the loss of only six U-boats all told.

[D3] It is a fact that similar trends actually were noticed by the Allies, though for slightly different reasons. On 19 April U-boat Command conceded that the strength of convoy defences was such that pack tactics were no longer practical. That month there was a decline in ships sunk (25) in proportion to U-boats sunk (16), brought about mainly by the greatly reinforced Allied forces and the latest weapons (see also fn 11 below).

[D4] In fact this signal, along with a whole series giving details of redeployment, was broadcast in Enigma cipher on 24 May. The delay adopted for this scenario is based on the difficulty the somewhat unimaginative Dönitz would surely have had in assessing the situation caused by delayed receipt of inadequate situation reports. The story of the real decisive May battles can be synthesised adequately from Anon MOD Vol III pp 104–13 and Hinsley Vol II pp 569–72.

Confirmatory footnotes:

1 Hinsley Vol 2 p 553.

2 *ibid* p 559.

3 *ibid* pp 552, 553.

4 *ibid* p 551.

5 *ibid* pp 549–55 including important footnotes.

6 *ibid* p 552 and pp 681, 682.

7 *ibid* pp 562, 563.

8 *ibid* pp 563, 564.

9 Anon MOD (Navy) Vol II pp 73–113 gives insight into the German point of view during the period up to and including May.

10 Hinsley Vol 2 pp 567–9.

11 *ibid* p 569. On 3 May there were more than 60 U-boats in the North Atlantic out of about 125 at sea.

12 *ibid* p 572. Revealed to the Allies through American Magic.

13 Anon *Füh* pp 331–6.

14 Anon MOD (Navy) Vol III pp 12–14.

15 These are actual figures based on the reasoning that, at this moment in this situation, Enigma could have been playing only a minor tactical role in anti-U-boat operations.

14.
Back to Intuitional Guesswork

Towards the close of the Tunisian campaign, Sir Stewart Menzies met with his closest SIS advisers to review the situation ahead of the forthcoming Trident conference between Churchill and Roosevelt and their chiefs of staff in Washington. After some six weeks managing almost without Enigma it was time to look at the current state of intelligence gathering and supply.

Already it was fairly obvious that the Battle of the Atlantic was swinging the Allied way, regardless of the loss of the accustomed flood of valuable tactical and strategic intelligence from Enigma. To compensate for this deficiency, C and his team noted the failure of the new flexible command and control system hurriedly imposed by the German U-boat Command. He realised that their need drastically to minimise encoded transmissions was creating a chaotic effect, simply because the U-boats could not operate decisively without a radio communication system that was guaranteed to divulge their positions.

Looking at air warfare, Menzies perceived a very different situation both in the defensive and offensive aspects. As was normal, prior notice of a renewed Luftwaffe offensive against England had been given via Ultra towards the end of 1942. Despite the heavy commitments to the intensive fighting in Russia and North Africa, bomber formations in France were being re-formed to start reprisals against the mounting terror being perpetrated by RAF Bomber Command against German cities. This forecast had been confirmed on the night of 17/18 January when 100 bombers attacked London. This raid was the overture to a series of sporadic night and day attacks, the latter by fighter-bombers against coastal and inland targets.

As was customary with nearly all raids, Enigma revealed little of tactical value; not that this mattered. The much improved British radar early warning system, enhanced occasionally by 'Y' Service intercepts of medium grade radio traffic, gave reasonable notice; except, that is, for low-level wave-skimming fighter-bombers: their undetectable depredations called for the mounting of standing fighter patrols to intercept. For the rest, the obsolescent German bomber aircraft, frequently manned by inexperienced crews, suffered badly at the hands of night-fighters and did but little damage.[1] All of this was duly noted by Ultra decrypts until the day arrived when they were virtually cut off by Schellenberg's Enigma ban in March.[D1]

From that moment Britain's air defence system relied upon intelligence supplied from a variety of traditional sources. Such as R/T conversations between fighter-bombers, the study of intercepted radio navigation beams of the *Y-Gerät* type, the interrogation of captured airmen, and agents' reports concerning the deployment of Luftwaffe units. These sources proved only partially effective since the night bombers were seldom engaged before dropping their bombs and the daylight fighter-bombers normally took the defences by surprise.[2] The results, however, were hardly worth the Germans' effort, as symbolised by a night raid on London by 30 fighter-bombers on 16 April. On that occasion only two bombs fell within the vast target area and six aircraft were lost (20%), including a trio which landed at West Malling in Kent in the belief it was in France.[3]

Likewise, Menzies concluded that, since Enigma had only rarely contributed significantly to the Bomber Offensive in the past, its forfeiture was no great calamity. Aerial photographic reconnaissance (PR) provided the best evidence of damage inflicted, along with reports from SIS and SOE agents, neutral diplomats and visitors to Germany from Spain, Sweden and Switzerland, articles in the European press, interrogations of prisoners and the reading of their letters from home, and occasional lax radio broadcasts. An increasing scepticism about the actual damage being inflicted compared with what was claimed by bomber crews sometimes happened from sheer lack of confirmatory evidence. Conclusions concerning effects on targets were based on comparisons with British experience of bombing in 1940 and 1941 and the results, gleaned from this and from operational analysis, were anything but encouraging since only a small percentage of bombers had found and hit their targets. As for the efficiency and methods of the German air defences, these were revealed to some extent by eavesdropping on the radio communications between German controllers and their fighter pilots, on the reports of returning bomber crews, and, disturbingly, the rising casualty rate after Air Marshal Arthur Harris's Bomber Command launched what already was known as the Battle of the Ruhr on 5 March — just a few days after Enigma went out of use.

As Menzies was aware, although the Ruhr was Harris's prime target, it was not the only one. The night bomber fleets, increasingly complemented by American B-17 and B-24 daylight bombers, also visited places connected with the Battle of the Atlantic, such as the naval bases of Wilhelmshaven and Bremen. What most concerned Menzies and others were the fluctuating trends of the attacks' results in terms of profit and loss. Although it was plain that the latest navigation and bombing aids, especially Oboe and H_2S, were producing far better accuracy than hitherto, there was nothing better than speculation to say how effective they really were. Bearing in mind the now proven gross exaggerations of the early days of bombing's effect (including those of the Germans), far more rigorous assessments than in the past were insisted upon. These indicated that neither German industrial production nor morale had suffered catastrophically. Indeed the former was rising impressively and the latter, at worst, was disclosing signs no worse than apathy.[4]

As for enemy defensive measures, there were already disturbing indications of deadly improvements in tactics. More bombers were being shot down than was prudently acceptable. True, the raid by 442 machines on Essen on 5 March was encouraging. Only 14 were lost (3.16%) and photographs showed that 480 acres of the central area of the city were destroyed or severely damaged. However, as the Germans knew (and Menzies did not), production was only temporarily reduced and soon recovered. Then there were the disasters, such as that of 16 April against Pilsen when out of 327 bombers 36 did not return (11%).[5]

Nevertheless, both Menzies and Harris were able to convince Churchill and Roosevelt and their Chiefs of Staff that, expensive in lives and material though the Bomber Offensive was, it was worth the attempt, if only to shorten the war and thus, perhaps, pre-empt any possibility of the enemy making an atom bomb that would change the balance of power overnight. Certainly there was every reason to fear this weapon and many another that the Germans might be developing because the limited intelligence about secret weapons still came mainly from interrogations, agents' reports and occasional lucky finds by PR. Even when in prolific use, Enigma had divulged but little of value.

* *

Regardless of the claims of airmen, such as Air Marshals Portal and Harris and the American General Carl Spaatz, that the war could be won by bombing, Menzies, the sceptical soldier, was naturally convinced that armies would be the ultimate arbiters of victory. Hence it was the analysis of the Enigma effect on land operations that most intrigued him — and the closing stages of the Tunisian battles were providing the surest guidelines to that opinion in his pre-Trident review.

Until the imposition of the Enigma ban, the Allies in North Africa in 1943 enjoyed intelligence galore from Army, Navy and Luftwaffe Enigma as well as SIS, PR and Long Range Desert Group patrols operating behind the enemy lines. In December 1942 the installation of a *Geheimschreiber*, known to Bletchley Park as Herring, a member of the Fish group, aroused considerable interest since, until then, only two such sets had been detected, both of them on the Eastern Front. Herring connected C-in-C (South), Field Marshal Albert Kesselring, in Rome with the HQ of General von Arnim's Fifth Panzer Army in Tunis, and assumed even greater importance with the elimination of Enigma. On Fellgiebel's directions, its main priority was the handling of the most urgent traffic generated within the High Command. For Fellgiebel assumed, on carefully considered advice, that the extremely complex *Geheimschreiber*, unlike Enigma, simply must be impenetrable. And even if it was not he was quite happy since it would have occurred to his tortured mind that, as yet another subversive war-shortening device, it was desirable for the enemy to remain privy to the thinking and plans of Hitler, OKW and the rest of the highest command hierarchy.[D2]

Awkward for the German communicators as the loss of Enigma was to their forces across the water in North Africa, the situation was far from wholly adverse. There remained useful and secure underwater cable links, beam radio and a fast, reasonably reliable air courier service to Sicily and Rome. The problem could largely be solved by rationalised signals discipline and the elimination of unnecessary chatter.

These things, above all the significance of Fish/Herring, were understood at once by Bletchley Park and by Menzies' SIS. Cracking Fish was a slow business and delays of between three and seven days were inevitable. In December 1942 it had been decided that a revolutionary high speed machine was needed to replace the existing laborious methods such as the use of calculating machines and even simple manual counters by

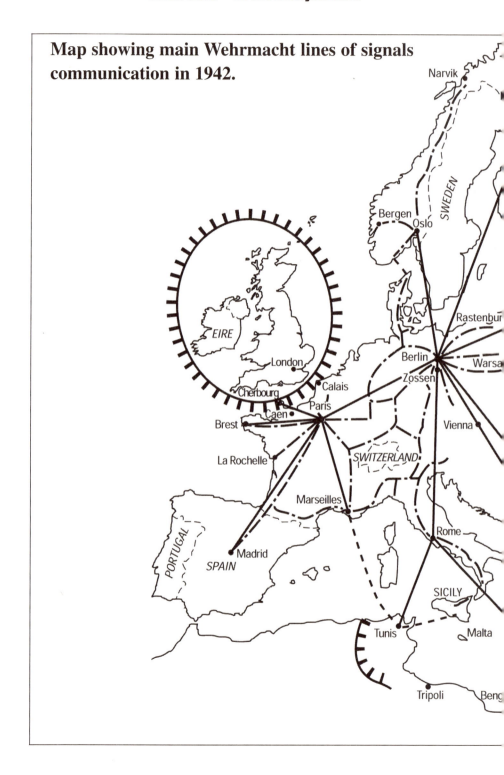

Map showing main Wehrmacht lines of signals communication in 1942.

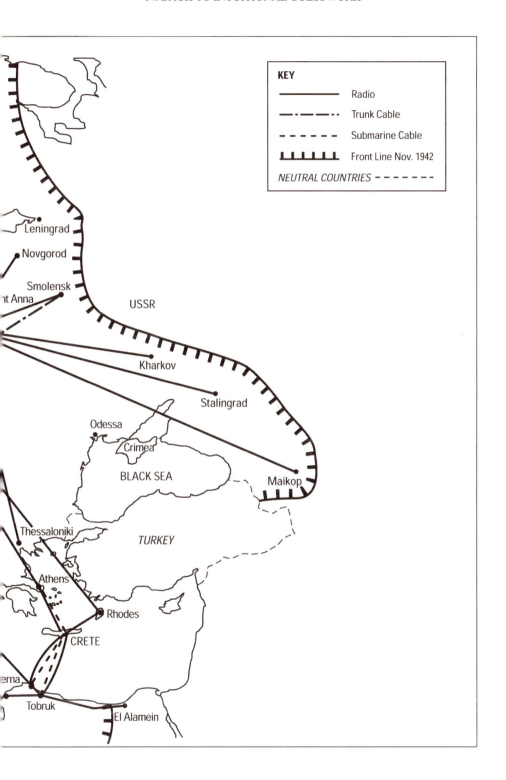

KEY

———————	Radio
—·——·——··	Trunk Cable
— — — — —	Submarine Cable
⊥⊥⊥⊥⊥⊥	Front Line Nov. 1942
NEUTRAL COUNTRIES — — — — —	

Leningrad

Novgorod

Smolensk

nt Anna

USSR

Kharkov

Stalingrad

Odessa

Crimea

BLACK SEA

Maikop

Thessaloniki

TURKEY

Athens

Rhodes

CRETE

erna

Tobruk

El Alamein

skilled, experienced, individual cryptanalysts.[6] By February, Turing and the others at Bletchley Park had devised a prototype, the lash-up called Heath Robinson. Churchill at once ordered that it should be given the highest priority. Even as he prepared his report, Menzies was aware that the GPO Research Station at Dollis Hill was on the eve of completing the first Heath Robinson. If found satisfactory, 24 copies were to be built.

In the meantime the Germans had won several spoiling battles in Tunisia in January and February, among them the overwhelming of the 1st US Armored Division at Sidi Bou Zid. This had acted as the prelude to a thrust through the Kasserine Pass which, momentarily, threatened to envelop the Allied armies in northern Tunisia. Possession of clear indications via Enigma had not prevented these disasters. The Germans had scored by application of superior tactics and combat ability against a numerically superior foe, even though the Allied commanders had been supplied with what amounted to a running commentary on German strategic intentions until Field Marshal Rommel and General von Arnim called off their counter-strokes on 28 February.

Almost the last decoded Enigma signals received by General Eisenhower, commanding the Allied Forces, showed that, although Rommel was short of fuel, he intended to attack General Montgomery's Eighth Army at Medenine on or about 4 March. The Battle of Medenine dissolved into a crushing defeat for Rommel from which the Germans never recovered in Tunisia.[7] Deprived thereafter of such priceless warnings that enabled ample time to prepare for the shock, the Allied intelligence staffs in future tended to be more cautious and make ever greater efforts to ferret out the enemy's intentions by other means. As very often they did, noted Menzies, usually through PR and hand-decoded, medium-grade 'Y' Service intercepts.

There was more to it than that, Menzies also surmised. With the initiative now firmly in their grasp, combined with superior numbers and crushing firepower, the Allies had little to fear in the future. Like Fellgiebel and many another, he dreaded only a prolonged war with commensurate loss of life. Lack of Enigma intelligence might well exacerbate that danger. On the other hand, there remained Herring which, though often beset by decoding difficulties, frequently gave useful longer-term strategic information garnered from the highest enemy level. In addition, analysis of the contribution made by PR, the 'Y' Service, ground patrols and POW interrogations showed the extent to which clear indications of enemy intentions — both strategic and tactical — could still be gathered.

Looking ahead to the day the Allies would land in Sicily, Menzies pointed out in his report that he saw no reason why, even without Enigma, adequate intelligence upon which to base plans with reasonable assurance could not be provided. Moreover, he declared, additional far larger sources of information would be tapped in Europe than in North Africa, where a significant proportion of the Arab populace (as well as some among the pro-Vichy French) had aided the Germans. In Europe, even in Mussolini's Italy, there simmered a multiplying number of frightened, angry people who were eager to see the back of the Germans.

Building on this unrest, Menzies emphasised the disenchanting effects of the compulsory transportation of people to Germany for labour which had begun in the summer of 1942. Previously in occupied Western Europe there had been a mixture of collaboration and live and let live between the populace and occupying forces. This was now changing most promisingly in that some people were taking to the hills and forests to form armed resistance groups. Those who remained at home in village and city were being organised and gradually armed by SOE agents sent in from Britain and Africa.[8]

Mostly the resistance from these growing home armies (except notably in Yugoslavia) was of the wait-until-the-time-is-ripe kind. Yet there was sporadic sabotage, perpetrated both by SOE and Admiral Mountbatten's Combined Operations amphibious raiders, which provoked ferocious acts of retribution by the Germans that tended to intensify mutual hatreds. These activities disturbed Menzies in his capacity as head of the SIS. He earnestly desired to tap for SIS purposes the spontaneous growth of innumerable informers angered by the German behaviour in order to increase the flood of intelligence that was so badly needed, but did not wish his agents and sources to be endangered by too fierce a German reaction being provoked. In an, at times, acrimonious debate starting in 1943, Menzies tried and failed to impose an embargo on raiding — the 'C ban' as it was called.[9]

In his summing up Menzies wrote, 'It seems to me that at sea we have profited rather more than lost from the new situation, and undeniably the Germans are far worse off as a result. In the air, on the other hand, things remain much as ever; Enigma never contributed much of value to operations, to evaluation of damage inflicted or to analysis of the nature and state of new technology. On land it seems to me that we have merely reverted, to some degree, to the old intuitive guessing game about what is on the other side of the hill. Regrettable as that is, it is not calamitous. We still derive considerable up-to-date and reliable strategic and tactical intelligence from long-established sources. Moreover, we are by no means wholly deprived of high grade information via radio. The Japanese continue to keep the Americans and ourselves supplied by Magic. No doubt, too, the Germans will soon allow their diplomatic service to resume using old-fashioned code books which we will attack with vigour. Most fruitful in the months ahead will be the Fish codes which the enemy appears to believe unbreakable. For that reason I anticipate a considerable increase in the number of links opening as the enemy endeavours to compensate for loss of Enigma.'

'I conclude that the post Enigma situation is not nearly as damaging to us as was at first feared. It is of the highest psychological significance that we now hold the initiative and need no longer worry excessively about what next the enemy will do. He knows we have a vast preponderant offensive capability. It is he who must react to us.'

'I therefore recommend that there is no need to recast any of our major future plans. Nevertheless, I counsel increased vigilance in company with the diligent development of new and improved means of intelligence gathering, synthesis and distribution.'

This paper was received with relief by the privileged few to whom it was addressed. They might have been surprised had they been aware that Menzies had contemplated a plot to sow seeds in the German minds that Enigma had not been penetrated after all, in order to revert to the old regime, but he had reasoned that not only had things gone too far to attempt that, but also that the present state of affairs was bearable. He was obliged to Fellgiebel (about whom he knew little) for continuing to employ Fish in so selective a manner. So he instructed Masterman to maintain contact via Garbo with

Canaris on the subject of Enigma, suspecting that German interest in this area was on the decline. He remained concerned that, in the coming summer, the double agents would have a leading role to play in the prospective diversionary activities which would accompany the invasion of Sicily and subsequent, as yet unresolved, offensives. And he brooded over the problems that might arise when lack of Enigma could make it extremely difficult to obtain confirmation that those diversionary activities were proving effectual — or quite the reverse.

The end in Africa came with startling abruptness on 12 May after authoritative intelligence had been received by Magic on the 8th from a signal sent by the Japanese Ambassador to Tokyo. He reported that Mussolini had said that evacuation of the Axis forces by sea and air was impossible. Indeed only 632 officers and men out of the 250,000 remaining got away at the last moment. It was a devastating blow, not only for the Germans and Italians but also for the Japanese who were suffering hard times and making it plain how much would depend upon the Germans to hold the fort in the coming year.[10] In addition, as part of the immense military loot seized in Tunisia were two most intriguing 3-foot-wide teleprinter-type machines of priceless value to Bletchley Park. They were nothing less than the 10-wheel *Sägefisch Geheimschreiber* machines known to GC&CS as Herring. With these in their possession it was possible for the technologists at Dollis Hill to design and build decoding machines of unprecedented power to crack Fish.[11]

One event of apparently minor importance, yet of immense future portent for Fellgiebel and the other disordered resisters, had occurred in Tunisia on 10 April when a staff officer of 10th Panzer Division was seriously wounded. He lost an eye, his right forearm and two fingers from his left hand along with other injuries. He had been flown back to Germany and, after a fashion, would recover during a six month convalescence. His name was Claus von Stauffenberg.

DEVIATIONS FROM HISTORY

[D1] This was not actuality, of course, but of little real importance since only rarely did Enigma and Y Service TA contribute to the early warning system and defence.

[D2] It is very likely that Fellgiebel, a close colleague of the more aggressively devious Oster, would have reacted in this manner, as will become factually plainer below.

Confirmatory footnotes:
1 Hinsley Vol 2 pp 509, 510 and Collier pp 312–17.
2 Hinsley Vol 2 pp 511, 512.
3 Collier p 316.
4 Hinsley Vol 2 Ch 18.
5 Terraine pp 518, 519.
6 Hinsley Vol 3 Pt 1 pp 480, 481.
7 Hinsley Vol 2 p 395.
8 Foot pp 233–5. Foot is most informative about the evolution of SIS and SOE relationships throughout the war.
9 Macksey *Commando Strike* pp 173, 174 and 185.
10 Hinsley Vol 2 pp 613, 614.
11 Lewin *Ultra Goes to War* pp 131–3. This is not mentioned by Hinsley and others.

15.
Purple and Fish

When Japan decided to attack America and Britain in 1941 it was in the knowledge that her greatest strategist, Admiral Isoroku Yamamoto, had claimed he could play hell for six months. After that, he said, his country would be in difficulties if her opponents were still on their feet. Unfortunately for the Japanese the period of playing unmitigated hell lasted a mere six months and her opponents were beginning to play hell in return at the 14 month mark. At the very moment in January 1943 when Germany was flung back on the defensive, Japan, too, was backed against the wall. The annihilation of four aircraft carriers with their élite aircrews at the Battle of Midway in June 1942, followed by the punishing attritional naval battles off Guadalcanal in the Solomon Sea had concluded in abject retreat. A withdrawal to defended island strongpoints throughout the length and breadth of the South-West and Central Pacific would be the prelude to a series of enemy amphibious offensives. These would concentrate on strategic points and by-pass the majority of the strung-out perimeter defences. The strong naval forces that Yamamoto's defensive strategy had prescribed as necessary to support these defences had instead been frittered away.

The emasculation of the Japanese navy and air forces in company with the penetration of the outer perimeter defences were but the preface to the nation's disaster and start of its lapse into inferiority long before her enemy's potential mighty strength was anywhere near mobilised. Unlike the Germans, the Japanese never suspected that the Americans had broken their equivalent (though not copycat) of Enigma, the Type 97 (Purple) cipher machine. Nor did they realise that their ordinary naval code books were also readily broken. Like Dönitz in the Battle of the Atlantic, Japan's admirals were fighting at a gross tactical as well as strategic disadvantage in the Pacific.

* *

Military logic alone suggested to the Allies that the Germans were incapable of a major offensive in Russia in 1943 but that did not take into account the politico-martial intuitions of Adolf Hitler which began to come to light via Fish in April. In fact by that time it was all too obvious to GC&CS that the Germans were activating an extensive network of *Geheimschreiber* stations radiating from exchanges in two places — Angerburg, near Rastenburg (*Amt Anna*) and Straussberg, near Berlin (*Zeppelin*) — to strategically placed terminals from which radiated cable lines to lower formations. In November 1942 *Amt Anna* had been connected by what GC&CS knew as Octopus to Army Group A on the Stalingrad Front, and in March 1943 was connected to Memel by Trout and to Army Group South in the Ukraine by Squid. Towards the end of May, in response to the threat to Italy, Bream started communicating from *Zeppelin* to Rome and Tarpon to Romania, followed in June by Turbot to Denmark. Also in June, *Amt Anna* connected Whiting to Army Group North in Russia. In the months to come more links would be created as Fellgiebel loaded the exchanges towards their limits.[1]

Originally the Fish links were intended principally for Army use· as a complementary system to Enigma. In addition, both the SS and the Navy possessed a few of their own, although the latter did not take these bulky machines to sea. However, under the new Schellenberg regime, Fellgiebel insisted upon greater sharing of the highest-level Army traffic with the Luftwaffe on an operational priority basis.[D1] In so doing he improved the chances of the British penetrating the *Geheimschreiber* system, while doubting their ingenuity to do so. How wrong he already was!

Faced by this not unexpected proliferation of Fish links, the successful trial of the prototype, faster Heath Robinson machine in May occurred not a moment too soon. At once C ordered high priority construction of 24 Heath Robinsons to occupy the floor space currently filled by redundant Bombes of both British and American make.[D2] Simultaneously the transfer and re-education of superfluous Enigma staff began. Some were being trained to deal with the anticipated advent of new code books to replace Enigma. (A task already touched on above, which began to take shape as successive departments, led by the Abwehr, introduced their own systems. And which enjoyed its successes as, for example, when the Naval code was broken through enemy operator error.)

Other operators were discovering apace how to cope with the expanding demands imposed by Fish, learning how best to manage and operate the considerable variety of calculating machines, some of them more demanding than a Bombe, for example. In consequence the Fish department, divided into two sections, evolved into competing parties, of cryptanalysts, on the one hand, and engineers and operators on the other — of whom, among the latter, more than half were Wrens.

* *

At the beginning of April 1943, shortly after Field Marshal von Manstein's counter-stroke lost momentum in thick mud to the north of Kharkov, the Russian high command began to receive intelligence of a possible German offensive in the vicinity of the westward-bulging Kursk salient, an all too obvious target it has to be said. Of convincing importance to Stalin was the proven validity of these reports which emanated from a well-established spy ring known as Lucy; this network had previously produced most valuable information, especially during the Battle of Stalingrad. Lucy was run by a fanatical anti-Nazi German called Rudolf Rossler who was based in Switzerland. He was convinced that, for the good of mankind, Germany must lose the war. His authoritative (though not always wholly accurate) information came from senior Wehrmacht officers of like mind (including Oster of the Abwehr). The method of communication was by encoded messages sent on Wehrmacht land-line to Switzerland, where they were decoded and re-encoded before being retransmitted to Moscow. It would have been very surprising indeed if Fellgiebel, using his private and personal code, had not been closely involved with, if not the perpetrator of, this slick operation. Whoever it was posed a major security threat which completely eluded Schellenberg and his SD minions.[2]

Not until the end of April did Ultra get wind of what was already known to the Russians as Operation 'Citadel', the projected attempt to envelop the Kursk salient. The Fish source was Squid and the long signal it unravelled was a comprehensive appreciation from Field Marshal von Weich's Army Group South of the operation and the formations to be involved.[D3/3] The combined contents of the Lucy reports and the quite independent British contribution indicated a massive enemy effort and had two important consequences. (Incidentally, there is no truth in yarns that the Ultra organisation collaborated with Lucy.[4]) It signposted where the German's sole main offensive effort would be concentrated in 1943, enabling the Russians to concentrate their own information-gathering and counter-measures with assurance against the threatened sector. It also persuaded the Russians to shelve any pre-emptive offensive of their own, although they stepped up the harassing by partisan operations in the forested German rear for intelligence as well as attritional purposes, even as they stood on the defensive and encouraged the enemy to exhaust himself with his own attacks. Then would be the time to launch their own major offensive.

As a result there was no strategic and not all that much tactical surprise either, when the Germans, after several postponements as a consequence of Hitlerian intuition, struck hard on 4 July. Nor did Ultra contribute anything during the battle. In fact, the most illuminating information about the fighting that was received in London came from the Russian high command via the British military mission in Moscow.[5] In effect, therefore, the most important assessments of the situation were based on conventional synthesis and standard military training enhanced by intuition founded on the garnering of battlefield evidence.

* *

In parallel with the preparations for Operation 'Citadel', the British and Americans were assembling strong amphibious forces for Operation 'Husky', the invasion of Sicily. Unlike Citadel in Russia, however, the Allies' strategic objective in the Mediterranean was anything but obvious. The Germans and Italians delved in the dark because there were so many places on their long and exposed 'underbelly' where the enemy might arrive. Thus they lay wide open to deceptions and were unable to decide with confidence where and in what proportion to station their limited forces of uneven prowess and morale. The Allies, for their part, could scheme cunningly to uncover their enemy's strategy and dispositions, besides projecting convincing deception schemes designed to confuse the Axis.

Most celebrated of the Allied strategic deception plans was Operation 'Mincemeat', the ingenious scheme to convey to the Germans a misleading letter supposedly addressed to General Sir Harold Alexander (Deputy Commander of Allied Forces in the Mediterranean) by planting it on a corpse which would be washed up on the Spanish coast. The hope that this letter would reach Axis hands was duly fulfilled and actually did implant in OKW's thinking the belief that Husky was the deception as a cover for the real thing, an invasion of Greece. To the delight of the Allies this 'reliable' intelligence was decrypted on Bream in a message to Field Marshal Kesselring in Rome in mid-May, leading in due course to Axis reinforcements being diverted to the Eastern Mediterranean. Nevertheless, after the capture of the island of Pantelleria on 11 June, it gradually became apparent to the Allies from various sources that Sicily was being reinforced significantly. Moreover, from a vulnerable medium-grade Italian naval cipher (C38m), it was learned that the event had been correctly calculated as scheduled for 10 July.

All too obviously surprise would not be achieved so it was assumed that the leading troops would have to fight their way ashore and that the enemy could concentrate and launch a counter-attack against the beachheads. Thus a conventional balance-of-forces calculation had to be made of likely Axis build-ups of air, naval and land forces over, off and on Sicily. Lacking old-time generous helpings of Luftwaffe Enigma, the basis of such a calculation of air strengths was dubious, based as it had to be only on PR and low- and medium-grade Sigint. The same applied to Italian naval dispositions since their high-grade cipher was unreadable.[6] All the Allies could do was strike at everything of air and naval value in sight and hope for the best.

The strength and dispositions of the German and Italian land forces were just as difficult to ascertain. Their armies' security was tight, although through Bream it was possible to register the arrivals of reinforcing formations in Italy without being able to pinpoint their eventual deployments and roles. SIS contributed nothing. At the end of April it admitted that 'Sicily must now be so closely guarded . . . that it would be wasteful to expend . . . trained agents on such a hot target.' So complete was the Axis police and counter-espionage system that it was impossible to extract any information from the island.[7]

Fortunately, letters to Italian POWs in Allied hands supplied a fairly accurate order of battle, though not where units were located. Information about the beaches was reasonably good, even though charts were out of date and the initial surveys in February by COPP (Combined Operations Pilotage Parties) in canoes had been nothing short of disastrous. Of seven officers taking part only two came back — doggedly, with sore backsides, paddling 75 miles to Malta. The job was completed later by more experienced RN Hydrographic Branch people in specially equipped landing craft.[8] Neither air reconnaissance nor PR revealed much about the strong Italian coastal defences, although it was assumed that the more powerful mobile German battle groups were held back for counter-attack. Therefore it was with a distinct lack of adequate intelligence about what opposition might be encountered that the landing craft, covered by fighters and supported by bombers and naval gunfire, approached the beaches on the 10th.

In the event, Axis air and naval interference was minimal, the pre-assault bombardments having done their job well. Sheer weight of numbers and metal were far too strong for inferior troops who stood thin on the ground. The two British corps (XIII and XXX) were quickly ashore and moving inland. The American II Corps, 45 miles to the west, also got ashore safely, though battered and sickened by rough seas and encountering stiffer opposition than their allies. Parachutists suffered badly when dropped into the sea by inexperienced aircrew. Many Italian troops exposed their defeatism even in defence of their own land by surrendering on call. Not until the 11th was a counter-attack launched by Germans against the Americans at Gela, only to be beaten off after a stiff fight. Thereafter the invasion proceeded according to plan until the island finally was most skilfully evacuated by the Axis on the night of 17 August.

Post-mortems of the service provided by Allied intelligence revealed that even when their commanders were made aware of what was impending (especially in relation to the evacuation), they did not have in readiness an overall plan to make full use of it.[D4]

Of absorbing interest, however, as the battle thundered in the vicinity of Mount Etna, was the news from Kursk that the Germans had called off their offensive on 13 July and that the Russians were advancing on Kharkov in overwhelming strength. This was an episode to be supplemented by the startling announcement from Rome on the 25th that the Allies had achieved their highest aim by bringing about the toppling of Mussolini, a drama which had been hinted at in December 1942 when SOE agents had been approached by dissident Italians; a probe, along with similar attempts early in 1943, which led nowhere when Churchill, Roosevelt and the Combined Chiefs of Staff decided to ignore the hints. The deposition of Mussolini therefore came as a complete surprise to everybody except those carrying out this really well-managed coup.[9]

Be that as it may, no sooner was Bream intelligence of the impending Axis withdrawal from Sicily received than General Eisenhower was authorised to proceed with the invasion of Italy. This had been decided upon during the Trident conference, although now there was total ignorance about what the new Italian government might do or how the Germans would react.[10]

DEVIATIONS FROM HISTORY

[D1] A perfectly logical deviation in the fresh circumstances and a very sensible way of overcoming the Luftwaffe's embarrassment due to shortage of signals capacity caused by lack of Enigma resources.

[D2] In the actuality, due to the intelligence aplenty delivered by Enigma, only three Heath Robinsons were built. For it was evident that this improvised machine, which examined binary data from a five-level punched tape and included only 100 electronic valves, might soon be supplanted by a much more sophisticated machine which would dispense with the tape by generating data exclusively with 1,500 valves. This revolutionary machine would be called Colossus I. In the non-Enigma environment of June 1943, however, prudence undoubtedly would have dictated completion of the Robinson production order, just in case Colossus I failed to come up to expectations or was delayed.

[D3] In fact the first hints of Citadel received by Ultra came early in April from Luftwaffe Enigma signals. With the Prime Minister's approval the substance of these was passed to the Russians, as was the import of the long Squid signal.

[D4] This represents the opinions of two postwar official histories produced before the Ultra secret was revealed. There is no reason to suppose that, without Enigma, things would have been much different. Hitler's orders to Kesselring over Bream and information on the arrival of more reinforcements would have been read just the same. Low-grade Sigint, once battle was joined, would have been revealing as it was. Italian C38m (decrypted in Malta by a special Bletchley Park team) would have been invaluable. Air and battlefield reconnaissance and observation along with interrogations of POWs would have contributed normally. Without Sigint, the relentless Allied pressure still would have been successfully and economically maintained since it is fairly obvious that the sheer weight of their attack was irresistible. Moreover, an OKW signal over Bream to Kesselring on 26 July gave notice that an evacuation of the slowly retreating Axis forces was impending.

Confirmatory footnotes:

1 Hinsley Vol 3 Pt 1 pp 478–82.

2 Jukes pp 45–8. I have not obtained direct confirmation of Fellgiebel's contribution, but it is entirely in character, and I can think of nobody else at that level who would or could have provided such a crucial and secure service.

3 Hinsley Vol 2 pp 624–6 which shows that not even GAF Enigma was all that informative prior to and during the battle.

4 *ibid* p 60.

5 Hinsley Vol 3 Pt 1 pp 78–80.

6 *ibid* pp 80–7.

7 *ibid* p 75 and fn.

8 Macksey *Commando Strike* p 187.

9 Hinsley Vol 3 Pt 1 pp 69, 70 and 101, 102.

10 *ibid* p 102 and fn.

16.
Dramas, Threats and Sideshows

The fall of Mussolini, foreshadowing the distinct possibility of Italy breaking away from the Axis and seeking peace, in addition to several more incalculable consequences, did not catch the Germans entirely by surprise. Ever since Italy entered the war in 1940, they had been suspicious of Italian loyalty, and had notoriously harboured reservations about the calibre of the Italian armed forces. Nevertheless, the actual events of 25 July were a complete surprise — as was essential to the success of those generals at Comando Supremo who, with the connivance of the King and the Fascist Grand Council, deposed the dictator.

Coming on top of the successful Allied landings in Sicily, the abandonment of Citadel and the onrush of the Russian offensive to Kharkov, the possibility of fatal damage to Hitler's regime was by no means entirely remote. Fellgiebel, in his dual roles of Jekyll and Hyde, was among those best informed of the atmosphere at OKW, in Berlin and in Rome. Doubtless he debated with himself and a few close conspirators the renewal of plans for a putsch, but it was in the knowledge that lack of a fireball leader in a key position made this impractical. What Fellgiebel undoubtedly studied most carefully was the stream of signals saturating the Bream channel as the German ambassador and Kesselring in Rome prepared for the worst — the likely absconding of Italy from the Axis partnership.

Plan Axis (*Achse*), secretly and hurriedly prepared by Kesselring to take over the country, was distributed most secretly orally and by hand. Meanwhile Kesselring engaged in subtle diplomacy in order to retain the Italians as comrades in arms and win time. Hitler, who seemed largely to have forgotten the banning of Enigma, suddenly became acutely code-conscience at the probability of the Italians reading or listening to all radio, telephone and telegraphic communications, raising that aspect repeatedly during his prolonged, agitated conferences on the crisis.[1] When this was referred to Schellenberg and Fellgiebel, it was decided to cease use of the Italian postal and telephone system and to encode in Enigma those diplomatic and Wehrmacht messages that were likely to be useful to the Italians, regardless of any assistance to the enemy. For, as Fellgiebel reasoned, as with all easily-broken ciphers the speed of events would quickly out-pace the demands of secrecy.[D1]

Even as the Italian crisis rumbled on, triggering the ordering of the evacuation of Sicily, events of equally shocking import were in train.

* *

On the night of 24/25 July, RAF Bomber Command unleashed the Battle of Hamburg with a stunning attack that was to be followed by four more, executed by 3,095 sorties, and supplemented in daylight by two US Bomber Command attacks amounting to 626 sorties. Losses to the RAF were only 86 aircraft (2.8%); and to the Americans 43. The damage inflicted was immense, notably on the night of the 27/28 July when a phenomenon known as a fire storm, with winds up to 150mph, raised temperatures to 1,000° Centigrade to suffocate and incinerate thousands of people. About 61% of living accommodation in the city was destroyed and the workforce permanently reduced by 10%.[2] There were those in the German government who feared that a repetition, inflicted on a few more major cities, would raise a wave of terror that could not be subdued. However, Hitler, engrossed with the Italian crisis and the land battle fronts, merely told Albert Speer 'to straighten it out', which, between them, the Armaments Minister and Josef Goebbels managed to do. They were helped in this by the failure of the Allies to achieve similar results against a few more cities at the moment when the air defences were in utter disarray due to the RAF's belated use of the Window radar counter-measure.

Window consisted of clouds of metallic strips dropped to create a 'smoke screen' effect on enemy radar. It could have been used in the spring of 1942 but was deferred for fear of premature disclosure to the Germans, followed by the complex repercussions of their counter-measures. The only evidence that they might know about its principles had come from an SIS agent in October 1942, but, as with so many German technological inventions, there was insufficient corroboration.[3] When used during the Battle of Hamburg the confusion Window caused to the fighter controllers and pilots (contentedly monitored by 'Y' Service) was all too evident, but, as so often, apart from PR and disclosures by foreigners and, in due course POWs, little about the effect of the bombing was revealed from German sources,[D2] though the Japanese were especially obliging when, through Magic, their Vice-Consul in Hamburg provided a graphic description of the devastation, the extremely high casualties, the panic evacuations of people and departments and the dread of a collapse in morale.[4]

* *

The German leaders were not the only ones in dread of future aerial threats. Since December 1940 the British had gradually been growing more concerned about impending attacks by secret weapons, among which rockets of unrevealed range and dimensions were high on the list.[5] Not until the end of 1942, however, did an accumulation of reports ring alarm bells. From SIS came conflicting signals of uncertain veracity and reliability, gleaned from a variety of sources (including conscripted workers from the occupied countries and POWs). They had to be taken very seriously even though neither Enigma nor Fish contributed to them.

Rapidly a picture began to appear of the existence of several kinds of rocket weapons and of a gun with a range of 120km. Some of the rockets were small and, arguably, intended for the anti-aircraft or anti-shipping roles. But initially of most interest was a very large, very long-range rocket with a heavy warhead. This rocket (a tail-sitter launched vertically which in due course became known as V2) held centre stage of SIS attention until April 1943 when Polish agents in France passed on intelligence to SIS of 'a bomb with wings'. Information from several sources, which multiplied in the next eight weeks, rapidly implanted in British minds the existence of a cigar-shaped missile fired horizontally from a ramp of some sort. This became known as V1.

Concurrently with the burgeoning intelligence about new weapons and, at times, the furious debate raging among British scientists as to their capabilities, went the discovery by SIS (confirmed or otherwise by PR) of various sites and factories throughout Germany where testing and manufacture went on. Principal among these was a large, dramatically expanding site on the Baltic coast at Peenemünde. This had first come to SIS notice in November 1939 as a testing ground for remote controlled rockets, but the well-informed Oslo Report which contained this vital intelligence was pigeon-holed. Indeed, it was not until January 1943 that reports began to increase significantly about this facility along with ample evidence of rocket testing.

In January 1943 Peenemünde (which had first revealed its extent to PR in May 1942) was photographed a second time to expose a considerable expansion and certain mysterious and unique installations. This was followed on 22 March, by way of most concrete confirmation, by the transcript of a bugged conversation between two captured German generals. They had talked about well-advanced rocket developments, some actually witnessed by one of them, General von Thoma. Henceforward investigations into V-weapons were given far higher priorities, reaching a turning point in April when Winston Churchill appointed Duncan Sandys as co-ordinator for the assessment of intelligence in relation to the long-range rocket threat, a task which was to be progressively (and controversially) broadened to include the V1 flying bomb, long-range guns, jet aircraft and all sorts of other novelties.[6]

Hurt as were several parties with vested interests, Sandys' appointment did have an advantage often lacking among the Germans. It brought together under one dynamic man the multifarious service and civil authorities with a contribution to make. Peenemünde was now frequently a target for PR. So, too, in July were certain peculiar sites in France which were located within 130 miles of London, and were objectives for SIS agents who highlighted a large and very strongly guarded underground bunker near Watten. In June Sandys, supported by R. V. Jones, had pressed for very heavy bombing by Bomber Command of Peenemünde, to which agreement in principle was granted on the 29th by the Cabinet Defence Committee. On 6 August, as further evidence suggested that a bombardment was imminent, he added Watten to the priority list. This was allocated to the American bomber command.

On the night of 17/18 August 597 RAF heavy bombers attacked Peenemünde most accurately and systematically. They smashed specific installations one by one, including the living quarters of the scientists, technologists and production workers. Forty bombers did not return but Dr Thiel, the director, and a senior scientist were among 700 killed.[7] Damage was extensive but not crippling. Delays to production were in the order of two months, but rocket testing was moved to an inland range in Poland and production to an underground factory in the Harz mountains.[8]

For the Germans, the bombing of Peenemünde was undeniable proof of their secret being out. For Canaris and his tottering Abwehr, and Schellenberg and his burgeoning

SD, it was verification that the enemy was far better supplied with intelligence than was good for the Third Reich; and for Fellgiebel it gave cause for a quirky satisfaction. For the Luftwaffe's Chief of Staff, General Jeschonnek, it was the end of the road. After writing a highly critical memorandum to Göring, setting down the failings of the Luftwaffe and suggesting that Göring should hand over to somebody else, he committed suicide to shield his master's reputation.

The bombing of Watten on 27 and 30 August was a further blow to Göring and Hitler's 'vengeance' weapons by totally reducing the site to an abandoned 'desolate heap', a state duly revealed by PR and SIS reports — nothing whatsoever came from Fish.[D3] In the meantime, however, the attention of the Wehrmacht in the West was already fixed intently on the mounting fury of enemy air attacks, allied to abundant evidence of a forthcoming major invasion or series of big amphibious raids anywhere between Norway and Brittany.

* *

These activities came under the code-name Operation 'Cockade', the major deception scheme which had been ordered by the Chiefs of Staff in April in an effort to compel the Germans to divert major forces from the Mediterranean theatre of war. Steered by General Sir Frederick Morgan's COSSAC headquarters, and in close collaboration with the LCS, a most elaborate and large number of notional and very ambitious operations were combined within it.[10] Based on a notional Allied order of battle of 39 divisions, with the requisite naval, air and supporting services (created by LCS), Cockade evolved into the simulation of Operation 'Starkey', a notional Anglo-Canadian assault on either side of Boulogne timed for early in September. This was to be followed by Wadham, another notional operation, but this time by an American corps against Brest. Subsequently it was intended that Wadham should be 'cancelled' and the Americans 'transferred' to take part in landings in Norway (Operation 'Tindall').

Many were the devices, real and insinuated, used to spoof the Germans, such as bogus radio traffic, confirmatory reports by double agents, the building of dummy camps as assembly areas, the phased concentration of shipping and landing craft in appropriate ports, and the actual movement of troops to the south-east of England. There was also the launching of intensified air attacks plus small commando raids, commencing in July, intended realistically to simulate the essential preliminaries for Starkey and Wadham.

Eagerly the British awaited proof that the Germans were hooked, and to begin with they were encouraged. A series of misinforming reports in May by double agent Tricycle to the Abwehr, describing the build-up of Allied forces throughout the United Kingdom, attracted questionnaires asking for precise orders of battle and assembly areas. Diligently Tricycle satisfied Canaris's eager requests.

In June the enthusiastic and utterly 'reliable' Garbo was drawn into the business as a matter of the highest priority. Consequently, so overloaded did he become that, in addition to committing all his 'agents' to the task, he also found it necessary, notionally, to visit in person many places where activity was supposedly intense. In fact, so busy did Garbo and his agents become that he felt compelled to ask permission to cease the seemingly futile attempt to find Turing and Jones, a request that Canaris agreed to, after consulting Fellgiebel, who now felt that very little might come of this line of enquiry.[D4]

Far less eager were German reactions to the small commando raids when they began on 3 July. Indeed the majority of a series of Operation 'Forfar' landings were anti-climaxes. Some failed to come ashore and the majority which did came and went without being detected.[11] The impression was obtained that the enemy defences (except in the highly fortified ports, of course) were amazingly supine. The fact of the matter was that, after 11 July when Husky started, OKW discounted a major Allied operation in North-West Europe. Instead they started withdrawing large numbers of troops to the Mediterranean, informing the C-in-C West, Field Marshal Gerd von Rundstedt, that they believed that, 'the *Schwerpunkt* of the enemy attacks on the mainland of Europe lies in the Mediterranean and in all probability will remain there'.[12] This message was not monitored by the British because, in the absence of a Fish link to his headquarters, it was sent by land-line. On 30 August, Rundstedt's staff also shrewdly rumbled Garbo's and Tricycle's reports as giving 'rise to the suspicions that the material was deliberately allowed to slip into the agent's hands', and had added a week later that the enemy's preparations were 'somewhat too obvious'.[13]

The mounting signs of enemy aggression in the West nevertheless convinced Fellgiebel that, as land-lines became overloaded and ever more likely to interruptions and tapping by the enemy, the time had arrived to provide C-in-C West with the *Geheimschreiber*. At the end of August, to the relief also of GC&CS, Jellyfish began transmissions, although it was not until mid-October that its code was broken by GC&CS.[D5] Therefore it missed providing insight into the initial thinking and actions of Rundstedt on 13 September when he explained his fear that, although his opponent had rigged an elaborate deception scheme, perfectly timed to divert attention from events in the Mediterranean, 'All the same the transition to a real invasion is possible at any time . . . '[14]

The British were extremely disappointed at the apparent failure of Cockade to fool the Germans. Yet, painful as was the snub when the Luftwaffe declined to rise to the challenge of combat and when the mine-sweepers clearing lanes towards Boulogne were ignored, it taught valuable lessons and achieved more than was at first evident. For Cockade, fiasco as it might appear, was the soft prelude to the loud and vital performances of 1944. There was a theme of continuity about Cockade pointing to the invasions ahead. It formed a composition which Rundstedt had clearly discerned and which he repeatedly emphasised to OKW over Jellyfish in the weeks to come.

However, as agents reported, Hitler (taken in by Operation 'Tindall') remained hooked on the likelihood of an invasion of Norway where he kept twelve divisions in idleness. It was Jellyfish which, in the nick of time, was able to translate the vital appreciations by OKW and Rundstedt between 30 October and 8 November denoting their belief that the Allies were capable of an imminent invasion, and Rundstedt who, on 30 November, went so far as to insist that, even in winter weather, an invasion was to be reckoned with. These assertions at last convinced Hitler that the West must be strongly reinforced before the end of 1944, no matter what was happening in Russia or in Italy.[15]

DEVIATIONS FROM HISTORY

[D1] This would have been a common sense, short-term emergency measure.

[D2] In fact Enigma did let drop a few hints when decrypts reported the stopping of servicemen's leave to the Hamburg area and the dispersal of factories to underground refuges.

[D3] Enigma was silent on the subject in actuality, except for diplomatic telegrams to Buenos Aires on 10 and 13 August hinting at terror attacks on Britain by big guns.

[D4] The activities of Tricycle and Garbo were real (see Hinsley/Howard Vol 5 pp 77, 78). It seems more than likely that C would have preferred to halt the German enquiries and that Fellgiebel would have concurred.

[D5] Jellyfish did not transmit until 6 January 1944 and was not broken until March (see Hinsley Vol 3 Pt 1 p 482). It certainly is plausible that, in the absence of Enigma, an earlier installation of *Geheimschreiber* would have taken place. Indeed at about this time consideration really was being given by the Army to spreading the allocation of *Geheimschreiber* below army group and army level to division, but because the machines were large and clumsy, and best installed in buildings due to their sensitivity, the idea was not adopted. Moreover, the chances of its transport being captured in mobile combat were so high as to make the risk of it falling into enemy hands unacceptable (see Hinsley Vol 3 Pt 1 p 481 fn).

Confirmatory footnotes:

1 Warlimont pp 354, 355 and 361.

2 Terraine pp 547–8.

3 Hinsley Vol 2 pp 517 19.

4 Hinsley Vol 3 Pt 1 p 292.

5 *ibid* Ch 40 pp 357–82. This shows that neither Enigma nor Fish were the slightest use in the initial search for intelligence about the rocket weapons.

6 *ibid* pp 336, 337.

7 Terraine p 541.

8 Hinsley Vol 3 Pt 1 p 433.

9 *ibid* p 379.

10 Hinsley/Howard Vol 5 pp 71–83 provides an excellent outline description of Cockade and its associated notional sideshows.

11 Macksey *Commando Strike* pp 200–2.

12 Hinsley/Howard Vol 5 pp 79–81.

13 Hinsley/Howard Vol 5 p 80.

14 *ibid* pp 82, 83, 108, 109.

15 ibid pp 83.

17.
Encroaching Nemesis

Out of sheer necessity leaders of the new Italian government had to act in deepest secrecy as they paved the way to desert their German ally. The initial approach to the Allies on 4 August, indicating their desire to pull out of the war, was clandestinely made by emissaries at Lisbon. Italian Sigint gave little assistance to the Allies in deciding how to proceed. German Sigint, on the other hand, was more helpful due to their decision to use Enigma in a limited way to deny information to the Italians.[1] Yet, although the details of Plan Axis were quite unknown to the Allies, by mid-August there was no doubt, from Italian Army officers and Bream, that the Germans had reinforced Italy and the Balkans substantially, and that they would attempt to disarm the Italians if necessary as well as strongly resist an Allied invasion.

By great good fortune there was a summit conference (Quadrant) in progress at Quebec where, on 24 August after much, at times, worried argument, the plan put forward by General Eisenhower was accepted. In the fairly confident belief that an armistice with the Italians was within reach, Allied forces were committed to a two-phase operation: first, a landing by General Montgomery's Eighth Army on the toe of Italy (Operation 'Baytown'); and second, a landing by General Mark Clark's Fifth Army in the Gulf of Salerno (Operation 'Avalanche'). These were to be the prelude to the capture of the Rome area and the islands of Sardinia and Corsica, prior to an advance into northern Italy.

Information from German Sigint reaching the Allies was patchy as the plot thickened. Bream, of course, was invaluable for its supply of the highest-grade priority material but the Army and Luftwaffe used mainly land-line and courier for the transmission of their most secret material and therefore divulged little except when employing medium- and low-grade codes on radio for tactical purposes. In July, on the other hand, evidence of the employment of new code books, in lieu of Enigma, was registered at Bletchley Park. First off the mark had been the Abwehr, followed by the Navy and the Diplomatic Service.[D1] Use of the new codes on radio was cautiously limited, since there was no saying if and when the enemy might penetrate them. The radio security discipline imposed by Schellenberg and Fellgiebel therefore still had an inhibiting effect, although the Navy, to a worrying extent, found it impossible to manage without it.

After Eighth Army had crossed the Straits of Messina almost unopposed on 3 September, enough had been divulged from various sources to show the Allies that the Germans anticipated a landing in the Gulf of Salerno with a view to capturing the Naples area. Therefore surprise was forfeit. But what Sigint never revealed were the actual defensive positions General von Vietinghoff's Tenth Army was taking up. Thus considerable anxiety was raised about the sort of reception the first wave of troops would receive as they came ashore. Also undisclosed were the likely repercussions if the Italians did surrender and Operation 'Axis' was activated. Crucially, it was not known that German troops would be extracted from Sardinia, and that several formations would be withdrawn to the vicinity of Rome to participate in the disarmament of the Italian forces.[2]

It was with some relief, therefore, when Fifth US Army got ashore against only light resistance at Salerno on 9 September. Worst off was Kesselring who had everybody (including an untrusting OKW!) against him. To begin with, he was mainly engaged in successfully coercing and bluffing the local Italian forces into an almost bloodless disarmament. Next, having accomplished that with amazing rapidity, he rounded most effectively on the enemy at Salerno, despite being totally ignorant of the enemy's intentions, lacking the initiative, being spied on by Italians and also being the target for a baffling mixture of enemy deception schemes. Yet, by sheer intuitive genius, he got his priorities and allocation of troops-to-task right in a masterly exhibition of generalship.

In the nick of time he managed to reinforce the Panzer corps at Salerno once its role in Operation 'Axis' had been completed. Then, throughout the ensuing week, he managed to apply such heavy pressure on Clark that, briefly, there grew great Allied anxiety that their bridgehead could not be held. Neither Sigint nor more conventional sources of intelligence were able to paint a clear picture of the German reactions, intentions and capability. At sea it came as a nasty surprise to the Allies when ships were sunk by unexpected radio-guided Hs 293 rocket bombs. On land the violent German counter-attacks threatened to seize decisive observation over the Salerno beachhead. Eventually, a week-long battle of attrition was brought to an end chiefly by heavy naval gunfire, bombing and German logistic overstretch. This led to a withdrawal as the arrival of Eighth Army compelled Kesselring to fear excessive casualties and the danger of Tenth Army's envelopment.

Allied intelligence about these high-level factors and events was, to say the least, inadequate. Vital signals sent via Bream on 14 September were not decrypted until the 17th and it was not until the afternoon of the 18th that Bream signals sent on the 17th were decrypted to disclose an enemy in retreat in all sectors. This was the prelude to a thorough German withdrawal, brilliantly executed by Kesselring, that was to establish his mastery of the most difficult of all operations in the art of war.[3/D1] In the weeks ahead, having imposed maximum delay, he brought the Allies to a halt on the prepared Gustav Line that ran from the Gulf of Gaeta to the Sangro River.

During the ensuing 18 months the Germans stolidly would economically deny every river line and piece of vital ground as they backed off against an enemy who usually was the better informed. For, unlike the circumstances in Sicily, where the Fascist regime prevented espionage by their own people, many among a populace who would be termed co-belligerents willingly passed copious information to SIS and SOE agents.

The work of Fellgiebel's well-trained Army signallers in these conditions has been much overshadowed by the more glamorous combat arms. Not only did their strict signal security deny much information to the Allies, but they also prevented the loss of invaluable material and stores with each step backwards, besides wrecking Italian facilities whenever possible. For example, in addition to crippling civil telephone exchanges, they would carry away or wind in extremely scarce copper wires, thus contributing to the logistic desert that was intended to make pursuit more difficult.

Similar techniques on a much grander scale were being practised in Russia where, to all intents and purposes, the poor indigenous land cable network had long since been eliminated and replaced by beam radio and poled overhead wire. There, in the aftermath of defeat at Kursk, the Germans recoiled grudgingly on a very wide front between Smolensk and the Black Sea. Massed Russian attacks rolled forward to take Kharkov on 23 August, Smolensk on 25 September and Kiev on 6 November, in the process crossing the mighty Dnieper and cutting off the Crimea. This was despite the mobile defensive operations brilliantly conducted by Field Marshals Manstein and Kluge — and habitually spoiled by Hitler's intuitive interventions. As in Italy, Germany's enemies were compelled to depend far less upon Sigint than other sources of intelligence. Lucy continued to contribute, courtesy of Fellgiebel; partisans collaborated with conventional army and air reconnaissance. The Germans, having isolated themselves by antagonising the populace through their murderous excesses, could neither place much reliance on spies nor upon air reconnaissance as the Luftwaffe was worn down.

* *

Germany was being pounded day and night by the misnamed Combined Bomber Offensive of the independently minded RAF and US Bomber Commands, which only occasionally co-ordinated their operations, yet still forced Göring's Luftwaffe to withdraw many fighters from the battle fronts, for the time being to exact stiff penalties on the raiders. Indeed, in the post Battle of Hamburg period of five months, the Germans enjoyed a distinct technical and security advantage over their tormentors. Their Sigint invariably picked up ample warning of impending operations from bombers testing their radios during pre-raid flights. Once battle was joined, their fighters had the benefit of being able to home onto the electronic emissions from the H_2S device that helped bombers navigate to their targets. Moreover, having once located their prey, fighters equipped with *Schräge Musik* (upward-firing cannon) could steal, unobserved to close range, to deliver the *coup de grace* from beneath. Not until May 1944 was firm evidence obtained by the British that the Germans were using H_2S for homing purposes,[4] and it was July 1944 before a POW let slip information about *Schräge Musik*, although it was another three months before this was disseminated by Air Intelligence.

Nor did the advantage obtained by Window over Hamburg last for very long. The Germans simply changed their tactics by loosening the previous tight control of fighters and having them, on outline instructions, without help of radar, follow the course of the bomber stream to make attacks on visual contact. The results were a distinct improvement on the old method. Bomber losses increased progressively, especially throughout the episode that opened with the first Battle of Berlin (from 23 August to 3 September) when 1,719 sorties cost 123 bombers (7.15%). This disastrous period was overshadowed by the second Battle of Berlin, which cost 1,047 RAF aircraft and wreaked appalling loss of life and colossal damage on Germany without stopping the rise of industrial production or cracking morale.[5]

This was a decisive defeat for the night bombers engaged in the campaign against area targets in Germany. One which, nevertheless, would be turned into victory by the Americans, despite the defeat in the autumn of their daylight precision attacks. Their formations, unescorted by fighters during attempts to hit targets deep in Germany, lost 175 bombers from seven operations (loss rates in excess of 20%), without shooting down anything like the number of fighters they claimed. Yet, they were on the threshold of making day bombing cost-effective, both in terms of strategic damage inflicted and fighters destroyed.[6] For, on 5 December, the debut of a deadly long-range fighter, the Rolls-Royce Merlin-engined North American P-51 Mustang, paved the way for the winning of Allied air superiority in German air space. They completely out-classed the German fighters and escorted the bombers to and from Berlin and other deep targets without excessive loss. So that, come the end of March 1944, a condition had been reached when, as a German airman remarked, 'the safest place over Germany is in the cockpit of an American fighter.'[7]

Then, as ever, Allied knowledge of results achieved by bombing was dependent on the usual non-Enigma sources previously mentioned in this book.[D2] Of considerable value, however, were American P-51 pilots' combat reports which commented upon a marked reluctance on their opponents' part to seek battle at a time when the Americans were also claiming highly exaggerated kills. In the last week of February, for example, they claimed 600 when the actual total was 225 — although the latter was bad enough for the hard-pressed Germans. Be that as it may, a bold policy of selecting targets in such a way as to compel the enemy to fight was adopted in place of the previous evasive routeing.[8]

Yet much valuable strategic information was denied the Americans as the result of tighter radio security and lack of Luftwaffe Enigma.[D3] It was the monitoring of tactical R/T conversations in clear between ground controllers and fighters which best enabled the Americans to exploit their technical and numerical superiority to the full.

✴ ✴ ✴✴ ✴

The wearing down of the Luftwaffe fighter arm in the defence of the homeland also had an indirect deleterious effect on V-weapon development due to the need to defend launching places. Despite the set-back at Peenemünde early in August, later in that month the Germans began widespread construction of the so-called 'ski sites' in France — named after the layout of the concrete launching ramps for the V1. Towards the end of October six had been found by SIS agents, and were soon confirmed by PR. Some were in the Cotentin peninsula within 140 miles of Bristol; the vast majority in the Pas de Calais within 170 miles of central London. An aerial photograph also detected a flying bomb on its ramp near Peenemünde on 28 November. The advanced state of the many sites under construction (a few were also being built for V2), and increasing knowledge of the nature and performance of the V-weapons, made counter-measures against this serious threat essential.

Bombing of the sites, to begin with, was by British and American medium and fighter-bombers, subsequently joined by heavies. It started on 18 December and continued unabated until August 1944 when they were mostly overrun by the Allied armies. For notwithstanding the vast tonnage of bombs dropped on the ski sites and their less visible and easier to construct successors, it was at a high price in aircraft lost to guns and fighters. Moreover, the Allied air forces were never able to discover and hit every launcher. Sigint contributed nothing about them. Neither PR nor the SIS was an infallible source of supply, admirable as were their numerous coups in locating targets — not a few of which were dummies.

* *

In the aftermath of the seemingly abortive spoof Operation 'Starkey' the intensive enemy air activity over the Pas de Calais continued to have a persistent and disturbing effect on the equanimity of Field Marshal von Rundstedt and of Hitler. Fish/Jellyfish decrypts throughout November 1943 showed that Rundstedt had convinced his Führer, even as late as the 30th, that a major landing must be expected soon. Operation 'Tindall', the notional landing in Norway, predictably fired up Hitler who was ever prone to threats of danger in that region.[9] Consequently, once the Italians in the Balkans had been rounded up and Kesselring had stabilised the Italian front, the flow of forces to the Mediterranean theatre was reversed. Substantial reinforcement of the Western Front was ordered on 3 November by Hitler in his Directive 51 — which laid down that the Pas de Calais was to receive the lion's share of divisions. Moreover, a new Army Group B soon was formed in France under Field Marshal Rommel, to be provided by Fellgiebel in January with its own *Geheimschreiber*, called Grilse by Bletchley Park.[D4]

Most significant of all from Cockade's spin-off was firm implantation of the notional Allied order of battle in Hitler's, Rundstedt's and OKW's intelligence assessments. The success of this deception was made clear by Bream and Jellyfish, and was to grow into fundamental importance as the real Allied plans for the invasion of North-West Europe in 1944 matured.

* *

The turmoil succeeding the collapse of the Abwehr group of resisters, along with Operation 'Flash', and the rapid encroachment of nemesis upon his beloved Fatherland, drove Fellgiebel to desperation. Because Oster was dismissed and Canaris neutralised and in a grapple for survival with Kaltenbrunner, the control centre in Berlin had to be shifted from the Abwehr. Furthermore, Henning von Tresckow's nervous breakdown and enforced extended leave at the end of May not only meant that immediate hope of retaining Kluge as an active Resistance leader was lost, but in addition Tresckow's enthusiastic driving power and influence were missed. Not one active service Field Marshal with popular appeal and prestige could now be rated suitable as a substitute for Hitler. This was another fortuitous benefit for a Führer whose propaganda image stole all the limelight by portraying him as the unchallenged military genius. Certainly neither Kesselring, Manstein, Rundstedt nor Rommel, who were duty bound by the Oath of Allegiance, were candidates for the appointment. They, like General Guderian, clung pathetically to the hope that something might yet be found to create, by military means, a situation that might make possible negotiations towards an acceptable peace before the Russians engulfed Germany. As for the suitability of retired or sacked and thoroughly embittered senior officers such as Field Marshal Erwin von Witzleben (Wehrmacht C-in-C designate) and Generals Ludwig Beck (head of state designate) and Erich Hoeppner (C-in-C Army), well, even though their commitment to the removal of Hitler was virtually absolute, they were forgotten men of little public standing whose sense of ruthless urgency had long since atrophied. Fervent revolutionary activity was never their forte.

Control of the resistance was switched to HQ Home Army in Berlin, commanded by General Friedrich Fromm, whose Chief of Staff was General Friedrich Olbricht. Fromm was no resister, though believed to be sympathetic to the cause if it turned out to be successful. Olbricht was an enthusiastic one and also well placed to take the lead, yet lacking the charisma or reputation to inspire revolutionaries. In any case, it was much more officially correct and safer for Fellgiebel to communicate personally and frequently with Olbricht than it was with Tresckow who was spending his leave in Berlin. Suspicious Gestapo agents would soon smell a rat if a prominent general repeatedly visited an unemployed lieutenant-colonel of dubious loyalty to the Nazis. For, though General Schmundt had blocked Himmler's latest attempt to have the 'irreplaceable' Fellgiebel replaced, he had also appointed a Colonel Ludolf Sander to have the extraordinary, and significant, task of ensuring that Fellgiebel did not meet a now highly suspicious Hitler in the *Wolfschanze*. No longer was Fellgiebel the Führer's 'most trusted General'.[10]

Olbricht's suggestion to Tresckow that Lt-Col Claus von Stauffenberg should be brought into the central planning group was made with Fellgiebel's approval, dating back to those dramatic meetings with Manstein and Stahlberg in February. Essential was the need for Tresckow and Stauffenberg (who also was on leave, recovering from his awful wounds) to meet clandestinely to draft Putsch-Walkyrie.[11] The original Home Army Operation 'Walkyrie' had come into existence in the spring of 1942 as an emergency plan in the event of internal unrest. Its purpose was to deal with any sudden outbreak of violence by the thousands of enemy POWs and the rapidly increasing number of conscripted foreign workers flooding the country. (In 1942 there were 2 million of the latter rising to 8 million in 1944.) Groups of combat troops were to be ready for action at six hours' notice. It had Hitler's approval and was first issued on 26 May 1942.

On 31 July 1943, on Olbricht's directions, Tresckow and Stauffenberg created a secret revised plan, known as Putsch-Walkyrie, designed to exploit an overthrow of the Nazi government. Beck, Olbricht, Tresckow, Stauffenberg and Fellgiebel agreed that there would be three phases: first, the assassination of Hitler; second, a period of perhaps three to four hours in which it would be necessary to seize control of the government by military action; and third, the exploitation of the military and political situation thereafter.

Fellgiebel was one of the strongest supporters of this plan, as justified by Tresckow's belief that, 'It is an historical duty of the General Staff Officer to prevent the certain loss of the war, to be expected under the present leadership, for the sake of the nation . . . '[12] There were two crucial steps in making all this work. First there had to be an announcement: 'The Führer, Adolf Hitler, is dead! An unscrupulous clique of Party Leaders, taking advantage of the situation, has attempted to seize power for themselves.' Coupled with this was the statement that the task of the legitimate power was to secure the signals communication centres, disband Schellenberg's SD and absorb Himmler's Waffen SS within the Army. The second step was referred to as 'letting the cat out of the bag'. This was the planned arrest of all the Nazi Gauleiters and any uncooperative leaders of the Waffen SS and the occupation of the offices of the SD and the Gestapo.

Within the Army hierarchy Fellgiebel held the essential keys to dissemination of information and orders. It was his task when Hitler was killed to ensure that the Nazis were deprived of their communications; this was known as the 'campaign of the telephone and telegraph exchanges'. Only by winning time in that manner was the implementation of the fundamentals of the plan by the Army possible. It was a tall order and a gamble (bearing in mind that Fellgiebel had no authority to give orders to the Navy, the Luftwaffe or the SS[13]), but one Fellgiebel was ready, in desperation, to undertake.

By consent of Beck's colleagues, Putsch-Walkyrie, signed by Stauffenberg on behalf of Field Marshal von Witzleben, was ready for activation on 1 September. It next remained to accomplish the assassination of Hitler, but that proved easier said than done. There were more than half a dozen schemes with willing volunteers prepared to undertake them — and as many cancellations. These included a plan to plant explosives with an extremely noisy fuse in the Führer's HQ; a shooting during a conference, which was aborted because the officers concerned would have been prevented by the SS bodyguards from getting close enough to draw their revolvers, let alone hit their target; and Operation 'Overcoat' for which an officer called Axel von dem Bussche volunteered to sacrifice himself while modelling a new style Army overcoat before the Führer. This young man was prepared to carry a bomb in a pocket and grapple with his victim long enough for the fuse to function and kill them both. That attempt, however, was foiled by an Allied air raid which not only postponed the fashion show but also destroyed the overcoat. Finally an attempt was planned by Stauffenberg, representing Olbricht on whose staff he now served, to plant a bomb at a Führer conference at Rastenburg on 26 December. This time the bomb, primed by a captured silent British SOE fuse, was contained in a briefcase. But although Stauffenberg reached the conference ante-room undetected, he was denied the opportunity because Hitler called the meeting off at the last moment.[14]

That man really did lead a charmed life!

DEVIATIONS FROM HISTORY

[D1] See Chapter 16 above. In actuality, Enigma was very useful in a confirmatory role of German thinking and intentions. The Abwehr was indeed very active in acquiring sound intelligence of Allied intentions and movements; and of course the Army and the Luftwaffe actually used Enigma to the full and provided excellent intelligence.

[D2] This is true of Fish but not of Enigma which really did produce encouraging information about pilot and aircraft shortages, training deficiencies, a reduction in the meteorological service, and the high wastage rate of fighters in combat with the P-51s.

[D3] See Hinsley Vol 3 Part 1 pp 317–20. In fact Enigma supplied extensive information including actual German losses at 10%, along with 40% wastage, plus meteorological data and the locations of fighter airfields and their support services ripe for strafing.

[D4] In fact Grilse was not activated until 9 June 1944.

Confirmatory footnotes:

1 Hinsley Vol 3 Pt 1 pp 106, 108–11, 114, 115.

2 *ibid* pp 108, 109.

3 *ibid* pp 111–14.

4 *ibid* pp 314, 315. Note that even evidence provided by Enigma only gave unconfirmed and inconclusive leads.

5 Terraine pp 551–7.

6 *ibid* pp 555, 556.

7 Anon *Luft* p 296.

8 Hinsley Vol 3 Pt 1 pp 317–19.

9 Hinsley/Howard Vol 5 pp 81–3.

10 Wildhagen p 295.

11 Wheeler-Bennett pp 580–9. W-B is somewhat vague about the timing of the drafting of Walkyrie, just as he seems unaware of Fellgiebel's prominent role in it.

12 Wildhagen p 289.

13 *ibid* pp 289–91.

14 Wheeler-Bennett pp 589–91.

18.
Fortitude to Overlord

The strategic problems facing both the Germans and the Allies as 1944 loomed ahead were not whether there would be an invasion of North-West Europe but when, where and in what strength. The question of when would tease both sides to the last moment. As to where? Well, the Allies, courtesy of Hitler and Jellyfish, were well informed about what the Germans expected. For had not Hitler advertised it in his Directive 51 when he signalled, 'I have decided to reinforce its [the West's] defences, particularly those places from which the long-range bombardment of England will begin. For it is here the enemy must and will attack, and it is here — unless all indications are misleading — that the decisive battle against the landing forces will be fought.' In other words, Hitler expected the attack to be on the Pas de Calais and the Cotentin peninsula, although he was very much alive to the likelihood of holding and diversionary attacks on other fronts.[1]

This was of the greatest assistance to General Eisenhower when, as Supreme Commander Allied Forces in Europe, his Supreme Headquarters Allied Expeditionary Force (SHAEF) came to absorb the COSSAC organisation and its plans in January. For it then was evident where best not to land in strength, and easy to concur with COSSAC (General Morgan) that Normandy was the right place. At the same time this inside knowledge of the enemy's intended deployment (even without Enigma but progressively confirmed by PR, SIS, Jellyfish and, in March, by Grilse) made it possible to calculate with some assurance the acceptable and critical balance of forces which would enable the Allies to prevail once ashore.

Indeed, regarding the performance of the SIS at this moment Menzies could genuinely congratulate himself and his staff upon the work of his agents. Reduced to virtual impotence in Europe by the debacles of 1939 and 1940, the SIS had arisen phoenix-like as a force to be reckoned with. With more than 2000 agents (British, Polish and Western Europeans) supplying over 150 reports per day by coded radio messages (sent with all the risks of detection by DF) and remarkably reliable carrier pigeon post, it was providing for Military Intelligence a reasonably comprehensible picture of the German deployment and order of battle. Admittedly some reports were delayed (by a month in some instances) and others were of dubious reliability, but when supplemented by interrogations of POWs, Jellyfish, Grilse and vast quantities of captured documents (including code books), they went far to compensate, along with the other sources, for what Enigma might have contributed if it still had been in use.[2]

Nevertheless, from the end of 1943, when it was accurately calculated that there were 182 German divisions in Russia, 31 in the Mediterranean theatre and 56 in north and western Europe, it remained a perpetual preoccupation of Eisenhower and his commanders that the Germans should be prevented from concentrating in greater strength and at a faster rate against Normandy than troops and resources could be put ashore. To accomplish this it was essential to deny the enemy the means to reinforce physically and also psychologically to deter him from the desire to do so. At the same time it was imperative to stifle the long-range V-weapons for fear they interfered decisively with the mounting of Overlord, and also generally undermined morale.

With those fundamental aims in mind, the prelude to Overlord would be dominated by efforts to isolate the Normandy front. Attacks would be aimed at both the enemy's land and signal communications, but would be governed to a large extent by an immensely complicated deception operation named Fortitude. Formulated by SHAEF's deception staff in collaboration with MI6 and LCS, and approved on 23 February, Fortitude's aim was to fix German attention on the Pas de Calais. In conjunction ran two complementary deception operations called Bodyguard and Zeppelin. Bodyguard's aim was to persuade the enemy that Overlord, the principal effort, would be preceded by minor operations, and would take place later in the summer. Zeppelin was a subsidiary of Bodyguard, designed to spoof the Germans into thinking that the large amount of shipping in the Mediterranean portended either a landing in southern France or a major operation in the Balkans.[3]

The ongoing development of Fortitude, Bodyguard and Zeppelin was monitored by Fellgiebel as best he could from the usual sources. Canaris, however, was now excluded because, 11 days before Fortitude was approved, he had finally lost the grim struggle with the vicious Kaltenbrunner. At last, by order of Hitler on the evidence of a damning report by Himmler, the Abwehr had been amalgamated with Kaltenbrunner's RSHA, and Canaris had been demoted. No longer could the little admiral and Fellgiebel share the cosy informative chats which in the past had yielded so much high grade intelligence. Henceforward exchanges between the head of Wehrmacht Signals and Intelligence and the RSHA were more formal, though thriving on Fellgiebel's friendly collaboration with Schellenberg, that unrelenting hater of Kaltenbrunner.

Be that as it may, Fellgiebel's interpretation of the accumulation of misleading intelligence presented by Fortitude coincided with the agreed assessment of OKW's staff, which amounted to this: no matter how many options might be offered (and there was hardly a valid deception prospect that was not) the Pas de Calais was the only objective likely to be adopted at some time or another. The advantages to the Allies of this choice were obvious: short sea passage, ease of maximum air support, and a direct route to the heart of Germany with its plethora of vital strategic objectives, including the V-weapon sites. No matter that the strength of the Atlantic Wall in that sector was at its most formidable, nowhere else was there an objective of such compelling strategic correctitude.

When discussing the subject with old Abwehr contacts in the weeks to come, Fellgiebel became as impressed as they by the conclusive assurance of the intelligence available; the majority of which came from those long-proven Abwehr (now RSHA) double agents, known to their British controllers as Garbo, Tricycle, Brutus, Cobweb, Beetle, Mutt and Freak. All the more indicative of the excellence of the flood of double agent reports were the actual corroborative acts to be witnessed. Real or convincing dummy concentrations of shipping and landing craft were seen on the rare forays made by Luftwaffe reconnaissance aircraft which managed to evade the highly efficient enemy fighters and anti-aircraft guns. There were unmissable signs of an ever larger army gathering in the south-east of England, poised for embarkation and transport to Calais and Boulogne. Camps were occasionally detected by PR and radio transmissions from new networks were detected and pin-pointed. The possibility that all these might be spoofs was discounted because the Germans were seeing and hearing what they actually expected.

Next, as the preparatory aerial bombardment began to mount in all its fury, it was noticeable how the bomb tonnage dropped on the Pas de Calais (excluding V-weapon sites) was something in the order of twice that on other sectors, yet never in a recognisable pattern to fit any one particular enemy intent. When occasional small raiding parties landed, or attempted to land by night (presumably for reconnaissance purposes), these visitations occurred along the length of the threatened coasts from Brittany to Belgium. Also it was recorded that, in the event of major movements of troops from one theatre or area to another, evidence was available to corroborate that something of the sort had taken place.[4]

Such overwhelming thoroughly confirmed evidence was, to a considerable extent, wasted on the Germans, partly because they rarely saw or received it but largely because it was superfluous. One central fact stood forth: the Germans never doubted that the Pas de Calais was the main objective. Almost to a man their officers deluded themselves.

But how could their enemies be equally sure that their tall stories were being believed? Not of course through Sigint to the extent some might have thought, even though all the German services were now using code books in lieu of Enigma. Nothing helped more to concentrate the minds of the Chiefs of Signals, even the once obdurate General Martini of the Luftwaffe, than the vital need to abstain as much as possible from using radio. For one thing they needed to shield their new and always potentially vulnerable code books from capture and penetration. For another, it took far longer to encode, transmit and decode hand codes than had been the case with the simpler to operate Enigma; moreover the chances of human error were greater. This was another reason, therefore, to use couriers (who, for fear of ambushes, had to be escorted) and encoded land-line teleprinter links (that frequently were tapped by SIS agents), plus 'secure' *Geheimschreiber*, for the passage of the hundreds of thousands of messages sent.[D1]

Therefore it was mostly by physical observations of German moves and locations that SHAEF's staffs and the LCS weighed the impact of Fortitude's intricate ploys. This was amplified to some extent at the highest strategic level by reading Jellyfish and Grilse — although these sources provided nothing like the amazingly detailed service once furnished by Enigma. Then, just as things were hotting up on both sides of the English Channel, in Italy and in Russia, there came a hiccup. All at once it was discovered that an additional cryptanalytical security device (initially noted briefly in March and February 1943 on Herring to Tunis and, beginning in December, in Russia) was in universal use. Heath Robinson and other machines could barely cope. In

February less than half the number of January's messages were decrypted. Only the delivery of the much faster, more capable, semi-electronic Colossus I saved the day in March. Colossus I's success prompted an instant demand for an improved Colossus II in readiness for the start of Overlord, a machine which would make history as the world's first programmable electronic digital commuter equipped with a memory.[5]

As SIS and PR indicated (and, to some extent, as did RSHA/Abwehr through its requests addressed to the double agents asking for specific kinds of information), Bodyguard was faltering. Nevertheless, Allied offensive operations in the Mediterranean (above all the hard-fought, well-concealed surprise amphibious assault at Anzio in January) showed beyond doubt that not all Allied plans were deceptions. As intended, the Germans were kept on tenterhooks, but so, too, were the Allies. After all, despite completely surprising Field Marshal Kesselring at Anzio and being in possession of sound intelligence of German dispositions, they had failed to take advantage of a golden opportunity to win a great victory, whereas Kesselring, lacking adequate intelligence of his opponent's intentions, had achieved a brilliant defensive success and thereby held intact the Gothic Line. This expensive set-back generated in Allied minds increasing concern following receipt of the news that the formidable Field Marshal Rommel had assumed command of the recently established Army Group B.

Rommel's presence in France had been disclosed on 13 December to GC&CS through the Magic in use by the Japanese military attaché in Vichy. His revelations in the weeks to come had tended to confirm that the Germans were very perplexed about where the Allies would land. Yet, worryingly, they suggested that Normandy might be an objective.[6] To make matters worse, a shift of forces into that sector gradually became apparent in February.

The reason for this shift was also revealed by the Japanese attaché after Field Marshal von Rundstedt's Chief of Staff, General Günther Blumentritt, disclosed on 17 February that it was the intention to hold Holland, Belgium and France 'firmly on the coast'.[7] Here was a complete reversal of Rundstedt's classic strategy. All along he had planned to hold the coastline thinly and retain inland his mass of manoeuvre, comprising the fast, mechanised armoured forces, with a view to launching a decisive counter-stroke once the enemy's true intentions became clear. There were political as well as military reasons for the radical change of plan, but it was Rommel who carried most weight in the, at times, heated debate that erupted with Rundstedt.

Forcibly, and based on bitter experience, Rommel argued that in face of the overwhelming effect of Allied air power, it would not be possible to assemble the counter-stroke forces in sufficient time and strength to carry out their task. He adhered to the opinion that if the invasion was not defeated on the beaches, the campaign and the war were lost. The matter was referred to Hitler who, politician to the fingertips, adopted a compromise. Some of the fast armoured forces would be held back under Rundstedt's command for a concentrated effort. The remainder could be spread along the coast, located close behind the most threatened beaches (including Normandy's) for instant counter-attacks against the leading assault troops.

Significantly, and as proof of the excellence of Army signal security, not one word about the controversial debate, the organisation and the chain of command of German forces or their intentions leaked out — except by inference in a Magic message sent by the Japanese Vichy attaché. So it was left to General Montgomery, applying his practical, close insight into Rommel's mind, to declare on 7 April that he expected Rommel to hurl his armour into battle, even though the Panzer divisions were being kept (as he was incorrectly led to believe) under Rundstedt's direct command. Acutely he observed that 'delay may be caused before they are released to Rommel . . . quarrels may arise between the two of them.'[8]

More to the point, it was already apparent just how right Rommel was in his dread of air power. By then the Allied transportation plan was demonstrating its awesome potential. Conceived expressly in 1943 as an essential measure to prevent Rundstedt's fast armoured groups intervening decisively against the Normandy landing area within the first week of the assault, the plan raised fierce political, humanitarian and military controversy. Shaped to disrupt land communications in north-western Europe, the aim was 'to deaden the whole system as to delay the concentration and reinforcement of the German forces . . . and weaken their fighting power.' Objections ranged from fear of the damage to diplomatic relations with France and heavy loss of civilian life, to doubts about whether the aim could be achieved. Eventually the plan was adopted. To begin with, the railway yards at Trappes, near Paris, were shattered by RAF Bomber Command on 7 March.[9]

The protagonists maintained their struggle about the effectiveness (or otherwise) of the transportation plan after 6 June, when the landing took place — and, indeed, for years to come — but it was the Germans who best understood what was happening. In a report dated 13 June, their Air Ministry admitted that all main railway lines had broken down, the coastal defences had been cut off from supply bases and transport of essential supplies for the populace had been completely stopped. Only the most vital military traffic was possible, with numerous delays and detours and only by night; large scale strategic movement of troops by rail was practically impossible.[10]

Lack of Enigma did not deprive SHAEF of adequate intelligence about the transportation plan's effect. Fish contributed a few encouraging items of news, telling of impending doom to add to numerous SIS, PR and SOE reports. At the start, however, there was almost a consensus claiming that attacks upon railways, to the exclusion of road and rail bridges (which were rated difficult targets to hit and destroy) were insufficient to achieve the aim. Not until the decision to bomb bridges, especially those over the River Seine, was taken and most successfully implemented, did the air assault bite hard.

Another crucial aspect of the transportation plan's effects, which seems to have eluded the Allied intelligence officers but certainly not their German counterparts and Fellgiebel's officers, was the concurrent destruction of the cables which carried the vast majority of signals traffic. Previously, sabotage by SOE resistance members of telephone and telegraph facilities (including the 11,000km of trunk cable installed by the Germans since 1940) had caused only a sporadic nuisance. Likewise, it was not until Allied bombing of German city centres and their environs had grown intensive in 1943, and seriously damaged the trunk cable network and technical installations, that communications in the Reich were disrupted. Until then the Reichspost, with Wehrmacht assistance, had coped adequately in maintaining home services. Now, in Germany, there was impairment of flexibility and numerous breakdowns. In France the widespread bombing of railway junctions and bridges, exacerbated by wire cutting by saboteurs (who tended to avoid well-guarded exchanges[11]) caused disruption on a colossal scale; occasionally cable communications between army groups were severed for days on end.

Reporting to Fellgiebel, General Praun listed how the French postal authorities were involved in sabotage, how inadequate were radio communications, how vulnerable were couriers and how weak and cumbersome was signals intelligence. He added that, as in Italy, tactical communications in forward combat areas were being destroyed by air attacks. He dreaded the prospects of what might happen if and when mobile warfare commenced in Italy or north-western Europe. In Russia, the enemy's winter offensive was inexorably forcing back the Wehrmacht towards Poland, and air attacks were not so intensive, so that matters, though difficult, were slightly less crippling.[12]

* *

Realisation of the serious deficiencies in the service which Fellgiebel regarded as central to operational effectiveness and survival only compelled him to strive all the harder to redouble his efforts to eliminate Hitler and the ghastly organisation that were the root causes of the wrecking of his beloved Fatherland. To Fellgiebel's regret, Henning von Tresckow was no longer a driving force at the heart of the resistance movement. When, at the end of 1943, through the Head of the Army Personnel Department, General Rudolf Schmundt, Tresckow had offered himself as a member of Field Marshal von Manstein's army group staff, the Field Marshal, unhappy about his political attitude, had refused to take him. Instead Tresckow was posted to an army HQ on the Russian front, thus removing him from a prominent role in the conspiracy.[13] Whereupon, and most fatefully for Schmundt, as well as for Fellgiebel and the conspirators, Stauffenberg stepped into Tresckow's shoes to become, with Fellgiebel, the dynamic force behind the adulterated Operation 'Walkyrie'.

On 11 February 1944, a spurious amendment to Walkyrie ordering the concentration of every available combat group into a Grenadier Regiment was signed by Stauffenberg on behalf of General Fromm, without the latter's knowledge.[14]

In effect, Stauffenberg was now acting as Fellgiebel's chief-of-staff with all the thoroughness of a top-grade member of the German General Staff serving his commander. And by no means insignificantly, like Oster, he was hazarding security by filing far too many compromising documents.

Fellgiebel was now in charge of the conspiracy pending the recruitment of an active, charismatic, nationally celebrated Field Marshal who would assume the leading role.[15] The vacillating Kluge was out of action due to a serious road accident. Rundstedt would have no part of it. As a known adherent of Hitler, Rommel was not approached at this stage, while Manstein, who had declared that 'Prussian Field Marshals do not mutiny,' was to be politely dismissed from command by Hitler on 2 April.

Yet, amazingly, despite the large number of people who were in the know, the secret was kept — indicating that support for the plot was present even though the willingness to partake was not. C (and therefore the British Foreign Office) knew something was afoot in March after Adam von Trott du Solz, a leading conspirator, had made contact with the British mission in Stockholm concerning opposition to the Nazis by unnamed senior Army officers. There were SIS reports from Lisbon in May that a plot to eliminate Hitler existed, but nobody took these seriously since there was no evidence of a valid organisation.[16]

With the approach of the (correctly) predictable co-ordinated major offensives in the Mediterranean theatre, in North-West Europe and in Russia, Fellgiebel, who was the conspirators' Postmaster General designate in their intended government, spread the word far and wide as he toured headquarters throughout the Reich and occupied territories. He made repeated and frequently successful efforts to drum up support from important personalities, including Army officers who were very close to Hitler and who realised only too well, as Fellgiebel himself put it, ' . . . it is already too late', remarking also, 'For such a good and just cause, paying with one's life is a just price.'[17]

DEVIATIONS FROM HISTORY

[D1] A deviation, of course, but one with its roots in fact since the foresighted Fellgiebel's policy was to expand the *Geheimschreiber* service as much as possible to reduce the load on other means of communication.

Confirmatory footnotes:
1 Hinsley/Howard Vol 5 pp 108, 109.
2 Hinsley Vol 3 Pt 2 pp 27–31 including some highly informative footnotes.
3 *ibid* pp 47–9.
4 Hinsley/Howard Vol 5 Chapter 6 for numerous examples.
5 Hinsley Vol 3 Pt 1 pp 479–82.
6 Hinsley Vol 3 Pt 2 pp 46, 47.
7 *ibid* p 66.
8 *ibid* pp 67, 68.
9 *ibid* pp 106–15.
10 *ibid* p 115 fn.
11 Foot p 350.
12 Adapted from Praun pp 45–7.
13 Wheeler-Bennett pp 588, 589.
14 Wildhagen p 290 and pp 323–6.
15 *ibid* p 287.
16 Hinsley Vol 3 Pt 1 pp 893, 894.
17 Wildhagen p 206.

19.
Surprise, Brute Force and Ignorance

W ith hindsight it can be argued how astonishing were the fears and doubts afflicting the Allies concerning the prospects of success for the amphibious landing in Normandy in June 1944. After all, even without the benefit of Enigma-supplied intelligence, they possessed an historically unrivalled insight into their enemy's intentions and deployment, plus an overwhelming superiority in manpower, equipment and material resources. Above all, they not only held the strategic initiative but were also in a position of reasonable confidence that the Germans would be taken by tactical surprise, as already they had been in the amphibious landings in North Africa, Sicily and Italy.

Yet, at the time, stirred by Churchill with his dark, personal recollections of the debacle at Gallipoli in 1915, and by every senior officer of good conscience (unlike some among their opponents) with ingrained memories of the horrors of World War 1's slaughters, they tended to be hosts to their own worst fears. They dreaded the slaughter of aircraft transporting airborne troops, the prospects of men being mown down on the beaches, and the danger of an immediate armoured onslaught on the left flank which might easily overrun the leading forces before they could be reinforced by tanks and heavy anti-tank guns.[1] Some even contemplated total failure, the possibility of being thrown back into the sea, or, failing that, the prospect of a stalemate brought about by the Germans winning the build-up race. Also they were apprehensive of the V-weapon menace in the knowledge that the Germans, despite the aerial punishment being inflicted on launching sites, still had the capability of pounding London and the cities and military bases of southern England.

In the event it was the Germans who had the most to worry about. Prevented from exerting any role of air power, the Luftwaffe could neither detect information of their enemy's intentions and movements on land, nor interfere to the slightest extent with shipping and with air formations. Numbers of available machines were being cut down by systematic bombing of airfields (enhanced by fighter intruder missions at night) and the supplementary interception of reinforcements flying in from Germany. Sigint played only a minor role in this Allied programme, except when revealing flight paths. The bulk of intelligence about airfields in use came from PR and SIS. After the heavy losses of the winter blitz over England the reduced Luftwaffe strength in the West was being remorselessly whittled away to well under 1,000 aircraft.[2] To make matters worse its radar early warning system and radio jamming stations began to come under heavy air attack on 10 May. Again Sigint provided next to no information to SHAEF, the principal evidence of results (which were better than regarded by assessors) being obtained by PR and by listening stations.[3]

Decidedly the Germans already had yielded the advantage of strategic surprise to the enemy through their own misconstrued concept of Allied intentions (reinforced by the lies of Operation 'Fortitude's' double agents) but they also stood on the verge of suffering from a decisive tactical surprise.

Many German commanders whose experience was mainly from the Russian Front still had no real concept of the crushing power of the US and British air and naval bombardment that would be thrown at them. None expected the waves of specialised armoured vehicles capable of wading ashore in the van of a landing to neutralise the defences ahead of the much more vulnerable infantry. Nor could they have foreseen the greatest, most fortuitous surprise of all, the false weather forecast (worked out by their meteorologists who lacked adequate data from the Atlantic because all their weather stations had been found and eliminated) that said the enemy would not assault in weather so bad as to make conditions too rough for parachutists and landing craft. This was a fatally misleading prediction which made it permissible for Rommel to absent himself in Germany to visit his wife on her birthday, and for General von Feuchtinger, commander of the 21st Panzer Division that was tasked immediately to counter-attack landings on the Normandy beaches, to be in Paris visiting his mistress.

Before either of these commanders (among others) had reached their holiday destinations, they were all too well aware of news from Italy announcing the fall of Rome on 4 June. Commanders of the Allied attack on the Gothic Line, which had been launched on 11 May, were well furnished with information from a number of sources, including Bream (which carried some very high-grade material concerning orders of battle and Kesselring's future strategy) and anti-German Italian co-belligerents. And, as was usual, once battle was joined, the ether became alive with encoded and plain language signals of high, medium and low grade which contributed jointly to a clear picture of German tactics and strategy. This undeniably helped economise in lives by enabling commanders to avoid butting expensively against strong opposition and instead seeking safer ways to their objectives. Yet, in point of fact, once the known German frontal positions had been overcome by carefully orchestrated deliberate attacks, the magnitude of victory was never in doubt due to the sheer brute force exerted by the attackers. It hardly needed Sigint to explain that Kesselring was in dire straits, though fighting a delaying action of commendable skill.[D1]

In theory the first lines of German defence against the invasion of France were provided by the Luftwaffe and the Navy. In practice the former was notable by its virtual absence over Normandy for the first three days of the landing, and thereafter made its meagre presence felt almost entirely at night because, by day, its few sorties were almost all ignominiously chased away or shot down. A similar fate, in a way, was in store for the Navy which, by force of deprivation, was compelled to depend far more on U-boats than on surface vessels. The latter, consisting of five destroyers (two in dock) and a few torpedo boats and 12 E-boats available at Cherbourg made but few sorties with minimal effect and disastrous losses.[4]

In the aftermath of 1943's disasters, the U-boat fleet had suffered further heavy losses without sinking many ships, either in the Mediterranean or the Atlantic. Still the hunted, its boats had failed utterly to make any positive impact off Sicily, Salerno or

Anzio. Not until January 1944 had it dawned on Dönitz's scientists that it was centimetric radar, not infra-red devices, that enabled the enemy to detect surfaced boats, and that *Naxos*, all along, was an effective detector of 10cm wavelength impulses.[5] Then came an undesired set-back when it was discovered from *B-Dienst* Sigint that the schnorkel, the 'breathing tube' which, when raised, enabled a U-boat to run when submerged on its diesel engines, was itself detectable by radar.[6]

On 4 June there was another, unsuspected, adverse development in store for the U-boat Command. That day off Bermuda, *U-505* was forced to the surface and compelled to surrender. Astonishingly, its commander failed to throw overboard the weighted bag containing secret material. This resulted in a present to GC&CS of an obsolete Enigma machine, the latest code books and a copy of the so-called 'address book' code. Equipped with these priceless gifts, especially the address book, ascertaining U-boat positions was greatly simplified and speeded up for the cryptanalysts at Bletchley Park.[D2]

On 5 June, as the mighty invasion fleet was approaching the coast of Normandy, not a single U-boat was positioned to harass it. Of the 58 available at short notice for anti-invasion duties, 17 were stationed at Brest and 19 formed a screen between St Nazaire, Lorient and La Pallice. As anticipated by the Allies, Sigint divulged a flurry of sailing instructions, though without details, not that this mattered. For one thing the inevitable (though much shorter than once upon a time) radio transmissions gave ample warning that boats on the surface (for the sake of speed) were converging on the English Channel like wasps to a honey pot, and for another, such was the extensive cover by air reconnaissance, they were almost bound to be spotted and attacked, either from the air or by ships that were patrolling in enormous strength.

The story of U-boat endeavours was a dismal one for crews who had been whipped up into a sense of the importance of their vital, if suicidal, mission. Negligible and of scant significance were their successes, catastrophic their losses. Out of 14 boats at sea on the night of 6/7 June two were sunk and six forced to return to port due to damage. Next day three went down and more were damaged, extinguishing the threat. A similar fate awaited reinforcements as they arrived piecemeal, any intention to operate in packs having long ago been abandoned.[D3/7] In the event, it was the E-boats and torpedo boats which made the most impact at sea — until the destruction of a very high proportion of their number by massive bombing of their shelters and docks at Le Havre on 14 June.[8] Once more sheer brute force aimed accurately at a strategic target, long since highlighted by intelligence sources, had paid off.

Distinct, if incomplete, tactical surprise on the beaches also made virtually unnecessary supplementary intelligence to that gathered prior to D-Day. The descent of massed airborne forces was totally unexpected by the Germans. Nevertheless that event inevitably alerted them to something larger than a mere raid or diversionary operation. It resulted in the broadcast of somewhat delayed warning orders with the manning of many coastal fortifications in readiness to greet the invaders. Yet only at one notorious beach — the American one code-named Omaha — was there such stiff resistance as to hint at the possibility of a repulse. The other four beaches were quickly seized and bridgeheads firmly established by nightfall, and at a far lower price in casualties than those anticipated by Winston Churchill, who was braced for 20,000 British and Canadians alone. Indeed, out of 155,715 Allied troops landed by air and sea on 6 June, total casualties were only 10,300, of which the higher proportion were American, mainly suffered on Omaha beach. Furthermore, losses might have been even fewer if only SHAEF intelligence had realised that the enemy beach pillboxes were sited in enfilade and not, as assumed, facing seawards.[9]

Only against the British left flank was any semblance of an enemy counter-attack attempted, the effort by 21st Panzer Division which really was feared as a result of intelligence's previous gross over-estimate of that formation's power and dynamism. Yet it was not expected at once by I (British) Corps which, seemingly inadvertently and certainly incorrectly, harboured the illusion that 21st Panzer was concentrated 20–30 miles south of Caen and therefore unlikely to intervene before Caen was entered; whereas, in fact, some of its artillery and infantry were positioned overlooking the coastline and its best armoured regiment was located within relatively easy reach to the south of Caen. In the event 21st Panzer's armour, due to its commander's absence, to a change of orders from above and to a succession of air attacks, did not hit the British and Canadians until 16.30. Tracked throughout the day by Sigint and air reports, its leading group nevertheless surprised the 3rd British Infantry Division because its leading elements, due to tardy transmission of information, had not been warned of the enemy's approach. Yet, once again, brute force decided the issue. Concentrated fire from artillery and tanks checked the group and the awe-inspiring appearance at 21.00 of a massed landing by gliders on his right flank persuaded the German commander to pull back. At the end of the day 21st Panzer had lost some 50 out of 127 tanks committed.[10]

Rommel's aim to throw the enemy back into the sea at once had been frustrated. The opportunity to do so would never recur.

In the days to come, as a bloody battle of attrition evolved in Normandy, the Allies benefited, as in Italy, from a plethora of intelligence of which that of high grade was only a minor proportion. Sigint there was aplenty, especially due to the load thrown on cable communications from bombing and sabotage. Jellyfish, Grilse and Anchovy (Luftflotte 3's *Geheimschreiber*) were in great demand and naturally receiving close attention from Colossus I and its far more powerful successor Colossus II which, due to the unsparing efforts of Bletchley Park and GPO Dollis Hill, was functioning with qualified success on 1 June.

Colossus II, with its 2,400 valves and limited capacity memory read photo-electrically from a perforated tape, was indeed revolutionary as the world's first programmable electronic digital computer. But neither the growing number of Colossi (eventually 10 Mark IIs, in addition to the original 24 Mark Is, were built) nor the rest of the enormous expanding assembly of 'Y' Service listeners, GC&CS staff and machines could wholly cope with the huge volume of Sigint being generated by the Germans. There had to be astute selectivity in choosing which nets to listen to.

To begin with, the task was complicated because of the characteristic discipline of German Army signal security; little material was disclosed for breaking until 6 June. Although the Colossi began well by breaking the Fishes, the results were neither wholesale nor timely. Worse still, after only a few days, Jellyfish (soon to be copied by the other Fish codes) was no longer decipherable when an additional safeguard was introduced, one that was not overcome until October.[11] It was the same with the other high-grade code books, many of which remained unbroken. Medium- and low-grade codes, which were used in vast quantities, did yield valuable cumulative returns.[D4] The fact remains, however, that the expert cryptanalysts of GC&CS did manage to master a number of code books to compensate for the lack of Enigma.[D5]

To reiterate, possessed of the strategic initiative and a colossal superiority in men, machines and firepower as they were, the Allies had but little need to worry about the possibility of being thrown off balance by enemy counteraction. Even if caught momentarily by surprise through a lapse of intelligence, they were far from being vulnerable to threats of a decisive reverse, though their losses might increase if the war was prolonged. Therefore in the pages to come, only those military events which impinged significantly on the course of a war approaching its inevitable end will be commented upon. First of these concerns the initial use of the V-missiles which, not unexpectedly, began with the V1 bombardment of England on the night of 12 June.

* *

Bearing in mind that as late as that date the Allies were uncertain of the height or speed of a V1 in flight, as well as ignorant of the positions of many launching sites, it was no mean achievement that, within four days, they had acquired sufficient data to undertake an effective redeployment of guns, fighters and barrage balloons to improve interceptions and destruction of the flying bombs. In the main it was ground and air observations that provided a basis for the operational analysis that made this possible.[12] What little Sigint contributed came chiefly through Japanese Magic in various reports indicating German disappointment at V1's performance even as a terror weapon. That performance was impaired by various adverse factors. First, because the sites in the Cotentin peninsula were overrun by the American Army before the launching of a single missile; second, because the latest, easier-to-construct and conceal post-ski-type launching sites in the Pas de Calais were soon found by agents and PR and therefore did not entirely escape air attack; and third, because the supply of missiles was hampered by the transportation plan's battering of railways and roads.

However, the Germans were never aware to any significant degree of the damage and morale effect being inflicted on their sprawling target. Pre-D Day censorship and the closing of communication links with the outside world prevented adequate reporting of where and when damage was inflicted and their effect on morale. In any case, the Germans believed they were already in receipt of high grade intelligence from the double agents, above all from Garbo. The truly remarkable implementation of disinformation conducted by the Twenty Committee and the Whitehall authorities did far more than simply report events, however. By skilful drafting of Garbo's ebullient messages, it managed to spur the Abwehr to submit questionnaires which indicated German concerns and provided opportunities further to mislead, besides confirming the success or otherwise of various devious ploys.[13]

At the heart of evolving intentions, as approved by Churchill and the Chiefs of Staff, was a policy of shaking the enemy's faith in V1. In this, as Japanese Magic revealed, they were to some extent successful.[14] Far more politically controversial were suggestions that the Germans might be induced into shifting the V1s' point of aim — thus dropping missiles on people who so far had escaped them!

In the event this policy was never implemented. For one thing, the idea was dubious, if only because the inaccurate V1s never achieved anything like concentration of impact on target.[15] For another, what once was referred to as 'the drizzle of V1s' from the Pas de Calais had ceased by the start of September when the last launching site was overrun by the advancing British and Canadian armies, by which time the combined efforts of SIS agents, PR, plotting of flight routes and lines of communication had helped locate launching sites and enabled bombers to reduce the number of launchings in any case. Simultaneously the introduction of American-made VT (radio proximity) fuses had greatly increased the rate of missile kill by anti-aircraft guns, in conjunction with interceptions by the latest fighters, including Gloster Meteor jets.

It has to be recorded, however, that Sigint had contributed very little of vital importance to the winning of these successes. Indeed, as was not unusual, the Germans had contributed to their own delusion. An amazing example was the misinterpretation of air photographs on 16 September (the first taken since January 1941) when the self-satisfied Colonel Wolff of Flak Regiment 155(W) claimed the credit for all the damage inflicted on London since then![16]

Nothing, however, was more indicative of the total delusion afflicting the Germans than the signal received by Garbo on 29 July from his controller in Madrid. 'With great happiness and satisfaction I am to advise you that today the Führer has granted the Iron Cross to you for your extraordinary merits.' Garbo's reply reflected the satisfaction of the Twenty Committee, 'I cannot at this moment, when emotion overwhelms me, express in words my gratitude.' For it was more than convincing evidence that their opponents were thoroughly deceived by the double agents. It proved beyond doubt that the Germans were operating in total ignorance of what their enemy was up to on the eve of the collapse of their front in France.[17]

DEVIATIONS FROM HISTORY

[D1] Hinsley Vol 3 Pt 2. Undoubtedly Enigma did provide its fair share of valuable intelligence, but it is equally clear that all the other sources and providers of information played significant roles without which Allied commanders at all levels might have been embarrassed.

[D2] Hinsley Vol 2 p 681 and Vol 3 Pt 3 p 852 including entertaining fn. It is reasonable to assume that when using code books in lieu of Enigma, the Germans would have continued to disguise U-boats positions with the address book code.

[D3] Hinsley Vol 3 Pt 2 pp 155–61. Enigma actually did reveal a number of boats' positions and orders from U-boat Command. Nevertheless it is most unlikely that the anti-submarine groups would have been baffled by the absence of this information, especially since, without Enigma, the Germans would still have used radio to some extent and thereby disclosed their presence to DF. And all the more so if, as assumed here, their code books had been broken.

[D4] Hinsley Vol 3 Pt 1 Appx 2 and Vol 3 Pt 2 provide invaluable insight into pre- and post-Normandy invasion Sigint developments, and include of course the valuable roles played by Enigma and the Bombes. Even so it is noteworthy that with Enigma (especially that used by the Luftwaffe) intelligence was by no means complete. On the other hand it is reasonable to assume that without Enigma, code books would have been used and might or might not have been broken as promptly as was some Enigma. In other words, this fiction might well not have been much different from fact.

[D5] Hinsley Vol 2 pp 631–42. In accessing the likely rate of success in breaking the German code books, comparison should be made with considerable German success against British codes throughout the war. True, they never broke the Typex machine code, but it was another matter with non-machine codes. By April 1940 30–50% of naval traffic was read without delay. From February until 15 December 1942 it amounted to 80% of British/US/Canadian traffic and, after a hiccup, was doing well again from February to June 1943. Similarly they enjoyed considerable successes against Army codes in other theatres (see also Praun pp 25–45).

Confirmatory footnotes:

1 Hinsley Vol 3 Pt 1 p 839.
2 *ibid* pp 115–8.
3 *ibid* pp 119–22.
4 *ibid* pp 161–5.
5 Macksey *Combat Errors* p 146.
6 MOD (Navy) Vol III p 67.
7 *ibid* Vol III pp 67–74 which describe the appalling difficulties and perils and the bravery of many crews.
8 Hinsley Vol 3 Pt 2 pp 162–6.
9 *ibid* pp 129–32.
10 *ibid* pp 139, 140 and pp 839–42.
11 *ibid* p 848.
12 *ibid* pp 533–5.
13 *ibid* p 536.
14 Hinsley/Howard Vol 5 pp 167–73.
15 Hinsley Vol 2 Pt 2 p 535.
16 Hinsley/Howard Vol 5 pp 179, 180.
17 *ibid* p 174 and amusing footnote dealing with the difficulties of awarding this medal to a foreigner.

20.
Breaking Points for Field Marshals

The inexorable build-up of Allied forces in the Normandy bridgehead had, by 17 June, produced a situation which both von Rundstedt and Rommel recognised as running out of their control. Until Grilse and Anchovy (in addition to Jellyfish) could no longer be read early in July, their reports to OKW had shown that the Germans' prospects of containing their enemy, let alone mounting a well-concentrated counter-stroke, were diminishing to the point of extinction. The ring around Cherbourg was tightening and its capture was only a matter of a few days distant. Fed by Fortitude and the double agents, the High Command clung to the belief that the main enemy offensive was yet to hit the Pas de Calais; with a vastly exaggerated margin of error they estimated 67 hostile divisions poised for action there. Night after night their air reconnaissance and their monitoring of radar and WT lent credence to the likelihood of fresh landings somewhere or other. Moreover, they persisted in the quite ludicrous assumption that the Allies were capable of putting ashore no less than 25 divisions in a single day, whereas on 6 June they had been stretched to send in the equivalent of ten, including three airborne.

Beguiled by these fantasies, on the 17th, Hitler, accompanied by his chief of operations, General Jodl, met the two field marshals and their chiefs of staff (Generals Blumentritt and Speidel) in the command bunker at Margival, which had been built as his command post for the invasion of England. It was to be an encounter between the disgruntled and the arch dissembler. The field marshals painted a gloomy picture, illustrating the impossibility of holding the ring against such an overpoweringly superior enemy and at the same time maintaining a reserve to deal with the main enemy landing when it came. Speidel, who was sympathetic to the conspirators, was intrigued to hear Rommel not mincing words 'in describing the inherent difficulties of the defence', and in due course demanding, 'My Führer, what do you really think of our chances of continuing the war?' To which Hitler had angrily retorted, 'That is a question which is not your responsibility. You will have to leave that to me.' Hitler monopolised the conversation over lunch with evasive intuitions and talk of new weapons.

The Führer's boast that the V1 would be decisive against Great Britain then was given an ironic twist when, following the departure of the field marshals, a V1, which had reversed course, crashed on the bunker. There were no casualties, but the Führer, shaken in more ways than one, promptly cancelled the next day's visit to HQ Army Group B and headed for the safety of Berchtesgaden instead.[1]

Twelve more days elapsed before Rommel was ready to launch his last attempt to stop the rot at the front with the oft-postponed counter-stroke by II SS Panzer Corps. On the afternoon of 29 June four SS Panzer divisions and two Army Panzer divisions (not one of them at full strength) plunged forward. Something of the sort had long been expected by General Montgomery. Already prisoners had revealed the presence of these formations whose passage to the front had been traced in the usual ways from the usual sources. To make matters crystal clear, a map and notebook found on a captured SS officer laid bare what was coming. Surprise there was none. Blasted by intensive naval and army gunfire directed from vital ground, ravaged from the air and decimated by concentrated anti-tank gun fire in close country, the counter-stroke was called off in disarray on the evening of the 30th.[2 & 3]

The commitment of these élite mobile divisions (bringing to eight their number in Normandy) might have suggested to SHAEF that Fortitude was blown, and indeed it was known to them on 1 July that only two Panzer divisions remained in reserve to German Fifteenth Army in the Pas de Calais. This continuance of the grand delusion far exceeded SHAEF's original expectations that the deception could not be prolonged beyond D+4. In any case, it had always been anticipated that those divisions which already had been moved to Normandy would have been transferred in that way. From the beginning SHAEF was prepared to settle for Fortitude holding in place only a small mobile reserve behind the fifteen static and three so-called mobile infantry divisions (with their dependence on horse-drawn transport and bicycles) garrisoning the coastal fortifications. It was beyond SHAEF's wildest dreams that this delusion had lasted so long, and too much to expect it to be prolonged, as it was, until 25 July.[4] In the meantime it had sucked into the Normandy vortex from Germany and other theatres several more Panzer and infantry formations to meet the mounting crisis.

Everybody with a grain of information and insight among the upper echelons of German government and high command knew that a breaking point had been reached, though few, outside the hard core of conspirators, had the temerity to say so to Hitler's face or take action to terminate his rule. But on 29 June, when the field marshals next met their Supreme Commander, that event was imminent. For not only was the news from Italy and France bad, so, too, was it appallingly grim from the Russian Front.

The sharing of information between the Western and Eastern members of the anti-fascist alliance had rarely been whole-hearted and usually self-interested. The West had never disclosed the existence of Ultra. The East was not in the habit of sharing its plans unless there was something in it for Russia. Long and tedious were the negotiations before the Russians at last fell completely in line with the West's grandiose deception schemes for 1944. The forthcoming Russian summer offensives had only been advised in outline as comprising an attack on one sector in mid-June, followed by developments at the end of that month leading to a general offensive in July.

In the event there was an attack on the Leningrad front on 10 June, followed by a huge offensive aimed at Army Group Centre on 22 June, which encompassed the destruction of that formation and caused a widespread German withdrawal along the length of the Eastern Front. On the 30th the Russians were within five days of crossing the Polish frontier. These developments were notified to the British and Americans by official communiqués and by special reports to the military missions in Moscow, though in nothing like the detail as those which advised the Russians about Overlord;

not that this deprived the West of the essential facts of the scale of German disaster, revealed as they were through Fish and other codes. They soon knew that 28 divisions in Army Group Centre had been destroyed and drew the logical conclusion that no further transfers to France were likely.[D1]

The next private meeting of Rundstedt and Rommel with Hitler, Field Marshal Keitel and Jodl, this time at Berchtesgaden on the 29th, again exposed the raw edges of their association. Asked to speak first, Rommel opened provocatively by stating, 'The whole world stands arrayed against Germany, and this disproportion of strength . . . ', whereupon Hitler interrupted by ordering him to confine himself to military matters. The field marshals, without yet knowing that their counter-stroke had been delayed, then insisted upon an immediate withdrawal to prevent destruction of Seventh Army in Normandy and the elimination of Fifteenth Army's capability to repel a landing in the Pas de Calais. This Hitler rejected. ' . . . we must not allow mobile warfare to develop, since the enemy surpasses us by far in mobility due to his air superiority and his superabundance of motor vehicles and fuel. Therefore everything depends on our confining him to his bridgehead by building up a front to block it off and then on fighting a war of attrition to wear him down and force him back, using every method of guerrilla warfare.'[5] Rubbish of this sort only made the field marshals more angry. At the end Rommel once more attempted to raise the question of Germany's prospects, whereupon an infuriated Führer ordered him to leave the room.[6]

Upon their return to France both field marshals metaphorically began burning their boats. On the evening of 1 July, when it was known that a desperate attempt by II SS Panzer Corps to renew the counter-stroke had failed, Rundstedt had exploded as Keitel wailed down the telephone, 'What shall we do? What shall we do?' The doyen of field marshals had snapped, 'Make peace you fools. What else can you do?' and had instantly been reported to Hitler. It just happened by chance that, at that very moment, the Führer was in conversation with Field Marshal von Kluge who was reporting for service after eight months' recuperation from a road accident. Hitler received Keitel's report calmly, at once told Kluge to take over as C-in-C West and wrote 'a nice letter' of dismissal to Rundstedt.[7]

Rommel demonstrated his concern in a very different manner. Until the 17 June meeting at Margival he had brushed aside approaches by the conspirators. Now he concluded that some form of direct action was necessary and this he communicated to General Beck along with the opinion that the Normandy front could not long be held.[8] Returning from Berchtesgaden he spoke with Fellgiebel-like frankness to several officers, including Speidel, about the need to end the war. On 15 July to Colonel Warning, an old Africa comrade, he said, 'I will tell you something. Field Marshal von Kluge and I have sent the Führer an ultimatum. Militarily the war can't be won and he must make a political decision.'

'And what if the Führer refuses?' asked the astonished Warning.

'Then I open the West Front. There would only be one important matter left — that the Anglo-Americans reach Berlin before the Russians.'

Politically unrealistic as this was, the involvement of the chronically hesitant Kluge was crucial. Unwilling at first to fall in line with Rundstedt's and Rommel's pessimistic appreciations of the situation in Normandy, he soon swung round to their opinion by counter-signing the ultimatum and despatching it by courier on the 16th,[9] thus once more obliquely signifying his support for the conspirators.

Meanwhile Rommel was focusing his attention on the open country, dotted with villages, to the south of Caen. On the 15th and 16th he visited the formations that were positioned in depth on either side of the vital Bourguebus ridge and warned their commanders that it was there that the numerically superior British armour would next attack in strength. But on the 17th Rommel was struck from the lists, severely wounded by an air attack on his car. If ever he did have any genuine inclination to become involved with the main conspiracy, this was now at an end along with the chances of Beck obtaining the inspirational services of a popular field marshal.

As for the British Operation 'Goodwood', which indeed was launched to seize the Bourguebus ridge on the 18th, this phalanx of armoured vehicles advanced in overwhelming force behind a deluge of air and artillery fire the next day, only to be stopped short of the ridge with the loss of over 130 tanks. This check retrospectively won for Rommel one last defensive success. It was a well-deserved local victory which might have been a defeat for him if the thrust by the three armoured divisions of VIII British Corps had been organised and handled in a better way. For it was not as if the British were short of the essential intelligence about the depth and quality of the German defensive position.[D2] Simply their organisation and methods were wrong. The fire support by air and artillery was incapable of defending the tanks all the way to and beyond the vital crest of the ridge to neutralise the known locations of enemy artillery and mortar batteries. Grouping was wrong, too; there was insufficient infantry allocated to capture the fortified villages which sheltered anti-tank guns on the ridge. Two days later, even though Operation 'Cobra' (the intended vast American breakout on the Allied right flank) had to be postponed repeatedly due to foul weather, this check palled to virtual insignificance when, at last, the conspirators struck.

DEVIATIONS FROM HISTORY

[D1] Hinsley Vol 3 Pt 2 pp 281–3. The absence of Enigma was not crucial since, until early in July when new safeguards were introduced by the Germans, various Fish channels provided the highest grade material.

[D2] *ibid* Appx 18, pp 869–71. This shows that the information 'was probably based mainly on aerial reconnaissance complemented, and perhaps prompted, by two important Ultra decrypts of 10 and 14 July, which, even allowing that code books (in lieu of Enigma) had not been broken (as very likely they would have been), those historians who have claimed that Ultra gave 'no warning of the multiple defence lines south-east of Caen' were treading shaky ground. For combined PR and routine artillery reconnaissance and flash spotting assuredly would have detected what was located there without need of prompting by Ultra.

Confirmatory footnotes:
1 Wilmot pp 366, 367.
2 *ibid* pp 379–81.
3 Hinsley Vol 3 Pt 2 pp 196–9.
4 *ibid* pp 177, 178.
5 Anon MOD p 398.
6 Fraser *Rommel* p 504.
7 Wilmot p 382.
8 *ibid* p 409.
9 Fraser *Rommel* p 507.

21.
Heroes and Bunglers

With Winston Churchill's approval, the German Section of SOE laid serious plans in 1944 to assassinate Hitler. Under the code-name 'Foxley' various fantastic options were studied. Among these was infecting the Führer with a dose of anthrax contained in spectacles, false teeth (if he used them) or a fountain pen, or perhaps blowing up his train, preferably in a tunnel. First favourite seems to have been by ambush while Hitler took his daily walk at Berchtesgaden, by using a sniper's rifle, or a hand grenade, or an anti-tank projectile fired from a PIAT. This plan was described in an extremely detailed document of 120 pages, complete with map, and was to be undertaken by intensely anti-Nazi Austrians and Bavarians, or maybe by Poles or Czechs.

The ambush was to be executed in June when Hitler was expected to visit Berchtesgaden. However, it was badly received by Churchill's advisers. Stewart Menzies most reluctantly promised help by MI6 agents. The head of SOE's German Section disliked the use of such 'low methods' which might be disastrous. He foresaw it canonising Hitler and giving birth 'to the myth that Germany would have been saved if he had lived'. The Chiefs of Staff also objected on the grounds that Hitler's incompetence as a military strategist was a priceless asset to the Allies, 'Hitler has been of the greatest possible help to the war effort'.

The plan was not activated, even though Churchill had supporters who thought Hitler's removal would be fatal to the Nazi regime. Instead the German resistance attempted to do the job with an almost equally fantastic scheme.[1]

* *

It is among one of the many incongruities of the time that on 1 June Stauffenberg trusted in a single item of misleading intelligence suggesting the Allies would not invade in force in 1944 and, if they did, might suffer such a catastrophic repulse as to persuade the British 'to negotiate with us'. Like Rommel, though in a different aspect, he, too, was amazingly out of touch with both the political and the military climate. After 6 June it took a typically inspiring letter from the sidelined Henning von Tresckow (still serving on an army staff on the Eastern Front) to restore resolve and momentum. 'The assassination must be attempted at any cost. Even should that fail, the attempt to seize power in the capital must be undertaken. We must prove to the world and to future generations that the men of the German resistance movement dared to take the decisive step and to hazard their lives upon it . . . nothing else matters.'[2]

This was in the spirit of the excluded Oster and, of course, the now hyper-active

Fellgiebel, but already, in fact, Stauffenberg's hand had been forced by a surprise stroke of luck which disallowed delay. On 1 June he was promoted Colonel and appointed Chief of Staff to General Fromm, C-in-C of the Home Army. Initially he accepted this appointment with reservations since, as he told Fromm, 'I do not think I would make you a good Chief of Staff as, quite frankly, my views on the military and political situation may differ from yours'. But Fromm persuaded him to take the job, which Stauffenberg accepted with enthusiasm when he discovered that periodically he would attend Führer conferences.[3] On 7 June he attended the first of such meetings and imbibed the frightening atmosphere of these gatherings with their ever present threat of murderous Hitlerian outbursts. On that occasion he decided that it was his duty to plant the bomb and realised that it was relatively safe since the SS bodyguard would not be suspicious of one so crippled.

Four weeks later, in the light of the disasters on the Russian and Italian fronts and the imminent collapse in France, the urgency of carrying out the putsch was irresistible. On 3 July at a meeting in the Obersalzberg house of General Eduard Wagner (First Quartermaster General) at which Generals Stieff, Fellgiebel and Fritz Lindemann also were present, it was resolved to strike at the earliest possible moment. It was also agreed that Stauffenberg would plant the bomb (which would be supplied by Stieff) even though this meant that he would be absent from Berlin during the first three crucial hours after the assassination.

Fellgiebel would be in charge of the conspirators' security and outgoing information, in unison with the inactivation of numerous headquarters in order to keep the opposition in the dark. This was to be the so-called 'revolution of the telephone exchanges' based on Fellgiebel's belief that ' . . . in modern warfare the highest leadership was totally dependent on the smooth running of the signals system. A fault in transmission even for a few hours robbed the leadership of effective action. A rioting army would not be as destructive of a war campaign as paralysis of signals for command stations. For overthrow of the government to have any chance of success inevitably meant seizing control of the signalling system during preparation and execution.'[4]

Courageously Fellgiebel set himself the highly risky and well-nigh impossible task of restricting (though certainly not, for obvious operational reasons, destroying) the highly complex and widely dispersed telephone, teleprinter and radio communications stations of his creation. Communications' control was imperative during the vital few hours of chaos which was anticipated after Hitler was killed.

It was also agreed that:

1. General Fromm's Home Army (its HQ located in the War Ministry on the Bendlerstrasse in Berlin) and run by Olbricht) was to bear the burden of the uprising — initially unbeknown to Fromm.

2. The Army telephone operators in the *Wolfschanze* would be controlled by Fellgiebel and his fellow conspirators. Control of the Navy and Luftwaffe was hardly contemplated in the initial phase of the putsch but, interestingly (and maybe through Schellenberg who was on the eve of absorbing the rump of the almost defunct Abwehr into the SD), Fellgiebel confidently relied upon his personal reputation to bind the SS

to his orders 'in the interests of the regime,' once news of the assassination had leaked out.

Although Fellgiebel thought he could control those local telephones and teleprinters which might disseminate news, it was another matter when it came to imposing control over key distant radio stations. These were spread wide from the Berghof in the Obersalzberg, the War Ministry in Berlin, Bad Recklenburg, Rhein, and the powerful *Amt Anna* at Angerburg and *Zeppelin*, adjacent to Army HQ at Lotzen. They were commanded by 'many senior gentlemen' who were not necessarily expert in the fine technicalities of switching on and switching off complex facilities, but for security reasons it was impossible to involve the junior officers and signallers in forward clandestine planning to cope with the crucial decisions of which messages to let through and which to block. That task had to be reserved only for élite conspirators who were thoroughly in the know.[5]

Meanwhile the political situation seethed in ferment. Rundstedt was sacked on 3 July and replaced by Kluge; who with but little delay, once he had assessed the hopeless situation in Normandy, sent a message to General Beck, by hand of Stauffenberg's cousin, Lt-Col Caesar von Hofacker, saying he would support a putsch the moment he knew Hitler was dead.[6] Naturally, those who knew Kluge took that with a pinch of salt.

On 11 July, accompanied by his ADC, Lt Werner von Haeften, Stauffenberg made the first attempt to blow up Hitler at Berchtesgaden, but aborted it because neither Göring nor Himmler were present, for it remained policy that they and the Führer must be eliminated in one go.[7] On 14 July Hitler returned to the *Wolfschanze*, having called another meeting for the 15th. Again Stauffenberg and Haeften prepared, this time assured that Göring and Himmler would be present. The conspirators gathered in Berlin and from the War Ministry Olbricht issued a warning order for Operation 'Walkyrie'. Nervous tension was at a peak, notably for General Beck and Field Marshal von Witzleben, neither of whom was in the best of health. Beck, aged 64, had undergone major surgery for cancer in the autumn of 1943 and was a shadow of his former self. Witzleben, aged 63, had also suffered from ill-health and, like Beck and Olbricht, had a reputation for indecision in a crisis.

Once more fate intervened, this time when Hitler cancelled the meeting at the last moment. Needless to say, Olbricht's consternation in the War Ministry knew no bounds. It took slick thinking and quick communicating to call off Walkyrie, luckily without arousing suspicion. Next day, Beck, Olbricht and Stauffenberg conferred. Stauffenberg set the tone. 'We have no choice now. We have crossed the Rubicon.' In a fatalistic state of desperation they resolved on two crucial changes in plan. First, that no further postponements were acceptable, even if Göring and Himmler were absent. Second, that the Walkyrie order should not be issued until a message confirming Hitler's death was received at the War Ministry.[8] Neither then nor at any time was there a declared course of action should Hitler survive the explosion.

On 17 July additional urgency was injected when a warrant for the arrest of Dr Carl Goerdeler (Chancellor designate) was issued, and this urgency was exacerbated when, in Normandy, Field Marshal Rommel was wounded, removing from the scales that weighty independently motivated conspirator (egged on by Speidel), with his simple unilateral aim of 'simply' ending hostilities. The loss of Rommel was a heavy blow. In a forlorn hope of replacing him by somebody held equally high in public esteem, one last attempt was made to recruit General Guderian. At the suggestion of Fellgiebel, through Caesar von Hofacker, Luftwaffe Colonel von Barsewisch, a member of the resistance since 1939 who had been Guderian's pilot in Russia in 1941, spent four hours talking to his friend as they tramped the woods on the 18th. Guderian refused to join in. He would not believe that Kluge or Rommel were involved in a local armistice and could not approve an assassination — though he undoubtedly surmised one was imminent. Yet he kept the secret and at short notice so changed his schedule as to be at home at Deipenholz within easy reach of Berlin, OKH at Lotzen and OKW at Rastenburg on the 19th; and out of touch with the telephone while walking his estate on the 20th.[9]

* *

Unannounced and earlier than usual on the morning of 20 July, Fellgiebel arrived at the *Wolfschanze* from his residence at Maurwald Camp near *Amt Anna* at Angerburg. His minder, Colonel Sander, had observed how for several days prior to the 20th, 'frantic telephone calls were made to many places by Generals Fellgiebel, Stieff and Olbricht without my knowing what they were about'.[10] Now Fellgiebel had no particular orders for Sander and clearly was waiting for somebody.

Stauffenberg and Haeften arrived shortly before 11.00, having flown from Berlin in a special aircraft. Stauffenberg was immediately involved in a 30-minute discussion with General Walther Buhle, the Chief of Army Staff designate as replacement for the exhausted General Zeitzler. Then they joined Field Marshal Keitel for a 45-minute meeting at which Keitel announced that the conference with the Führer was advanced from 13.00 to 12.30 because of the scheduled arrival of Mussolini by train. Neither Göring nor Himmler was going to be present.

Unexpectedly pressed for time, Stauffenberg and Haeften retired to the nearby bedroom of an officer called John von Freyend, ostensibly for Stauffenberg to change his shirt but in fact to re-pack the briefcase with the explosives. They were engaged in this when an Oberfeldwebel intruded with a message asking Stauffenberg to telephone Fellgiebel and please to get a move on. Having failed to speak to Stauffenberg, Fellgiebel now asked Sander to telephone the Gastebaracke, where the conference was to be held, and ask the orderly officer to tell Stauffenberg to go to Sander's office after the conference. This message, duly passed on, was intended to provide Stauffenberg with an excuse for leaving the conference room.[11]

The Gastebaracke was a wooden building with three windows. Officers sat round a large table, 12.5 by 5 metres, heavily supported at each end, and covered by maps. Stauffenberg carried in the primed briefcase, placed it near a support close by Hitler, and then, leaving his hat and belt behind, departed to make the telephone call. Unfortunately for the conspirators, a Colonel Heinz Brandt found the briefcase was getting in his way and pushed it farther under the table, putting it beside the support and thus effectively shielding Hitler.

Meanwhile an agitated Haeften had entered Sander's office, where Fellgiebel was already waiting, to arrange transport immediately for himself and Stauffenberg to the airfield. A few minutes later they were joined by Stauffenberg who had walked the 200 metres from the Gastebaracke. At once he, Haeften and Fellgiebel, followed at a distance by Sander, walked towards the car park. At 12.50 came the sound of an explosion. Sander noticed how startled Stauffenberg looked and heard Fellgiebel say, 'Good Lord, what was that?' Sander explained that it happened frequently; probably somebody out shooting deer had stepped on a mine. Without tarrying, Stauffenberg and Haeften departed for the airfield, the former having registered the intensity of the explosion and assumed '. . . hardly anybody can still be alive'.[12]

Telephones were ringing; the battle of the exchanges had begun. Sander was told, 'Attempt on Führer's life. Führer is alive and orders you to send for the Reichsmarschall and Reichsführer. Not a word is to leak out.' These orders he relayed to Fellgiebel, who was engaged in passing the 'good' news to his Chief of Staff, Colonel Hahn, at *Amt Anna*. For a fraction of a second Fellgiebel revealed uncertainty,

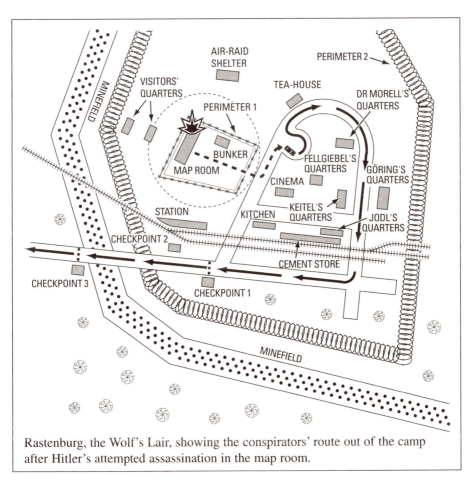

Rastenburg, the Wolf's Lair, showing the conspirators' route out of the camp after Hitler's attempted assassination in the map room.

yet he instantly ratified Sander's prompt actions which, fortuitously, admirably matched the conspiracy plan's requirements. Sander had been told to stop all telephone and teleprinter communications from the *Wolfschanze* by ordering switchboard operators to disconnect all calls. All conversations were severed and postal personnel ordered to cease deliveries. He contacted Göring and Himmler and told them, despite obstruction by the former's ADC, to come at once. A news blackout was imposed. No news of the bomb attempt was to reach Mussolini's train in Rastenburg station. When asked by Hitler, Sander told him that the earliest a radio announcement could be arranged was 18.00, possibly later.[13]

Having satisfied himself that Hitler was still alive, Fellgiebel made the brave decision to proceed with the action, even though totally preventing top officers like Keitel and Jodl getting the news out was never possible.

Things began to get out of hand. Fellgiebel failed in an attempt to contact General Fritz Thiele, the Chief Signals officer and his own contact in the War Ministry, because Thiele was temporarily absent from his office. When Sander made a connection with Thiele's secretary, Fellgiebel ordered her to find him. There was a short delay before contact was made and Fellgiebel was enabled to impress on him (in guarded language) the vital necessity of carrying out the prearranged measures, as if Hitler was dead.

Now fully committed, Fellgiebel next spoke forcefully to Hahn at *Amt Anna*. 'Something terrible has happened, the Führer is alive!'

'What shall we do?'

'Block everything'.

Fellgiebel evidently still believed that success was still possible even though time was fast running out. Confusion at the *Wolfschanze* still prevailed and Fellgiebel exacerbated it by insinuating that a partisan had got in to plant the bomb.[14] To General Warlimont he shouted, 'That's what happens when you put the HQ so near to the front!'[15/D1]

However, the main business of seizing the reins of political power was now out of Fellgiebel's hands. Control, such as it was, had passed to Beck, Olbricht and General Hoeppner in the War Ministry building in Berlin. Thiele (who was thoroughly loyal to his revered, long-time mentor Fellgiebel and understood that Hitler had survived) did not think he could begin to implement the disruption plan by ordering the shutdown or restriction of *Amt Anna*, *Zeppelin* and the other stations without authority from Beck, Olbricht and Hoeppner. This trio returned from lunch at 13.15 in time, as they thought, to deal with events after the explosion without knowing that the Rastenburg meeting had been advanced by 30 minutes. Then they deferred executive action due to Thiele's worries about what was actually happening at the *Wolfschanze*.

Olbricht and Beck dithered and dallied. Not until 13.55 did Hoeppner activate the signals plan and it was 15.30 before Olbricht authorised transmission of the prearranged orders announcing Hitler's death and the assumption of power by Beck, by which time Thiele had fatally weakened the plan by inexplicably permitting communications with the *Wolfschanze* between 15.00 and 16.00.

At 16.00 Olbricht told General Fromm that Hitler was dead. This was another fatal error since Fromm's immediate reaction was to check with Keitel at the *Wolfschanze*, a telephone connection made immediately possible by Thiele's lapse. Naturally Keitel's vehement denial of the Führer's death led Fromm to order the cancellation of Operation 'Walkyrie'. No sooner was a dismayed Olbricht back in his office than he discovered first that his assistant, Colonel Ritter Mertz von Quernheim, had already issued the order and troops were on stand-by, but second that he had not correctly authorised and graded the signal. To compound the difficulties and impose further delay, it was learnt that it would take two signals girls at least three hours to encode the numerous vital messages to the out stations. Nobody had thought to encode the messages in advance, and in the crisis nobody thought of risking breaches of security by using the telephone — that is until Stauffenberg arrived at 16.45.

In fact, between 18.00 and 21.00 several messages were transmitted (including orders to arrest concentration camp commandants), but mainly with no effects on the recipients.[16] Indeed, only in Paris was there a positive response. There General Karl-Heinrich von Stülpnagel, the Military Governor, after being phoned by Stauffenberg at 17.00, did act by ordering the arrest of some thousand Gestapo and SS officers and men in the city and throughout France but this was not carried out until 23.00, by which time the situation in Berlin had changed fundamentally.[17]

In the main, executive action was deferred until Stauffenberg reached the War Ministry at approximately 16.45. The delay was caused by lack of a car to meet him at the airfield when he landed at 15.30 — yet another elementary communication failure. Nevertheless, it had been Haeften's indignant telephone call from the airfield, announcing with conviction that Hitler was dead, that at last overcame Olbricht's indecision. Stauffenberg's belated arrival restored a whiff of momentum. Boldly confronting Fromm, he insisted untruthfully that he knew the Führer was dead. 'Keitel is lying as usual. I myself set off the bomb and I myself saw the Führer's body carried out of the hut', to which Olbricht coolly added that Walkyrie was in operation, despite Fromm's counter-order.

But really the game was up by 18.00 as a flood of telephone conversations poured from the *Wolfschanze*, spreading the word that Hitler was alive. Stauffenberg's and Mertz's phones were tapped and all signals were blocked at 20.00.[18] Meanwhile, at 19.00 a radio announcement initiated by Goebbels (and copied in London by the BBC) informed the world that Hitler was safe. At that same moment, too, Goebbels took a firm grip in Berlin. Contacting Major Otto Remer of the 500-strong élite *Grossdeutschland* Guard unit (which had been ordered under Operation 'Walkyrie' to seize the Government quarter), he arranged a personal telephone conversation between that officer and Hitler, who convinced Remer that his duty still lay with his Führer and not the conspirators.

Remer's troops entered the War Ministry building shortly after 22.00. There was no resistance and only a few random shots, of which one hit Stauffenberg in the back. By then Field Marshal von Witzleben (who had spent most of the day twiddling his thumbs at Army HQ at Lotzen), had departed for home with the words, 'This is a pretty mess'. And the hard core of conspirators, led by Beck, who had released Fromm from arrest, were preparing for the end.

Fromm, intent on his own survival, now administered rough justice. He handed

Beck a pistol which Beck used to end his own life, at the second attempt. Hoeppner, who was offered a similar exit, declined — perhaps to his regret in the few days of life left to him. Olbricht, Stauffenberg, Mertz and Haeften (among other conspirators present) were summarily condemned to death and immediately taken to a courtyard where, in the glare of a truck's headlights, they were shot. Thus, as Goebbels aptly later put it, 'It was a revolution of the telephone that we crushed with a few rifle shots. But with just a little more skill behind it and the rifle shots would not have done the trick.'[19]

* *

With control of communications firmly in their hands, swift were the reactions of Hitler and his henchmen and rapid the arrest of those thought to be connected with involvement in the conspiracy. Witzleben, Hoeppner, Stieff and Fellgiebel were among the most senior suspects soon rounded up to suffer thorough Gestapo investigation under the directions of Himmler and the even more bloodthirsty Ernst Kaltenbrunner. Evidence there was aplenty in the files which Olbricht, Stauffenberg and others most unwisely maintained in abundance; let alone what emerged from harsh and brutal interrogations.

Hitler was demanding the liquidation of anybody even slightly suspected of involvement, including their families, but more practical considerations finally held sway. After all, it was pointed out, the Army could hardly go on fighting effectively if deprived of a great many highly qualified key officers. So the list of those to be tried and condemned by civil courts was restricted largely to ringleaders, civil and military.

To begin with, however, the rebellious soldiers had for legal reasons to be stripped of their military status before facing a civil court. On 4 August Hitler appointed a Court of Honour consisting of Field Marshals Keitel and Rundstedt, and Generals Guderian (who had been appointed acting Chief of the General Staff on 20 July), Schroth and Specht. They did their work swiftly and included among those expelled the officers who had committed suicide — such as Beck, Tresckow (on the Eastern Front) and Wagner.

On 7 August the first batch of eight accused were arraigned before the First Senate of the People's Court, presided over by that vulgar and hectoring Nazi zealot Roland Freisler, to whom the rule of law was made to be broken. The trial was of the showy, propaganda sort, fully recorded on film, radio and phonograph. Already the victims of Gestapo interrogation methods, the accused were humiliated as cowed, pliant and guilty nonentities, stripped of their uniforms and past dignity, unshaven and shabbily dressed,[20] with one notable exception, that is: Erich Fellgiebel. Boldly retaining his dignity, he glared angrily at Freisler with contempt and at one memorable moment snarled, 'Well hurry up with the hanging, Mr President, otherwise you will hang before we do.'[21]

The farce lasted but one day. All eight were found guilty and condemned to death. Seven were executed on the 8th by hanging, suspended by thin wire or cord from hooks and slowly strangled. The grisly scene was filmed and shown to Hitler that day and later to an audience of officer cadets. Hitler's sadistic joy may be imagined. The horrified reaction of the cadets was such, however, that the performance was never repeated. All copies were destroyed on the orders of both Hitler and Goebbels.[22/D2]

The eighth 'guilty' general who did not appear on that film was Fellgiebel. For him the end of the trial was but the overture for more horrors to come. Fettered hand and foot, he was subjected to four days of crippling beatings and torture with thumb screws aimed at forcing him to divulge the names of his assistants and help in the tracing of signals to other countries, including Switzerland. On 12 August (three weeks after arrest) he broke, incriminating both General Thiele and Colonel Hahn along with many more members of their staffs. A situation unfolded so dire for the Wehrmacht and Germany that Fellgiebel's successor, General Albert Praun, felt constrained to declare that if so many members of his staff were withdrawn and threatened he would no longer be able to maintain communications.[23]

In consequence only Thiele and Hahn were tried, condemned to death and, in company with Fellgiebel, executed on 4 September. They joined the growing list of those already done to death, though more were to follow. Among them was Kluge who, defeated in the West and guessing that his complicity with the plot would be discovered, chose suicide. Rommel, too, was later to be coerced into suicide on the understanding that he would be granted a funeral with honours and that his family would be spared punishment such as already was being imposed upon the wives and children of known conspirators.

Predictably the Fellgiebel and Stauffenberg families were among the principal sufferers. Ejected from their homes, stripped of their possessions, reduced to beggary and split up while being transported from one notorious concentration camp to another, they lived in constant fear of execution by the SS or Gestapo.[24] Unlike Canaris and Oster, however, the 'families of 20 July', as they called themselves, were rescued by the Wehrmacht or the Allied armies and spared, during the war's last weeks, the outbreak of vengeful killings indulged in against key witnesses of Nazi iniquity.

DEVIATIONS FROM HISTORY

[D1] See Wheeler-Bennett pp 643 and 658, where he criticises Fellgiebel for not blowing up the *Wolfschanze* telephone exchange. He displays his total ignorance of the large amount of explosives needed, of the diversity and functioning of the total signals system, and how vital it was to keep that system working for the purposes of the conspiracy, let alone for command and control of the Wehrmacht in the field. Unhappily this led Wheeler-Bennett most unjustly to denigrate Fellgiebel's competence and resolve, a libel which many historians (including, to his shame, the present writer) have uncritically compounded to the detriment of Fellgiebel's outstanding character and genius.

[D2] Wheeler-Bennett p 682. Clearly he was neither aware that only seven were hung that day, nor informed of Fellgiebel's stand under torture and his fate, for there is no mention of his gallant behaviour under stress at the trial or after.

Confirmatory footnotes:

1 This information was recently released by the Public Record Office and is based on articles in *The Daily Telegraph* of 23 July 1998.

2 Wheeler-Bennett pp 626, 627.

3 *ibid* p 625.

4 Wildhagen pp 286, 287.

5 *ibid* pp 291–3.

6 Wheeler-Bennett pp 629, 630.
7 *ibid* p 633.
8 Manvell pp 92, 93.
9 Macksey *Guderian* pp 183, 184.
10 Wildhagen p 295.
11 *ibid* pp 296, 297.
12 *ibid* p 298.
13 *ibid* pp 299, 300.
14 *ibid* pp 301, 302.
15 Warlimont p 441.
16 Wildhagen pp 302–9.
17 Wheeler-Bennett pp 665–70.
18 Wildhagen p 309.
19 Wheeler-Bennett pp 657–62.
20 *ibid* pp 674–83.
21 Wildhagen p 315.
22 Wheeler-Bennett pp 683, 684.
23 Wildhagen pp 310, 311.
24 *ibid* pp 317–20 and letter from Stauffenberg's son, Major-General Berthold von Stauffenberg, to the author.

22.
A Foregone Conclusion

It was General Montgomery's original intention on 18 July that Operation 'Goodwood' would be followed on the 20th by Operation 'Cobra', a massive blow by First and Third US Armies breaking through the German lines to strike southwards towards Avranches. Then they would peel off westwards into Brittany and simultaneously wheel eastwards to complete, in conjunction with Second British Army, the envelopment of Seventh German Army. Bad weather, however, caused several postponements of Cobra. Not until the 25th did it unleash its immense power. If the postponements were of mixed advantages and disadvantages to both sides, the final outcome was inevitable — a crushing foregone conclusion of defeat for the Germans, regardless of the lack or otherwise of Enigma and Fish.

For the overbearing factor in the balance of forces was the sheer weight and superiority of Allied numbers and firepower which generated an irresistible strategic initiative and momentum. It was of almost academic interest to Generals Montgomery and Bradley that they knew with fair certainty how their weakened enemy was disposed. In addition to radio messages of varying quality from higher grade code books, down to transmissions in clear speech, Sigint contributed its share of intelligence along with extensive PR, air and ground reconnaissance, POW interrogations and reports from SIS and SOE agents. The Allies simply could not help but rapidly blast their way through and, at last, open the way to a state of untrammelled manoeuvre warfare. Such a condition would compel the Germans virtually to abandon all pretence of signal security in order to control by radio their overstretched mobile forces. At the same time Field Marshal von Kluge and his masters at OKW came to realise, and made clear to their enemy by their own decisions, that it was no longer rational to retain the last two Panzer divisions backing Fifteenth Army in the Pas de Calais.[D1]

Henceforward, therefore, this account deals only with those few episodes when the Germans momentarily held a vestige of strategic initiative, and when possession or lack of high-grade Sigint was of crucial importance to the Allies.

The first such rarity concerned the counter-strokes launched first by Kluge and subsequently enlarged by Hitler to sever Cobra's deadly penetration beyond Avranches. The predictable convergence of mobile forces against the Americans required no special service by high grade Sigint to forewarn Bradley's armies of dangerous threats against their extending left flanks. Routine intelligence synthesis founded on military common sense and a plethora of reports from numerous sources were sufficient to disclose the enemy's intentions, and bring down upon him massed air attacks and artillery bombardments to check each threat as it appeared. The anticipated last gasp attempts by the Luftwaffe to intervene in the land battle were almost invariably intercepted at a distance from the front and, as had been so frequently the case on the ground elsewhere, whenever mechanised forces endeavoured to redeploy they were detected, attacked, delayed and seriously damaged.

Subsequent to the 31st, as General Patton's Third US Army swung right into Brittany, signs emerged of a strategic shift of German armoured weight to their left, with the intention of driving westwards to the sea at Avranches. As of this moment, when Hitler and Kluge were compelled to abandon static defence and 'go mobile', there inevitably occurred such a stupendous rise in the use of radio by the German Army that its every move, both at the front and in rear, could be plotted.[1] Sufficiently forewarned, the Americans were relatively easily able in hard fighting to throw back each thrust as, in uncoordinated confusion, the Panzers lurched into sight from the dense bocage terrain. It mattered not that the Allies were unaware of Hitler's insistence that the repulsed attacks should be renewed. General Bradley's orthodox handling of his forces made sure that they would stand firm, with or without strategic insight into the Führer's intuition or the professionalism of his finest troops.

The ultimate destruction of Seventh Army in the Falaise pocket and the pursuit of a defeated Wehrmacht into Holland and to the German frontier followed as a matter of certainty, with Sigint playing an important role, though in a significantly changing manner, induced by the extensive cutting of German signals cables and wrecking or loss of exchanges. Then it was that radio *Geheimschreiber* came into its own to help cope with additional traffic at the very moment when it was unable to be penetrated by GC&CS. There was a tightening of German Sigint security which was further improved as the Wehrmacht withdrew into friendly home territory. For henceforward Allied intelligence would be denied the massive benefit it had enjoyed from agents and the hostile people of France, Belgium, Luxembourg and liberated southern Holland. On the other hand, it was inevitable that in the utter confusion and terror of the retreat, there would be instances when overrun headquarters yielded code books which were of immense assistance to hard-pressed code-breakers at Bletchley Park and in the field.

Though victory in Normandy and the ensuing headlong pursuit of the routed Germans relieved the Allies of the V1 threat, as their launching sites were overrun, London's freedom from long-range bombardment was short-lived. Quite literally out of the blue on 8 September began the next ordeal by a terror weapon, the crashing on London of a powerful though wildly inaccurate V2 rocket fired from Holland. Long awaited by the extremely anxious authorities, accurate intelligence of the weapon's characteristics was at a premium and very largely conjectural, based on a melange of conflicting reports. R. V. Jones was eventually to deduce from these with commendable accuracy (10 days before that first V2's landing) the rocket's size and performance. Not until the middle of July had it been discovered that the rocket was launched from a simple platform which might be difficult to find as well as destroy. This shattering revelation was confirmed by capture of detailed drawings and documents in Normandy on 7 August, and confirmed by POWs who guided investigators to prepared sites.[2]

Without warning, and in the total absence of intelligence on the location of firing points, the control systems and the logistic support for this revolutionary weapon, the Allies had to acquire information from scratch by a variety of methods (including radar tracking and Dutch agents). Among those sources, however, Sigint was for some time a notable absentee. Not until November did the 'Y' Service begin to detect low-grade radio signals associated with organisational command and control of V2. And that was about all Sigint ever contributed to the fight against a weapon which, until the sites were cut off in March 1945, neither threatened decisively in a strategic sense nor by sustained terror.[3] Although there was no defence against a V2 once it had been launched, V2 lacked the terror effect of the V1 since its approach could neither be heard nor seen due to its supersonic speed. It was a lurking menace which people gradually learnt to live with, without becoming demoralised.

Necessarily, though, Operation 'Market Garden' (Montgomery's ambitious airborne attempt to open a corridor from Eindhoven to Arnhem) was regarded as of strategic importance for its potential to sever the supply lines to the V2 launching sites in western Holland, and it did temporarily stop firings until that operation was abandoned. Market Garden's fatal flaws lay in misinterpretation of highly revealing information from Dutch Resistance people and from POWs who provided valuable reports of the presence of refitting Panzer formations adjacent to the dropping zones. This intelligence was not only underestimated but also left unconfirmed because of unnecessarily meagre PR sorties to investigate it. The result of this economy of effort allowed the over-confident Allied commanders concerned to draw false assessments of the balance of forces prior to the operation which began on 17 September.

Then it was that, through a variety of causes, two under-strength SS Panzer divisions (in conjunction with a good infantry division) outmatched lightly armed airborne infantry who, through poor communications, were inadequately supported by artillery, let alone tanks. Moreover, once begun, Operation 'Market Garden' received little assistance from intelligence of any sort, let alone from the handful of decrypts from Sigint which were received too late even to be of tactical advantage to generals who certainly made their share of faulty decisions.[4]

The check at Arnhem gave the Germans breathing space to restore their static defences and combat power. Now it was that the superb communication and security system built up by Fellgiebel, and presently controlled by General Praun, contributed significantly to the essential nervous system for the forthcoming surprise Operation 'Watch on the Rhine', Hitler's last major counter-stroke in the Ardennes which was launched in winter fog on 16 December. Despite the inexorable damage to Germany's prewar cable system by a mounting bomber offensive, it was possible for the Germans to operate with the flexibility, economy and security that had ruled in 1940, before Enigma was compromised. Now it was that Praun, following in the footsteps of Fellgiebel, expanded the cable services by erecting emergency overhead wire links and used *Geheimschreiber* increasingly on both cable and air. At the same time he employed secure beam radio links such as had been done in Russia, in effect making encrypting machines virtually obsolete.

Simultaneously, though, the German war effort was being progressively wrecked by the pulverising air offensive against the Wehrmacht's sinews, the internal road, rail and waterways system, and its life-blood oil. There had been nothing like this combined paralysing campaign in 1940. So, in defence of both German and Allied commanders, it has to be said that they shared a mutual sense of incredulity about the possibility of a major German offensive on any front in the foreseeable future. To any competent general, Hitler's over-ambitious intention to cut the Allied armies in two by a thrust to Antwerp totally lacked credibility. Indubitably it was in this spirit of incredulity that SHAEF intelligence officers tended to brush aside the mass of clues suggesting anything larger in scale than the kind of local counter-attacks which had taken place since Arnhem. Furthermore the good news in mid-October that GC&CS had once more managed to break the Fish codes, was confidence-generating to the tiny, select élite who were in the know.

Of course the Allies could not be aware of the secret strategic planning of Operation 'Watch on the Rhine' which took place under the strictest radio silence. Virtually all communications were person to person, in conferences, by courier or by Fish-encoded land-line. The reports of German troop and aircraft movements which did come to hand could more readily be attributed to improvements in the defence of the West Wall rather than any major attempt to leap westwards. In addition, decrypts of Japanese Magic provided abundant evidence that, far from being fit for an offensive, the Germans were on the verge of collapse and might soon sue for peace.[5]

These Japanese sentiments were of cold comfort. After all, were they not themselves, in the aftermath of the devastating naval defeat at the Battle of Leyte Gulf, in poor state to continue against the overwhelmingly strong Americans who, in 1945, would be poised to invade their homeland? And had not the Japanese (unwittingly) themselves contributed to the heavy defeats at Coral Sea, Midway, the Solomon Islands and the Philippines by their over-confident, prolific use of the Magic-broken codes? A use which, courtesy of their broken diplomatic and naval codes, had provided vast quantities of intimate state, strategic and technological information to the Allies.[6]

In Europe neither Sigint nor the other 'usual sources' were of any assistance in divining German intentions. Such high grade messages as were decrypted divulged conflicting views of what was in the wind and were part and parcel of deception schemes.[7] Without indulging here in a detailed study, it is apparent that the accumulation of minor Sigint intelligence which came SHAEF's way (including significant reports of the imposition of radio silence on important formations), was not well synthesised and failed to alert its experts to what was impending. All this culminated in a remarkable prediction of enemy intentions by Field Marshal Montgomery on the very eve of Watch on the Rhine, ' . . . his situation is such that he cannot stage major offensive operations. Furthermore, at all costs he has to prevent the war entering on a mobile phase; he has not the transport or the petrol that would be necessary for mobile operations, nor would his tanks compete with ours in the mobile battle.'[8] All of which looked perfectly sound and reasonably correct to a trained military mind, but took no account of Hitler's megalomania and the total inability of his cowed generals to bring him to order.

What relatively limited success Watch on the Rhine achieved was gained chiefly by surprise, therefore, and the exploitation of prolonged foul weather which severely restricted the use of air power either for bombing or strafing or (most important of all) PR. The crisis had been passed and the Germans were in retreat before the Luftwaffe attempted what should have been tried as a prelude to Watch on the Rhine. On New Year's Day between 750 and 800 fighter-bombers struck with complete surprise under radio silence at low level against sixteen Allied airfields. They achieved remarkable success, destroying 150 aircraft, damaging 111, killing 46 men and wounding 145, of whom only six were pilots. On the other hand, their losses in aircrews and machines were disastrous: 260 men lost along with 270 machines and 40 damaged.[9]

Surprise had been achieved by General Dietrich Peltz at a heavy price due to a classic case of over-security allied to unrehearsed techniques that induced an excess of errors and blunders by inexperienced airmen. To make matters far worse, the demands of strict secrecy which delayed briefing of leaders until the previous evening, denied many crews any sort of proper information so that they were vague about targets. There was confusion and there were mid-air collisions. Some machines failed to reach targets whose anti-aircraft defences were unready for action.[10 & 11] As General Galland wrote, 'The Luftwaffe received its death blow at the Ardennes offensive.'

It was the end for Germany, too. Soon the *Wolfschanze* and the vital *Amt Anna* and *Zeppelin* communication centres would fall into Russian hands, making the passing of information and orders extremely difficult. Yet, throughout a ridiculous prolongation of hostilities, Hitler (prior to committing suicide on 30 April) was enabled by the faithful signallers to stay in contact with the remnants of the Wehrmacht from his besieged bunker in Berlin through radio *Geheimschreiber* messages.[12]

DEVIATIONS FROM HISTORY
[D1] Hinsley Vol 3 Pt 2 pp 225–50 describes the sequence of events from the start of Cobra on 25 July until the final collapse of the German counter-stroke on or about 10 August. It is plain that even without help from the undecipherable Fish message containing Hitler's vital strategic order to Kluge on 3 August, all types of other Sigint were of immense assistance to the Allies. Yet it is clear, too, that, in actuality, prolific decryptions of Enigma messages were only complementary to other sources — and of diminishing value once the strategic movements of Panzer divisions had been detected and correctly interpreted by the Allied intelligence officers prior to the fighting entering its predominantly tactical phase. Medium and lower grade codes, which tended quickly to be overtaken by events, plus instantly helpful clear speech Sigint, soon gave the game away to effective monitoring and reporting by 'Y' Service. Cumulatively these would have provided Montgomery and Bradley with sufficient information to eliminate strategic errors, even if Enigma had not been in use.

Confirmatory footnotes:
1 Hinsley Vol 3 Pt 2 pp 238–50.
2 *ibid* pp 551, 555.
3 *ibid* pp 564, 569.
4 *ibid* pp 382–9.
5 *ibid* pp 402–17.
6 Hinsley Vols 3 Pt 2 *passim*, and Lewin *The Other Ultra passim*.
7 Lewin *The Other Ultra*. This unique volume remains a standard work on the influence of codes and ciphers in the defeat of Japan.
8 Hinsley Vol 3 Pt 2 pp 418–20.
9 *ibid* pp 421–38.

10 Terraine pp 675, 676.
11 Anon *Luft* pp 379, 380.
12 Hinsley pp 731–3.

23.
The Riddles

To evaluate the extent to which the Enigma effect has been exaggerated it is important to be aware of the sequence of events leading up to its emergence in the public domain some three decades after the war's end. For no sooner was the war over than, for pressing major political and security reasons, a wall of secrecy was built around the activities of Bletchley Park and GC&CS as a whole, along with everything to do with Ultra, the code-breakers and the machines and methods they employed. Ex-employees and other people in the know were sworn to complete secrecy and threatened with dire consequences if they breathed a word about what went on. Many machines were broken up, including most of the Colossi. Mention of Ultra and its functions were banned in the official histories. As a result undue praise was sometimes accorded to the select handful of top commanders (such as Eisenhower, Montgomery and Bradley) whose egos sometimes were burnished by credits for an intuitive genius they could not genuinely lay claim to; it was praise that some relished in reflected glory when writing their Enigma-free memoirs.

Strict security measures also were taken in the USA but, in that country of constitutional freedom of speech, these began to leak rather sooner. The tap was turned on in 1966 when David Kahn, an amateur American cryptologist and journalist, published his 1,164-page book, *The Code-Breakers*. This history of cryptology, which took over four years to produce, emerged as a work which, without mentioning Bletchley Park, Ultra, GC&CS, the Bombes, the Colossi and related functions or effects, opened the eyes and ears of discerning historians and journalists to a cornucopia of subjects ripe for bountiful research and speculation, and financial as well as intellectual enrichment. I well remember the intense interest generated in publishing circles by *The Code-Breakers*, and the discussions that followed with my friend Ronald Lewin, whose contacts with people with knowledge of Ultra, through the BBC and publishers, excited his vibrant inquisitive imagination.

In due course the British government, concerned about the spectre of potentially damaging books about Ultra and related matters, decided to relax security and allow some of the secret story to emerge. As a first step they encouraged Group Captain F. W. Winterbotham (who as Chief of the Air Department of the SIS from 1939–45 had set up the handling system for Ultra in 1940) to write a book to be entitled *The Ultra Secret*. It was composed in some haste from memory and without access to official documents, and published in 1974. Flawed as it inevitably was, it would have been even more inaccurate had not Ronald Lewin been brought in to tidy up its historical perspective and content. Naturally it created enormous interest. Overnight Bletchley Park and Ultra became household terms because, to the mass of uninitiated writers and the general public, it seemed as if those organisations had been the real revolutionary providers of victory for the Allies, a story that the media enhanced by thorough-going guesswork and conjecture.

In the years to come would appear two species of stories about Ultra and Enigma: initially by authors who, lacking access to official documents, tended to let rip their imaginations in order to write exaggerated yarns about the Enigma effect; and later between 1979 and 1990, successive volumes of Professor Sir Harry Hinsley's official *British Intelligence in the Second World War* with their almost (but not quite complete) access to public records. Of those in the first category, Ronald Lewin's *Ultra Goes to War* was the best informed and most authoritative. Although, in fact, he did have access to the first releases of Ultra material at the Public Record Office, he was not able to make much use of it, for, as he told me, the sheer volume of paper demanded research far beyond his means. Gradually, of course, Lewin's book was overtaken by the scale, detail and breadth of scope contained within Hinsley's massive work. Yet, inevitably from the very reputation won by *Ultra Goes to War* with its concentration on Ultra and Enigma, and virtual overlooking of the Y Services and their vital contribution to Sigint grew the myth of their omniscience since it largely understated the colossal contributions made by all the many other sources of intelligence. Yet Lewin's work retains a useful place in the literature of intelligence, if only because it is complementary to Hinsley's deliberately impersonal format by breathing life into the vital people involved in the higher echelons of command and control.

Nevertheless, the glamorising of Ultra and Enigma by some writers has led to a distortion of history through the obscuring of the fact that, along with Sigint as a whole, their contribution was only one facet of the highly complex gem that was cut by the Allied intelligence community in their battles with formidable opponents. As readers of this book will be aware, Ultra's place in the scheme of things was circumscribed by the fact that it could detect only what was sent by radio, and even then by no means everything that was transmitted. It should also be apparent that, in the absence of Enigma, GC&CS still would have been provided with a mass of decipherable Sigint from Fish, higher-grade code books and medium- and low-grade codes. In other words, Enigma was far from irreplaceable.

In the Preface to Volume 1 (p ix) of his official history Hinsley indirectly draws attention to the essential mass and importance of non-Ultra sources of information. He writes of the sheer complexity and vastly spread dimensions of the complementary sources of which Sigint and Ultra were merely a part. This included the work carried out, often in hazardous conditions, by service intelligence officers with fighting units and by the people who were responsible in the field for signal intelligence, for reporting to the SIS and SOE, for examining enemy equipment and for undertaking photographic interpretation, POW examination and many similar tasks. There were also the contributions of the many men and women who carried out essential routine work at establishments in the United Kingdom and overseas — who undertook the continuous manning of intercept stations or of the cryptanalytic machinery, the maintenance of PR aircraft and their cameras, the preparation of target information for the RAF or of the topographical information for all three services, the monitoring of foreign newspapers, broadcasts and intercepted mail, and the endless indexing, typing, teleprinting, ciphering and transmitting of the intelligence output. Only occasional references to all this have been possible in an account which sets out to reconstruct the influence of intelligence on the major decisions, the chief operations and the general course of the war.

What, then, of the importance of Enigma machines and their like to the Axis? What of Fellgiebel whose genius had created the superb, all-embracing German communications and intelligence system which had been the key to the overwhelming triumphs won between September 1939 and November 1942? That he was deeply concerned about the dangers of enemy penetration of strategic codes is left beyond doubt by his strict imposition of security on the Army's signallers and his persistent search for improvements to the safeguards built into Enigmas and *Geheimschreibers*. Likewise there was his long-standing objection to inherent Luftwaffe insecurity, especially its lavish use of encoded radio messages to the exclusion of other less vulnerable means of distribution. Because Fellgiebel had spent a lifetime with communications developments in two world wars and knew how likely it was that codes would be broken (as Germany was breaking her enemies' codes) he was never able to drop his guard.

In this respect he was as one with the Navy (which had suffered badly due to radio insecurity in World War 1 and had been first to adopt Enigma) in its perpetual anxiety about cipher security. This concern was also exhibited, as we have seen, in Dönitz's queasy suspicion in January 1943, that Enigma might have been broken, and which would prompt Fellgiebel three months later actually to institute an investigation into the reliability of Enigma. The investigation also drew a blank, perhaps because the investigators were people who had designed Enigma and who therefore had a myopic vested interest in the matter.

Or is it just possible that Fellgiebel, intent on selling Hitler and his gang down the river even to the shorter term detriment of the Fatherland, was cunningly engaged in undermining the Wehrmacht's nervous system and capability of waging war with maximum efficiency? Highly controversial and impossible to corroborate as is this suggestion, it fits with his character and behaviour in those horrendous days. Also it poses a valid question about the value or otherwise of Enigma to Germany. To what extent was the German addiction to Enigma machines justifiable?

On the credit side it undoubtedly helped reduce operators' errors and enabled them to work faster than people using code books. On the debit side, unlike *Geheimschreiber*, it was incapable of encipherment at speed and therefore could only be transmitted using the much slower morse code, a characteristic which increased the length of time spent on air and made more likely the chances of successful DF by the enemy. To the Army and Luftwaffe this disadvantage was threatening. To the U-boats it was fatal, as we have seen, once the opposition had developed effective DF equipment and procedures.

From another aspect the German addiction to Enigma was a real menace to themselves since their false belief in the absolute invulnerability of machine codes (reinforced by the fact that they failed to break the British Typex machine) positively spawned slack signal security. We have seen how, without Enigma, they would have been compelled to place far more emphasis on *Geheimschreiber* and to tighten up all their radio security procedures.

Readers of this book must make up their own minds about the relative merits of Ultra's and Enigma's contribution to both sides. And if they have doubts and the time, perhaps settle to a rewarding study of Hinsley's great work in order to verify his conclusion, founded on profound examination as well as on practical experience at Bletchley Park, that the Enigma effect has been exaggerated. Or, as he also evaluated it, 'not a war-winner' but a 'war-shortener'.

Bibliography

Anon *Fuh*, *Fuehrer Conferences on Naval Affairs 1939–1945*, London 1990. (Abbreviated in footnotes as Anon *Fuh*).
Anon *Luft*, *The Rise and Fall of the German Air Force*, USA 1969. (Abbreviated in footnotes as Anon *Luft*).
Anon MOD (Navy), *The U-Boat War in the Atlantic*, London 1989.
Brooks, G., *Hitler's Nuclear Weapons*, London 1992.
Collier, B., *The Defence of the United Kingdom*, London 1957.
Foot, M. R. D., *SOE in France*, London 1966.
Fraser, D., *Alanbrooke*, London 1982.
     Knight's Cross, London 1993.
Hinsley, F. H., and others, *British Intelligence in the Second World War*, 5 Vols, London 1979.
Ed Hinsley, F. H., and Stripp, A., *Code-breakers — The Inside Story of Bletchley Park*, Oxford 1993.
Hodges, A., *Alan Turing*, London 1983.
Hohne, H., *Canaris*, London 1976.
Jones, R. V., *Most Secret War*, London 1978.
Jukes, G., *Kursk — The Clash of Armour*, London 1968.
Kahn, D., *The Code-Breakers*, London 1966.
Lewin, R., *Ultra Goes to War*, London 1978.
     The Other Ultra, London 1982.
Macksey, K., *Military Errors of World War Two*, London 1987.
     Commando Strike, London 1990.
     From Triumph to Tragedy, London 1996.
     Guderian: Panzer General, London 1975.
     Kesselring, London 1996.
Manstein, E. von, *Lost Victories*, London 1958.
Manvell, R., *The Conspirators: 20th July 1944*, London 1971.
Masterman, J. C., *The Double-Cross System*, London 1972.
Pujol, J., *Garbo*, London 1986.
Reynolds, N., *Treason was no Crime*, London 1976.
Schellenberg, W., *The Schellenberg Memoirs*, London 1965.
Speidel, H., *Invasion 1944*, Chicago 1950.
Stahlberg, A., *Bounden Duty*, London 1990.
Terraine, J., *The Right of the Line*, London 1985.
Warlimont, W., *Inside Hitler's Headquarters*, London 1962.
Welchman, G., *Hut 6 Story*, London 1982.
Wheeler-Bennett, J.W., *The Nemesis of Power*, London 1953.
Wildhagen, K.H., *Erich Fellgiebel*, Germany 1970.
Wilmot, C., *The Struggle for Europe*, London 1952.
Winterbotham, F. W., *The Ultra Secret*, London 1974.

Unpublished
Praun, A., *The Signal Services in the service of OKH during World War II*, Neustadt 1947.

Index

Abwehr 7, 14, 17, 25, 31, 67, 101, 114, 134
  Department Z 49
Address book code 79, 123
Aircraft
  American
    B17 86
    B24 Liberator 80, 86
    P51 108
  British
    Gloster E1 58
    Gloster Meteor 126
  German
    BV222 54
    He 177 55
    Heinkel jet 58
    Messerschmitt jet 58
Alexander, Gen Sir Harold 95
Algiers 30, 42
American air force
  Eighth 60
American Army
  Fifth Army 105, 106
  First Army 143, 144
  Third Army 144
  II Corps 96
Amt Anna 72, 93, 94, 135-8, 147
Anchovy 124, 129
Angerburg 72, 135
Anzio 116, 122
Ardennes 145-147
Arnhem 145, 146
Arnim, Gen Jurgin von 41, 44, 90
Atlantic, Battle of 43, 55, 57, 77 passim
Atlantic Wall 114
Atomic explosives 60
Avalanche, Op 105
Avranches 143, 144
Axis, Plan 99, 105, 106
Azores 83

Babbage, Charles 22
Bad Recklenberg 135

Barsewisch, Col von 136
Baytown, Op 105
B Dienst 12, 15, 77, 82, 123
Beam radio 106
Beck, Gen Ludwig 49, 50, 69, 110 passim,
    131, 135 passim
Beetle 114
Belgium 115, 116
Berchtesgaden 129, 131, 133, 135
Berlin, Battles of 108
Bevan, Col J. M. 64
Bletchley Park 25, 28 passim
Blumentritt, Gen Gunther 116, 129
Bodyguard, Op 49, 50, 68
Boeselager brothers 49, 50, 68
Bogue 80
Bombe, The 8, 26, 94, 149
Bomber Command, US 100, 101, 107, 108
Bomber Command, British 71, 85, 86, 99,
    101, 107, 108, 117
Bomber Offensive, Combined 60, 87
Boulogne 102, 115
Bourguebus ridge 132
Bradley, Gen Omar 143, 144
Brandt, Col Heinz 69, 136
Bream 94, 96, 99, 105, 106, 109, 122
Bremen 86
Brest 102, 123
Bristol 108
British Army
  Eighth Army 90, 105, 106
  I Corps 124
  VIII Corps 132
  XIII Corps 96
  XXX Corps 96
British Union of Fascists (BUF) 31
Brittany 102, 115, 143
Brooke, Gen Sir Alan 58-65
Brutus 114
Buhle, Gen Walther 136
Busshe, Axel von der 111

C

Carllo   25
Reactions to enemy awareness of Ultra
    25-30, 85, 87, 90 passim
and double agents   27, 31-34
briefs the CIGS   57-65
and Fish   94
C38m cypher machine   96
Calais   115
Caen   124, 132
Cambridge University   21
Canaris, Adm Wilhelm   11, 12-23, 32, 41, 67,
    68, 91
Career   17, 49, 74, 101, 109, 114
connections with German Resistance   17, 71
death of   141
Carrier pigeon post   113
Casablanca conference (SYMBOL)   27, 57,
    60, 64, 65
Chemical weapons *see Gas*
Cherbourg   122, 129
Churchill, Winston   21, 25, 27, 28, 57, 64, 85,
    87, 96, 124
and Fish   90
and Hitler   133
and rockets   101
'Citadel', Op   94, 95, 99
Clark, Gen Mark   105, 106
Cobra, Op   132, 143
Cobweb   114
Cockade, Op   102, 103, 109
Code books   7, 74, 91, 94, 105, 113, 115, 123,
    125, 126 and 125 footnotes
Codebreakers, The   149
Colossus I   97 footnote, 116, 124, 149
Colossus II   116, 124,
Comando Supremo   99
Combined Operations   91
Combined Operations Pilotage Party (COPP)
    96
Communist Party of Great Britain (CPGB)   31
Concentration camps   139, 141
Convoy Code (British)   77, 83
Coral Sea, Battle of   146
Corsica   105
COSSAC   65, 102, 113
Cotentin peninsula   108, 113, 125
Crete   64
CVE (light aircraft carrier)   80
Czechoslovakia   49

DF (Direction Finding)   59, 78, 80, 113, 151

Dieppe raid   64
Directive No 51 (Hitler's)   109, 113
Dnieper River   41, 48, 107
Dohnanyi, Hans von   71
Dönitz, Adm Karl   23, 35, 37, 78, 81, 151
Reactions to breaking of Enigma   51
Relations with Hitler   53-55
Dutch resistance   145

E-boats   122, 123
Eisenhower, Gen Dwight   90, 96, 105, 113
El Alamein, Battle of   11, 114
Enigma machines   passim
History of   8, 17, 19, 20
Effects of their penetration   15, 21, 33, 59-65
Summing up   149 passim
Essen   86

Falaise   144
Fascist Grand Council   99
Fellgiebel, Gen Erich
Career and philosophy   7, 17, 18, 73, 151
Collaboration with Oster   47-52, 69
Collaboration with Schellenberg   69, 105
Leading part in Resistance to Hitler   8, 35,
    37, 71, 99, 110, 111
Reactions to suspicions that Enigma is
    penetrated   11-15, 37, 41-45, 53-55, 78
Trial of and death   140, 141
and Fish   87, 103
and Lucy spy ring   94, 95
and Operation Walkyrie   10 passim, 118, 133
    passim
on 20 July 1944   133 passim
Felssenest   72
Feuchtinger, Gen Edgar   122
Fish   63, 64, 87, 90 passim, 117, 130,
    143 passim
    See also code names (Tunny etc)
'Flash', Op   49-52, 68, 69, 109
'Foxley', Op   133
'Forfar', Op   103
'Fortitude', Op   114, 115, 122, 129, 130
Freak   114
Freisler, Roland   39, 140
Friedman, William   75 footnote
Fromm, Gen Friedrich   110, 118, 133, 138-140

Gallande, Gen Adolf   147
Gallipoli   121
Garbo   25, 27, 28, 31-33, 91, 102, 114, 125
Career   32, 126

Attempt to find Turing and R. V. Jones   33, 103
Gas   58
GC and CS   25, 30, 83, 103 passim, 149
Geheimschreiber   61, 87, 115
   Its history, technology and functions   44, 45, 47, 48, 63, 144, 151
   in Allied hands   92
   see also Fish
Gela   96
German Air Force *see Luftwaffe*
German Army
   Army Groups
      A   93
      B   109, 116, 129
      Centre   48, 68, 130
      Don/South   11, 35, 95
   Army
      Home   134 passim
      Fifth   87
      Sixth   11, 35, 36, 38
      Seventh   143, 144
      Tenth   105, 106
      Fifteenth   130, 131, 143
   Corps: II SS Panzer   129, 131
   Division
      10th Panzer   92
      21st Panzer   122, 124
Gestapo   18, 49, 71, 111, 139-141
Giesler, Paul   38, 39
Goebbels, Dr Josef   100, 139, 140
Goerdeler, Dr Carl   50, 135
Goodwood, Op   132, 143
Göring, RM Hermann   19, 22, 49, 52, 55, 69, 72, 73, 102
   and Walkyrie   135, 136-138
Göring, Frau   73
Gothic Line   116, 122
GPO Research Station   63, 90, 124
Graf Spee   54
Greece   64
Grey mice   73
Grilse   109, 113, 115, 124, 129
Guadalcanal, Battle of   83
Guderian, Gen Heinz   50, 51, 68, 110, 136, 140

H2S   86
Haeften, Lt Werner von   135-137, 139, 140
Hahn, Col   137, 138, 141
Halder, Gen Franz   18, 49
Hamburg, Battle of   99, 100, 107

Harris, AM Sir Arthur   86, 87
Heath Robinson *see Robinson*
Hedgehog   79
Herring   87, 90, 92, 115
Heusinger, Col Adolf   36
Himmler, Heinrich   18, 19, 49, 67-69, 114, 135 passim
Hinsley, Prof Sir Harry   7, 9, 31, 78, 150-152
Hitler, A.   11, 15, 18 passim
   Assasination attempts   50, 69, 133 passim
   and Enigma   44, 45, 52-55
   and Dönitz   35, 37, 38, 53-55, 82
   and Manstein   36, 48
   and Raeder   22
   and Stahlberg   35
Hitler Youth   38
Hoeppner, Gen Erich   110, 138
Hofacker, Lt Col Caesar von   135, 136
Holland   116, 144
Horton, Adm Sir Max   77, 80, 81, 83
Huber, Prof Kurt   38, 39
Husky, Op   95, 103
Hydrographic Branch, RN   96

Infra-red   83
Irish Republican Army (IRA)   31
Italy   94 passim

Jan Mayan incident   14, 42
Japan   93
   Communications with   74, 75
Japanese Navy   84
Jellyfish   103, 109, 113, 124, 125
Jeschonnek, Gen Hans   23, 42, 55, 102
Jodl, Gen Alfred   45, 53, 55, 129, 130, 138
Jones, Dr R. V.   21, 27, 33, 47, 101, 144

Kaltenbrunner, Ernst   67, 109, 114, 140
Kalvi   23, 42
Kasserine Pass   41, 90
Keitel, FM Wilhelm   69, 82, 130, 136, 138-140
Kesselring, FM Albert   11, 14, 87, 96, 99 passim
Khan, David   149
Kharkov   41, 71, 96, 99, 107
King, Adm Ernest   82
Kleist, FM Evald   11
Kluge, FM Hans von   50, 68, 107, 109, 118, 131 pasim
Knox, Dillwyn   26
Kursk, Battles of   71, 94, 95, 107

La Pallice   123
Le Havre   123
Leigh light   80
Leningrad   130
Lewin, Ronald   9, 149, 150
Leyte Gulf, Battle of   146
Lindemann, Professor Frederick   21, 28, 47
Lindemann, Gen Fritz von   134
London Controlling Station (LCS)   64, 102,
     115
Long Range Desert Group   87
Lorenz Co
  SZ 40 machine   48
Lorient   123
Lotzen   135, 136
Lucy spy ring   94, 95, 107
Lützow   55
Luftwaffe   71, 73, 80, 103 passim, 143 passim
  Poor Sigint security   73, 94, 96, 115
  Attacks on London, 1943   85, 86
Luftflotte 3   124

MAGIC   91, 100, 116, 117, 125, 126, 146
  History of   27
Magnetron valve   80
Malta   30, 96
Manstein, FM E. von   11, 35-37, 48, 51, 94,
     107, 110, 118
Manstein, Frau von   35
Margival   129
'Market Garden', Op   145
Martinez, Gen H.   11-15, 23, 41-43, 115
Masterman, John   27, 32, 33, 36, 91
Maurwald camp   136
Medenine, Battle of   90
Memel   93
Menzies, Sir Stewart see C
Mertz von Quernheim, Col Ritter von   139,
     140
METOX   80, 81
Midway, Battle of   93, 146
'Mincemeat', Op   95
MI5   25, 28, 31-33
Montgomery, Gen Sir Bernard   30, 90, 105,
     117, 130, 143, 145
Morgan, Gen Frederick   65, 102, 113
Moscow   94, 95
Mountbattten, Adm Lord Louis   59, 60, 91
Munich University   38
Mussolini, Benito   90, 96, 99, 136
Mutt   114

Naiad   14
NAXOS   80, 123
Nerve gas   61 footnote
'New Year's Day 1945', Op   147
Norsk hydro plant   58
Norway   102, 103, 109
Nuclear: see atomic explosives

Oboe   85
Octopus   93
Oil offensive   145, 146
OKH   11, 36, 37
OKL   11
OKM   11, 23
OKW   11, 21, 36, 45, 87, 99 passim
Olbricht, Gen Friedrich   110, 111, 134, 135,
     138-140
Omaha beach   123, 124
One-Time-Pad   27
Oshima, Ambdr Hiroshi   55, 82
Oslo Report   101
Oster, Gen Hans   41, 43, 109, 141
  in reststance   47-52, 68, 71, 94, 133
Overcoat, Op   111
Overlord   114 passim
Oxford University   147

Papen, Franz von   35, 48
Pas de Calais   65, 108, 109, 113 passim, 143
Patton, Gen George   144
Paulus, Gen Frederick   35, 36
Pearl Harbor   27, 75
Peenemunde   58, 101, 108
Peltz, Gen Dietrich   147
Petrie, Sir David   25, 27, 57
Philippines, Battle of   146
Photographic Reconnaissance (PR)   86-90, 96,
     100 passim, 150
Playfair system   8
Poland   8, 101, 108
Portal, AM Sir Charles   59, 60, 87
Pound, Adm Sir Dudley   59, 60, 83
Praun, Gen Albert   11-15, 41-45, 53, 72, 118,
     141, 145
Prisoners of War (PR)   90, 96, 100 passim, 143
     passim, 150
Pujol, Juan see Garbo
Purple   75 footnote, 7 footnote, 93
Puttkamer, Capt von   53

Quadrant   105
Quebec conference see Quadrant

Radar 59, 80, 83, 85, 100, 107, 123, 129
Raeder, Adm Eric 18, 22, 36-38, 54
RAF Bomber Command *see Bomber Command (British)*
Rastenburg 36, 68, 72, 93, 111, 136 passim
Red Cross, German 73
Reich Signal Security Agency (RSSD) 67, 69
Reichspost 73, 118
Remer, Maj Otto 139
Rhein 135
Ribbentrop, Joachim von 49, 55, 68, 74
Robinson (Heath) 63, 64, 90, 94, 115
Rockets 58, 100, 106
Rome 87, 99, 105, 106, 122
Rommel, FM Erwin 11, 14, 30, 41, 90, 109 passim
  and Walkyrie 135 passim
Roosevelt, Franklin 27, 85, 87, 96
Rossler, Rudolf 94
Rote Kapelle 67
RSHA (Reichsicherheitshauptamt) 67, 114, 116
Ruhr, Battle of 86
Rundstedt, FM Gerd von 103, 109, 110, 116, 129 passim

St Nazaire 123
Sägefisch see Fish and Geheimschreiber
Salerno 105, 122
Sander, Col Ludolf 110, 136-138
Sandys, Duncan 101
Sangro river 106
Sardinia 105, 106
Scharnhorst 55
Schellenberg, Walter 67-70, 74, 75, 85, 95, 101, 105, 111, 114, 134
Schlabrendorff, Fabian von 68
Schmundt, Gen Rudolf 18, 110, 118
Scholl, Hans 38, 39
Scholl, Sophie 38, 39
Schräger Musik 107
Schroff, Gen 140
Schutz Staffeln (SS) 7, 8, 67, 73, 135, 140, 141
Scotland Yard, Special Branch 31
Secret Intelligence Service (SIS) 31, 86 passim, 113, 143 passim, 150
Secret Writer *see Geheimschreiber*
Seebohm, Lt 14
SHAEF 113, 114, 121, 124, 130, 146
Sicherheitsdienst (SD) 95, 102, 111, 134
Sicily42, 60, 64, 87, 90-92, 95, 106, 122

Sidi Bou Zid 90
Siemens, Co
  T 52 machine 48
Sigint 96, 105 passim, 121 passim, 143 passim, 150
Signals Equipment
  Telegraph 19, 99
  Telephone 19, 99, 107, 117, 118, 134 passim
  Teleprinter 19, 99, 107, 117, 118, 134 passim, 151
Snow 31
Solomon Seas, Battle of 93, 146
Solz, Trott du 119
Spaatz, Gen Carl 87
Specht, Gen 140
Special Operations Executive (SOE) 58, 86, 91, 106, 117, 133, 143, 150
Speer, Albert 37, 71, 100
Speidel, Gen Hans 129, 131, 136
Squid 93
Stahlberg, Capt Alexander 35-37, 48-50, 110
Stalingrad, Battle of 11, 25, 35, 36, 38, 94
Starkey, Op 102, 109
Stauffenberg, Col Claus Graf von
  As member of Resistance 35, 110
  Assumes leadership of Resistance 118
  On 20 July 1944 133 passim
  Plans Operation Walkyrie 110, 111, 118, 133 passim
  Wounded 71, 92
Stieff, Gen Helmuth 69, 134, 136, 140
Straussberg 93
Stulpnagel, Gen Karl-Heinrich von 139
Stummel, Adm 11-15, 20, 23, 42-45
Summer 32

Tabun 61 footnote
Telephone and Telegraph Exchanges, Battle of 134 passim
Thiel, Dr 101
Thiele, Gen Fritz 138, 139, 141
Thoma, Gen Ritter von 101
Tindall, Op 102, 109
Tirpitz 55
TORCH, Op 12, 22, 32, 42
Tracking Room (U-boat) 77, 79
Transport offenisve 117
Transport Plan 117
Tresckow, Lt-Col Henning von
  As leader of Resistance 35, 48, 50, 68, 69, 109-111

Plans Operation Walkyrie 111, 118, 133
  death of 140
Tricycle 102, 103, 114
Trident conference 87, 96
Triton Enigma 20, 42, 77
Trout 93
Tunis 87, 115
Tunisia 11, 41, 42, 60, 71, 87, 90
Tunny 63
Turing, Dr Alan 22, 25-28, 33, 44, 47, 63, 77,
  90
Turing machine 22
Twenty Committee 27, 30, 32, 125, 126
Type 97 Japanese encoding machine:
  see Purple
Typex machine 27, 29, 151

U-boat Command 71, 77 passim, 122, 123
U-67 42
U-110 58
U-111 42
U-459 23, 42
U-505 123
  Supply boats 83
Ultra
  Creation of and function 8, 25, 28, 85
  and Lucy 95
  Summing up 149 passim
  See also GC nd CS and Bletchley Park
Ultra goes to War 150
Ultra Secret, The 149

V1 101, 108, 114 passim, 125, 125, 129, 144,
  145
V2 100, 109, 144, 145
Vietinghoff, Gen Heinrich von 105
Vinnitsa 53
VLR (Very Long Range aircraft) 80

Wadham, Op 102
Wagner, Gen Eduard 134, 140
Waffen SS 111
Walkyrie, Op 110, 118, 134 passim
WANZE 80
Warlimont, Gen Walter 82, 138
Warning, Col 131
'Watch on the Rhine', Op 145, 146, 147
Watten 101, 102
Wehrmacht 11 passim, 118, 141, 151
Weichs, FM von 95
Wheeler-Bennett, Sir John 19
White Rose Letters 38, 48
Whiting 94
Wildhagen, Karl 72
Wilhelmshaven 80, 86
Window 100, 107
Winterbotham, Gp Capt Frederick 149
Witzleben, FM Erwin von 110, 111, 135, 139,
  140
Wolff, Colonel 126
Wolfschanze 11, 36, 118, 134 passim, 147
Women signallers 73
WRNS (Womem's Royal Naval Service) 94
W/T (Wireless Telegraphy) 129

Yamamoto, Adm Isokuru 93
Y Services 27, 28, 60, 85, 90, 100, 124, 145,
  150
Yugoslavia 91

Zaparohze 48, 53
Zeitzler, Gen Kurt 36, 136
Zeppelin 72, 93, 94, 135, 138, 147
'Zeppelin', Op 114, 116
Zossen 72